To Al, John, Martha, Paula,
and Bud & Delores

A Note from the Publisher:

The economy. Everybody talks about it, but who really does something about it?

Entrepreneurs and brand-builders, that's who.

One of the most critical skills for the American economy – any economy really – is "the creative class," those who create value, jobs, profits, and economic growth by creating businesses and brands.

So now you know why we are so pleased to be publishing this important book.

It's important because of you.

It's important because the skills you learn and develop are the ones that will help you be part of "the creative class," the people that grow America.

We wish you luck in your journey and hope that the brands and businesses that you help build will play their part in your future, and the future of the American economy.

The Copy Workshop
Chicago USA

If you are a

… college student planning a marketing communications campaign for yourself, a class project, or a client…

…a college professor coaching students for a client or competition…

…an entrepreneur educator working with students to build marketing strategies and creative elements for their enterprises or brand…

…a high school teacher working with FBLA, Junior Achievement, or DECA student groups…

…a not-for-profit or nonprofit organization needing to raise funds, recruit members or employees, spread the Good News of your organization and make it more successful overall…

…a sports marketer, sports information department, or event planner needing to build an integrated marketing communication plan for your center or various teams, events, or tournaments…

…an agricultural group diversifying your operation to include sustainable activities, new product or service lines…

…artists and artisans looking for a way to bring your creative work to market…

**this book will benefit you.
Because each of you needs to build your brand.**

Table of Contents

Chapter 8: GOAL SETTING

Chapter 9: MESSAGING: BUILDING A CREATIVE STRATEGY

Chapter 10: MESSAGE WINDOWS 1: Marketing Communications, Media, and Evaluation

Chapter 11: MESSAGE WINDOWS 2: Creative Executions

Chapter 12: THE PITCH

PREFACE

Welcome to the *Brand Builder Workbook*. I've been thinking about this book for probably 15 years – maybe 20. It was only when I began a proposal for a sabbatical that it became clear what I should write. I needed a 'how to' book that students could use to analyze and build a communication campaign for the kind of projects we have at Morningside College in Sioux City, Iowa.

The result? *The Brand Builder Workbook* – a step by step guide to help a student team or a local entrepreneur get started on building their brand. I was in Chicago for a young entrepreneurs conference and called publishers Bruce and Lorelei Bendinger to discuss my project and their possible interest in publishing this book. As it turned out, they were looking for much the same thing.

Over the years, I've used a number of campaign planning books. My favorite is Jim Avery's *Advertising Campaign Planning*. The strength of Jim's book is his knowledge from his time in the agency business working with a host of national brands. His book is written with great insight for the American Advertising Federation (AAF) competition teams – typically at larger universities with larger resources in terms of marketing instruction.

My background happens to be with smaller and more entrepreneurial brands – the kind of projects that tend to show up at small to mid-sized universities. Along with that, our teams and class-size are quite a bit smaller as well. So I believed a book that addressed smaller brands with smaller resources would relate to my students, and the clients we were serving in the classroom.

Initially, I envisioned a manual to accompany another book we use, *Advertising & the Business of Brands* also from The Copy Workshop (as is Jim Avery's book). However, the longer we worked on the idea, the more clear it became that we needed to write a book specifically aimed at student ad teams and entrepreneurs. It reminded me of an important lesson – know your target audience.

Big Competitions and Small Clients.

We've learned a lot over the years by competing – with some success – in the American Advertising Federation's national competitions. We have also competed in the National Cadillac Case Study competition sponsored by EdVenture Partners. There, our teams were national winners two years in a row, pitching ideas at the top of the Renaissance Center in Detroit to a room full of GM and Cadillac executives and their agencies. Great fun.

But there was another important place where I wanted our students to win – right here at home. That's a mission that all of us who work to prepare students in our local regions and communities share. The test group was a summer class of eight that teamed up to prepare a campaign for a local non-profit music group – the Sioux City Chamber Music association. The approach worked - and it was music to everyone's ears. The entire branding campaign plan was adopted for immediate use.

Over the next two years we continued to accept local clients and to develop student consultants. Students feel much more connected and an integral part of the process when they work on a local or regional brand. Not only that, but those local and regional brands are more likely to adopt the fruits of student labor.

So here we are – with a book designed for local markets, with local and regional businesses, non-profits, and other community groups as your focus. You may want to use this as part of an entrepreneurial course or in a campaigns course as I do.

As Dorothy says in The Wizard of Oz, "There's no place like home." We hope the process you'll experience in the Brand Builder Workbook serves as inspiration for you to develop your brand where you live.

Begin with the End in Mind.

That's right, start at the end – just the way Steven Covey advised in *Seven Habits of Highly Effective People*, Habit 2. After reading the first chapter, review Chapters 11 and 12. They provide insight on what the 'end' looks like – and how to get there.

Chapter 11 describes team duties. Chapter 12 describes how a semester schedule plays out as you work your way to The Pitch – where students present their recommendations and prepare a book and (often) a CD for the brand decision maker(s), as well as for their own portfolio. If an entrepreneur is doing this for themselves – well - they'll figure it out. That's what entrepreneurs do.

The Instructor's Manual.

For faculty who adopt the book, we've prepared an instructor's manual with a variety of support – plus a website, which is for everybody:

Website Support – www.brandbuilderworkbook.com

The website supports both students and faculty through the brand building process. Blank documents are available on our site as pdf files so that you might reproduce them as you see most useful. In addition there is a gallery of brands – you'll find a variety of samples here. There are pdf files of the PowerPoints and plans books to help you visualize how a branding campaign is executed – how it gets from research to strategy to creative messaging.

I'm so pleased that you are using the book to build brands and develop your student's creative skills. In today's economy, it is important to recognize faculty's effort and their attention to the process as well as the product. Please keep us posted on your progress. Ask questions if you have them. And send us examples of your team's brand-building success!

Pamela L. Mickelson
Morningside College, Sioux City, IA
July 2011

CHAPTER 1:
INTRODUCTION TO BRANDING

We're all consumers of brands and brand messages.

Every day we see and hear hundreds of messages that ask us to buy, enroll, vote, select, donate, click … you get the idea. In virtually every case, those messages come from a brand – it's a product, it's a service, or perhaps it's an event, a referendum, a local politician, or a local business.

All those different things – each one of them – is a **Brand**. And, if we're familiar with them, each in their own way has achieved some sort of **Brand Identity.**

In today's business marketplace, that's the way we talk to each other. When done well, it's pretty effective. We pay attention to brand messages, and, if that message seems useful to us, we just may respond. When you add it all up, it's really pretty simple. On the surface, it's like a coat of paint – but it goes deeper than that.

A Brand is a promise to deliver a benefit that will serve you or yours. And that extra bit of identification that helps you remember who is offering that benefit is what we call **branding – or brand identification.**

Branding helps us remember, and it helps us organize our communication. If we're familiar with the brand, we're often more disposed to respond. Why not?

Over the years, lots of people have teamed up to develop lots of brands – some big and some small. And, over the years, they've developed some methods for doing that job effectively. That's what this workbook will help you do – we'll help you think it through.

We'll help you build a new brand, or make the most of an existing brand. Then, we'll help you develop and deliver messages for that brand. And, if we do it right, we'll help build that brand with successful programs and effective messages that help grow that brand in the marketplace.

First, let's take a look at what we're going to learn in this chapter.

LEARNING OUTCOMES

As we start each chapter, we're going to try to give you a "sneak preview" of what to expect. This chapter will help us get started. After studying this chapter you will:

1. have a basic understanding of marketing, promotion, advertising, and branding;

2. understand the various types of brands;
3. illustrate the elements of a brand building matrix;
4. identify characteristics of integrated marketing communications; and
5. understand the different elements of a brand building campaign.

Ready? Let's go!

MARKETING, PROMOTIONS, ADVERTISING, BRANDING – WHAT IS THE DIFFERENCE AND WHY IT MATTERS

Once upon a time, most brand messages were merely advertising in paid media. Today, brands have many more windows – opportunities to connect with the target.

Advertising is marketing messages in paid media. You might already know that. Advertising is one of the elements within the "Big P" called Promotion in the Marketing Mix.

Marketing is the broader activity that an organization practices to bring their products or services to market.

Advertising is just one of the things that we do in Marketing. And, while this isn't going to be a marketing course, we think you need to know just a little about what's involved. Advertising is part of the "P" called Promotion, which is part of the marketing mix – also known as the 4 P's.

So take a look at this chart (Figure 1.1). It's **The 4Ps of Marketing**.

The **Four P's are product, price, place, and promotion**. Incidentally, they are usually stated in that order.

Makes sense when you think about it. You need the right product and it needs to be offered at the right price. Once you figure that out, you have to figure out where to sell it or how to get it to the customer in some other way. That's Place, another word we use for Distribution. Got it so far?

Now, see how those Four P's are all clustered around a circle in the center – our Target Market. That needs to be at the center of our brand-building thoughts.

Figure 1.1 The Marketing Mix – Product, Price, Place and Promotion (4 P's)

We have to build our brand with the Target Consumer in mind.

Now there are a lot of other things we have to think about. For example, our overall Business Goals – maybe we have a Mission, that's OK. You'll find that there are a lot of things to think about.

After you determine what you want to accomplish for your brand, you will be developing messages that help you accomplish those goals. Those messages will come from an understanding of the Target.

It's a building process. Just as The Four P's are the building blocks of marketing, we'll be taking you through a process of building the program that will build your brand.

A Few Definitions:

It will be helpful to define a few terms. Some words have more than one definition – the word "target" for example. If we were at an archery range, we would be talking about something different – even though the concepts are related.

"Brand" for example has an interesting origin. It began, literally, with branding the manufacturer's name on the wooden crate that contained the goods – before that, it was a way of telling which cattle in the herd were yours.

Today, here's what we mean.

Brand – We discussed brands a bit earlier as a promise for a benefit to be delivered to you in a certain way. Let's get a little more formal with other definitions.

> 1) **a name, term, symbol, or design** in someone's head – often it's a combination of these elements, intended to clearly identify and differentiate a seller's products from those of a competitor.

> 2) **a conceptual entity** that focuses the organization of marketing activities – usually with the purpose of building equities for that brand in the marketplace.

> 3) **a verb (branding)** representing activities – usually marketing activities – on behalf of the brand.

> A brand is not just a product, it is a product that comes with a name, identity, and meaning different and unique from others in the same market. Subway is unique; a sub sandwich is not. I can make a sub sandwich in my kitchen. I cannot make a Subway sandwich.

Goals – OK, now what do you think your brand can accomplish? Goals are a vision – sort of a way you want to think about and talk about where you're going. If you look under the hood, those goals are driven by a combination of your brand, your objective, and your strategy – how you're going to do it. If you're asked about your brand, you'll often talk about your goals.

But you won't say, "my objective is to become a leading entertainment venue with a 30% market share in the local teen-age retail entertainment market with a strategy of high-profile anchor events and customer relationship marketing."

You're more likely to say, "We want to become the #1 rock concert venue, and also THE PLACE where teens want to hang out."

Simply put, Goals will mean Business Goals – even if you've a non-profit.

Also, you're going to have **Short-Term Goals** and **Long-Term Goals.**

One should help the other – though they may be logistically and strategically very different. Getting lots of publicity and goodattendance for the concert is one thing; getting a nice relaxed crowd for the CD signing by the local singer/ songwriter with a low-cost e-mail campaign is something else. Each will help you reach your long-term goal, though they may be very different marketing activities.

Objective – This tends to be a bit more specific. It is a description of what you plan to accomplish. Your goal helps you set the general direction. Now you will need some very clear idea of what you have to do. It is important to have a clear statement in mind for your brand and for your brand-building program.

As they say, "when you don't know where you're going, any road will get you there." While you may have some ambitious long-term goals, you will still want to accomplish something specific in the short term. These are usually stated as objectives. Some students ask if goals are different than objectives. That's a good question with many different answers. Successful brand-building usually has both in mind. A long-term goal or mission, and a specific objective for a specific program or short-term task to be accomplished. We may want to win the championship, but we still have to take it "one game at a time."

We will cover objectives in Chapter 8.

Strategy – this is an overall description of how we will get there. It's an important word, but you may be surprised to find it has a number of different uses. As we work to build a brand, you may well discover that we actually have a number of strategies and sub-strategies.

For example, as you work to determine your messaging, you will develop a Creative Strategy that will help you focus on the best thing to say. When you go over the Marketing Plan, you may see that your Creative Strategy is part of a larger Marketing Strategy. And, as you talk about finances, you may find yourself dealing with a Pricing Strategy. In each circumstance, a person may correctly be using the word "strategy" but talking about something that is very different!

In our Brand-Building process, we'll usually be talking about a Strategy for crafting the right message – a Communication Strategy or Creative Strategy. Then again, we might be talking about a program that works to get our Target Customer to do something – something that might require an incentive – like a "Buy One Get One Free" coupon. Know what that is? It's a Promotional Strategy. And, if we're looking at different media options, well guess what that is. Right, it's a Media Strategy.

The focus of Chapter 9 will be Strategies.

Situation Analysis – this is a document that helps us understand where we are as a brand. Even if we're a brand new brand, with no history at all, the Situation Analysis can help us understand the marketplace, the market for our product or service, what the Target Customer is like, and everything else we can discover to see where we are – the situation we're in. You'll find that we spend a lot of time pulling this together. You'll also find that this can be time well-spent.

Chapter 4 covers the Situation Analysis.

SWOT: Strengths, Weaknesses, Opportunities, Threats – Ever hear of a SWOT analysis? It's a very interesting process where we add up all the good news and the bad news and throw in a little bit of crystal ball. The SWOT analysis is conducted as part of your Situation Analysis. The company's internal strengths and weaknesses are determined as well as the external environments opportunities and threats.

Target – Who will be the source of your brand's business? In most cases, that's your Target. Though, of course, if you have a store that specializes in baby clothes, Moms will be your target even though the product is used by someone else.

There are a number of ways to describe your target. We'll go through them in more detail later, but here's a snapshot of the different ways we can look at the people we want to connect with your brand. Target Audience will be discussed at length in Chapter 7.

Demographics – This is a statistical description of your target. For example, *Women with children 18-35* or *Household income $50,000 plus.*

Psychographics – This is a psychological description of your target. Think about it. Two families may be neighbors with similar incomes and family size, but be very different in their outlook and in things such as media habits. For example, *Mothers who like to see their children wearing the latest fashions.*

Usage/Behavior – There are other things that can define a target. If you have a store that sells eyeglass frames, your target may be as simple as "people who wear glasses." "Theater-goers" or "Concert-goers" may be helpful, though you'll still have to find out other things about these people. After all, you have to reach them *before* they go to the theater or the concert.

OK, now we're on the trail of **who** and we'll have to figure how we connect with them – usually it's with some sort of message. Let's look at how we'll talk about this area.

Media – This is a plural term used to refer to all means of communication channels that can be used to speak on behalf of a brand. **Traditional media** include newspapers, magazines, radio, television, outdoor, Internet, and Yellow Pages. **Nontraditional media** can include everything from floor mats to fruit stickers. **Social Media** includes the use of YouTube, Twitter, Facebook, LinkedIn, etc. as part of your branding strategy.

Medium – Single form of those terms used to refer to forms of communication channels such as radio , television, etc. It can get confusing. Want to get more confused? A specific TV station, radio station, or newspaper is a media *vehicle.* Don't worry about it, just be sure people know what you mean.

You'll find Media as the focus of Chapter 10.

Message – this is, quite simply, what we say about the brand. Sometimes it is the most unique thing about the brand that will speak directly to the target in a meaningful way. "Fresh, organic coffee beans. For more flavor and a greener environment."

Then again, sometimes it's practical and functional. Like "We open at 6:30 so you can grab a fresh hot cup on your way to work."

Message (or Creative) Elements – The graphics, colors, designs, film, photography, words, and phrases used to bring the brand's message to the target. You'll often find that your Brand is building a library of message elements that will come in handy as you build new programs and upgrade old ones.

Message Window – This is a term we like to use to indicate all the places where your brand messages can be placed and communicated. For example, television, radio, internet, Google, Yahoo, YouTube, magazines, newspaper, outdoor, floor mats, t-shirts, telephone poles, subway posters, packages, menus, etc. Remember, your Brand might have some unique message windows.

For example, if you're involved in a church group, your church program can be a unique message window. If you're selling pizza, it's the pizza box. In general, we think you should look for Message Windows that are unique to your Brand and your Target. They often offer a wonderful opportunity.

Message Windows are a key part of a new model we use that is simple and easy to remember – we call it the Brand Builder Matrix. Your brand will most likely have a message that is cast in this large net and you will no doubt have a number of windows from which to choose – ranging from traditional mass communication to new forms that are more social in nature.

UNDERSTANDING DIFFERENT BRANDS

Before we discuss additional definitions and concepts, we want your brain to take a deep breath. OK? I want you to do this activity. Because as we learn to build brands, we're also going to be building our brains. You'll be discovering new ways to think.

Many Different Brands.

For your first exercise, we're going to pick a brand. But before we do, let's think about all the different kinds of brands there are out there. We can categorize them in a number of different ways, but here's an easy way to think about them.

- **Familiar Brands**
- **Brand New Brands**
- **Entertainment Brands**
- **Retail Brands**
- **Non-profit Brands**
- **Other Kinds of Brands**
- **National, Regional and Local Variations**

  Briefly, let's take them one by one.

- **Familiar Brands.** These may be brands you put in the shopping cart, they may be the car you buy every few years, or the gas you put in it. We don't have to tell you a lot about these brands, because you've known them for years.

- **Brand New Brands.** Every once in a while a new brand comes onto our radar screen. A few years ago, it was mobile phones. Now we're seeing new models almost every week. There are all sorts of electronic gadgets, and online brands like eBay and Facebook, and maybe a new store at the mall. These brands provide a new – or brand new – kind of challenge. It's fun, because you're working with a "blank slate," and it's frustrating because, "nobody knows nothin'."

- **Entertainment Brands.** This could be a famous rock band like the Rolling Stones, the movie coming out next week, a local sports team, or the place they play. These brands can be a lot of fun because you're selling entertainment. And they can be quite a challenge, because you have a lot of noisy competition.

- **Retail Brands.** Retail stores, including restaurants, are their own unique kind of brand. Sometimes they carry other brands, and sometimes, like a McDonald's, they have a lot of their own mini-brands – a Happy Meal for the kids, a healthy salad, and your favorite burger and fries. Mc Donald's is a company that's been very good at managing their brand and, whether or not we have lunch there, they have a lot to teach us about branding.

- **Non-profit Brands.** We live in a country with a tradition of giving a little bit extra to our communities, our church groups, and our schools. Think of national programs, like the United Way, the Red Cross, and Friends of the Earth – they're brands, too.

- **Other Kinds of Brands.** They're everywhere. The political candidates that come out every election year, the radio stations that want our ears and all the places that want to become the destination for our next vacation. They're all brands in one way or another.

- **National, Regional and Local Variations.** One other interesting thing is that sometimes brands can contain other brands. Think of a big national brand, like the NFL.

Geographically the NFL – the National Football League – is known throughout the United States market (and many international markets as well).

Regionally, The Pittsburgh Steelers and Dallas Cowboys are brands of keen interest in Pennsylvania and Texas, respectively, as are football teams for state schools like Austin's University of Texas or private schools in a large metropolitan market like Chicago's Northwestern University.

Then there's the local high school or college team that wants a nice crowd on Friday or Saturday. Go team!

In every **category**, you can usually find examples of brands that contain other brands.

Okay, how are we doing? By now, you should have an understanding of some of the things that go into marketing. So, can you name all four P's?

You should also have an understanding of different types of brands.

Now let's exercise our brand brains a little more. Let's work on identifying different brands.

BRAIN-BUILDER EXERCISE 1.1: Identifying Brands

The purpose of this exercise is to identify various types of brands

Note: You'll find additional worksheets at www.brandbuilderworkbook.com.

Keep in mind the various brands that were previously discussed – retail, non-profit, new brands, etc. Let's fill out a simple worksheet with some of those brands. (Hint: a big national brand – like an automobile – has local brands, like car dealers, and they'll usually have a regional dealer group.)

Use a variety of "search engines" – your local newspaper, a drive down the street, a quick google session, channel surfing on your TV, or paging through a magazine – to help you with this assignment.

Don't worry if you can't fill in every blank – the regional one can sometimes be hard. The purpose of this worksheet is to get you to start to identify brands – the obvious ones and the not-so-obvious.

Here goes.

What kinds of brands interest you? As you go through this worksheet, think about the types of brands you'd like to get involved with. You'll probably find that you're attracted to some area – maybe a local sports team, or a national charity. It could be a brand new idea, your idea, or an old favorite that you think needs some new energy.

Keep that in mind as you choose the brand(s) for the next exercise.

We all swim in a sea of brand messages. So, we can end up taking a lot of these messages for granted. Now, we want you to pay a bit more attention.

There's a worksheet on the next page. Print out a few copies from www.brandbuilderworkbook.com

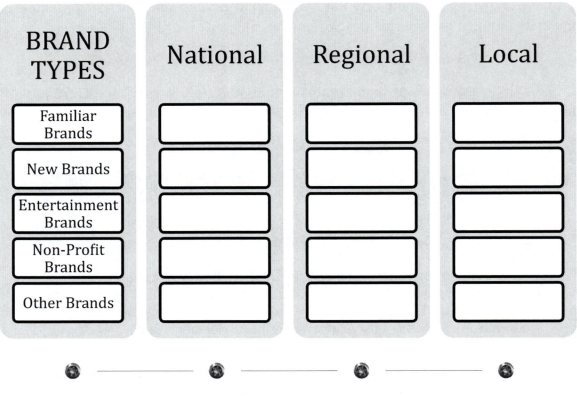

THE BRAND BUILDER MATRIX

Now we want to introduce a simple conceptual model that reflects how to think about building a brand. You'll recognize the terms. And now you'll see them working together – it's simple – but it's memorable. "Simple and memorable" helps us remember.

We call it The Brand Builder Matrix. Here's a simple graphic that illustrates the brand's pivotal relationship to four critical elements – Business Goal(s), Target(s), Message, and Message Windows (Figure 1.2).

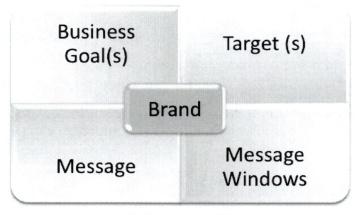

Figure 1.2 The Brand Builder Matrix

But, in practice, you'll probably find it more practical to think in terms of subheads and bullet points. Like this:

Brand: Name of brand

Business Goals: State basic business goals simply and clearly.

Targets: You may have more than one. Use bullet points and a clear description.

- Main Target
- Other key Decision makers in the Value Chain
- Interesting Secondary Target that needs to be developed

Message: Core brand message. You may need to add a few more with bullet points – but, again, try to keep it clear and simple.

Message Windows: On judgment, the best places to place your messages.

We'll be covering each of these factors in more detail throughout the book, but let's start by getting our heads wrapped around the basic concepts. Our little graphic places "Brand" in the center to illustrate its close relationship to the four other elements. If you have a clear and effective view of what is needed for the brand in each of the quadrants, you should be able to build a successful brand.

Business Goal(s): An enterprise or entity will probably have a long-term business goal. For example, the enterprise called The Study Break has a long term business goal to be the leading student gathering place. They also have a series of short-term business goals, i.e. to introduce freshman and transfer students to The Study Break and collect e-mail addresses for additional relationship marketing. Some non-profits may simply have Goals, and that's okay, too. Your local sports team has the goal of a winning season. Goals help us focus on where we're headed and what we have to do to get there.

Target(s): The better an organization understands who makes up its market, the more effective its messages will be. More than one Target might exist: for example, a business's own employees may also be a Target (although secondary in nature to its primary target market). The primary Target audience for The Study Break would be students (freshmen and transfer students), and the secondary Target audience would be its employees (or members). Knowing the Target audiences (both primary and secondary) will also help the organization establish appropriate Goals – for example, to establish the service staff of The Study Break as friendly and up-to-date on campus events.

Message: The Message is what is being said. Sometimes building a Brand means having a message that is saying one thing over and over – like Bounty (the paper towel) is the "Quicker Picker-Upper." Sometimes one can develop a conversation that is welcomed by the Target. Leo Burnett said it best: make it simple, make it memorable, make it interesting.

We would add to that by recommending matching the Brand's character and making it deliverable. That's often easier said than done. We want to understand the most unique thing about the brand that, when said, will speak directly to the target and, done right, will provide the Target with the information, or the motivation to act.

By the way, that unique thing has to be important to the target customer. If they get our message and just sort of say, "that's nice," chances are we haven't accomplished what we need to accomplish. You might be putting a unique mint on the pillow, but what's important to the customer is exceptional service. Or maybe it's price. If so, skip the mint.

Message Windows: A Message Window includes all traditional paid media – TV, radio, newspapers, magazines, direct mail, and outdoor boards. But today, it includes all the unpaid and nontraditional forms of communication that have entered the mainstream of what people see and how they make decisions.

Now there is "The Big Window," the network of computers, with e-mail, Google, Facebook, and all the other windows that just might make sense for a Brand.

For example, a local restaurant might pay attention to all the hungry people (the Target) that are within a few blocks. A restaurant that delivers (think pizza), might try to post a menu on the doorsteps of everyone in the market area – or, better yet, a magnet for every refrigerator. The restaurant itself can be a message window, and every customer in every booth is a target with the potential for a return visit.

THE CAMPAIGN: PUTTING IT ALL TOGETHER.

When we put all these elements together in a coherent and effective way, we generally call that effort a "campaign." That campaign may be a short blast of activity before a certain date – like the publicity before a concert. Or, it may be a long-term effort that builds a relationship, with repeat purchases and a growing connection with the Target.

That said, let's talk a bit more about campaigns, with a tip of the hat to Jim Avery – much of this next section is adapted from his insightful work in *Advertising Campaign Planning* and *Advertising & The Business of Brand*s.

Military and Political Campaigns

We have talked about brands and building brands. Now it is time to understand the concept of campaigns. Traditionally in the world of advertising you hear the term ad campaign. But where did the word come from and why did advertising pick it up?

The term campaign has roots in the military. A military campaign occurs when armed forces work towards a desired goal. Extended and extreme military campaigns are declared wars. It's also helpful to remember that, just as military campaigns usually had someone fighting on the other side, our brand-building campaigns may also have an "enemy." Sometimes it's a competitor with similar offerings, and sometimes our "enemy" is simply lack of awareness or the inertia of doing things the same way instead of trying something new.

Political campaigns have similar characteristics. The political campaign's purpose is to elect a person to office. The campaign is designed to reach voters in specific geographic locations.

Here in Iowa, we're very aware of this every four years. During a presidential election year, the Iowa Caucus means that virtually every presidential candidate will visit our Iowa campus at Morningside College, as well as many small towns. In 2007, we got a close-up view watching (then Senator) Barack Obama build his brand. He appeared in the college gym. Soon-to-be First Lady Michelle Obama visited schools in towns and nearby communities.

Their strategy and message was clear and consistent at every visit. Did you vote? Do you remember the message? Senator Obama's use of non-traditional and social media with a specialized message to the young as well as minority voters made a big difference in his success. His campaign slogan, "Yes we can," hit the sweet spot with many Iowa voters.

The upcoming election will most likely be as memorable. Political campaigns and branding campaigns are very related.

Now that you understand brands better, let's work your brain a bit.

BRAIN-BUILDER EXERCISE 1.2:
Understanding Ways A Brand Can Communicate

The purpose of this exercise is to help you understand how a brand communicates and how that translates into building a brand.

Note: Additional worksheets are provided at brandbuilderworkbook.com, and you have our permission to make copies of the worksheets in this workbook.

You might want to do this exercise more than once.

Or, if you're serious about building a certain kind of brand, you might want to examine more than one brand in your chosen category.

Ready? Let's go.

Step One.

Select Three Brands

Instructions: You will need to choose three brands to study. They might be brands that you know and like. More than likely you identified at least one of them in Exercise 1.1.

Discussion: Before you build a new brand, think about brands you have already experienced. Successful brands can teach us a lot.

One very successful brand is Apple. It combines well-designed and extremely useful products with a whole range of engaging brand messages that are usually as well-designed as the products: entertaining TV commercials, cool outdoor boards, and even great-looking packaging.

Apple is a company that really understands messaging. When Apple has a new product, you know about it in the news, because Apple is also good at obtaining news coverage through Public Relations. Finally, when we go online – we are able to find Apple easily and can purchase one of their many products.

Apple uses a whole range of Message Windows to get us involved.

Now it's your turn to learn. What three brands should you choose?

Here's a thought-starter. Pick a retailer you like, a new product, and one of your old favorites – a brand you've liked for years.

You don't have to stop there. If you're involved in community activities, you might want to pick a non-profit, maybe a theater or local music group, or your favorite place to hang out.

Step Two.

Start your collection, organize your work.

Instructions: Find at least three examples of communication for each brand. There should be at least two examples from paid media or "collateral" (brochures are an example of collateral).

Where to look: you most likely will choose a brand from Exercise1.1. If you wish to search a bit more, check out adsoftheworld.com and YouTube.

The worksheet is a good place for you to begin to list the activities of your brand(s). However, there will not be enough room to capture all the ideas in your collection. That's why paper clips and folders were invented.

Collect material on each of the brands you pick: print-outs of Web pages, ads from magazines or newspapers, brochures, news stories, and anything else you can collect.

You'll want two kinds of folders:

- an electronic folder for URLs and YouTube videos, and

- a regular folder for print ads (we call them tear sheets – for obvious reasons) and for news articles, reprints, brochures, and anything else that seems appropriate.

For example, you might select Verizon Wireless as your brand. The two media you find are one print ad and one television spot. For TV commercials, you may just describe the spot in a few sentences, though you'll learn more if you can record it and write down the entire script. You may want to stop by a Verizon store and pick up a brochure or two. And you may Google Verizon – and be a bit surprised at what you find. Verizon on the ski slopes. Oh, and if you haven't seen the T-Mobile in the train station event, take a look. Different brand, but cool event.

Don't feel like you have to stop there. You could find mention in the news or a seasonal promotion for a gift with a purchase. Take notes.

Step Three.

Research brands and the competition

We're not done yet. You might also want to add another clip file of articles on the brand or the product category. You'll be pleasantly surprised at the articles and industry information you can find on the Internet. And, you might want to save examples of interesting material from the competition.

Now, if you picked a local restaurant, that doesn't mean you should save every single coupon and special meal deal flyer – you'd be ready for a paper drive in a week – but you should keep an eye out, and save the things that you think are particularly well-done.

Good brands and good work have a lesson to teach us.

After you've filled in the worksheet, answer the questions. ***This is a Workbook – feel free to write your answers right on the pages.*** For many of you, this will be your first glance inside the world of Brands, and it will help you to start thinking about how you're going to promote your own brand someday.

TIP: Keeping everything organized and in files and folders will help you with future assignments. Here's an example of how we might fill out the worksheet using the original Apple iPhone as an example.

Brand-Builder Worksheet – Example: Apple iPhone

BRAND (Name of company, product, or service) Apple iPhone™	TARGET (Describe who the advertisements are written for – describe the "who" as much as you can)	MESSAGE (What is the primary message of the ad? Maybe a headline, listed claims, and/or call to action.)	MESSAGE ELEMENTS (Note any designs, illustrations, photography, logos, symbols or color elements.)	MESSAGE WINDOWS (In what media did this advertisement appear?)
Ad 1 iPhone 3GS	**Demographic:** 18 – 35 year old, male and female **Psychographic:** Tech-savvy, like the latest gadgets **Behavior/Usage:** Mobile phone users and/or AT&T subscribers	"Introducing … The fastest most powerful iPhone yet."	iPhone Pictures, links to details of the phone, black phone with white background, Apple logo at the top muted in gray tones, much more on website	www.Apple.com TV spots, in-store displays, print ads, out-of-home, outdoor boards.
Ad 2 article	Techies and tech readers	"With the iPhone 3GS, Apple solidifies its leadership position in a crowded smart phone landscape." by Melissa J. Perenson, *PC World*	Picture of phone and article	Pcworld.com June 23, 2009
Ad 3 TV commercial showing iPhone with apps on face of phone	Someone who already owns an iPhone, or is considering switching to one	"There's an app for that."	Applications are highlighted, phone is highlighted, scrolls of pages are shown, phone sits in hand, icons, speed, easy to use	Prime time network television, weeknights, October

OK, now here's a blank grid. We've included these as pdf and .doc files at www.brandbuilderworkbook.com

INSTRUCTIONS: Just a reminder – you are to select three brands – one per worksheet. For each brand, find three examples of ads or communications that have been aired, printed (and most likely paid for) in the mass media or published as news articles. Dissect the communication pieces according to the grid.

BRAND (Name of company, product, or service) _____	TARGET (Describe who the advertisements are written for – describe the "who" as much as you can)	MESSAGE (What is the primary message of the ad? Maybe a headline, listed claims, and/or call to action.)	MESSAGE ELEMENTS (Note any designs, illustrations, photography, logos, symbols or color elements.)	MESSAGE WINDOWS (In what media did this advertisement appear?)
Ad 1				
Ad 2				
Ad 3				

Questions to answer:

Now it's time to give this all a bit of thought.

Here are some starter questions…

1. Of the three examples you selected, which piece of Messaging do you think best matched the spirit of the brand, and why?

2. Consider one of the brands you used. Do you see Messages that, if changed, would change the way you feel about the brand? If so, what are those changes? How would you feel about the brand if they were changed?

3. Did one Brand do something exceptionally well? If so, what was it?

4. Did one Brand do something poorly? What was it? How would you fix it?

5. Do you feel that any brand was particularly effective at selecting Message Windows to connect with the Target Audience?

6. Refer to the Brand you selected in Question 3. Do you believe the series of communications achieved any of their Business Goals? If so, why and how?

THE 4ᵀᴴ P AND THE MARCOM MATRIX

Remember that Fourth P? The one we called promotion.

That very large and very important "P" covers a whole range of promotional activities – from advertising to PR to event marketing and more. It even covers a promotional activity called Sales Promotion and – guess what – this often causes confusion.

To ease that confusion, we have a new matrix for you – this one will help you make the most of how your brand communicates. It's the MarCom Matrix.

The MarCom Matrix deals with Marketing Communications. After all, MarCom is short for, you guessed it, Marketing Communications.

A related term, Integrated Marketing Communications (IMC), was developed to address the growing range of activities and the need to keep things organized.

Now, a new phrase has entered the vocabulary – **Strategic Communications**. As more and more non-business entities – say a non-profit or a government health initiative – have adopted these same principles, some felt a need to include these types of activities without calling it "marketing."

It's communication with a purpose – it's strategic. You'll find this term used more and more. StratCom for short.

Here are the major pieces of that "Big P." How they're budgeted and prioritized is often called the "promotional mix." The major disciplines are Advertising, Sales Promotion, Public Relations, Direct Marketing, and New Media.

and more.

Two examples of "and more" would be Event Marketing – including all the marketing activities that revolve around an event – and Promotional Products – things ranging from the ball point pen and calendar from your local bank, to much more elaborate "business gifts," which might be used at a meeting for key customers.

Naturally, with all those things to choose from, *you're going to need to do some strategic prioritizing*. We may see a big budget marketer like McDonald's do something in almost every area of marketing. But, as a smaller marketer, you'll have to make tough choices.

So, the first thing you need to do is get your arms around your overall marketing objectives. The Four P's and the Brand Builder Matrix will help you do that.

Then, you'll want to have as many great ideas as possible – even though you won't have the budget for all of them. And, finally, you'll have to prioritize and make some more specific decisions about which MarCom programs – activities in that "fourth P" – will do your brand the most good.

The MarCom Matrix is a good place to start. It lays out all the basic types of Marketing Communications to help you think about the things you need to do.

A "Conceptual Model."

The MarCom Matrix is a "conceptual model" – a way for you to think about the range of options that are available to you. It's a starting point. And, as you learn more about each aspect of the matrix, you'll be able to make better decisions and do better work.

Now, let's take a quick look at each of the major MarCom areas – with a brief definition. You'll recognize many of the terms – as we've discussed them earlier.

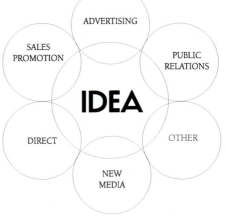

Figure 1.2: MarCom Matrix

Advertising: This is the part of the "P" that you're most familiar with – paid messages in familiar media: TV, radio, newspapers, magazines, outdoor, etc. For years, this was how the majority of brands spent the majority of their money. But now, there are many more options.

Sales Promotion: Simply put, it's the use of incentives to stimulate (promote) a certain behavior that will result in more sales. It may be a program to get your grocer to build a display in the store with a special on your favorite soft drink, or it may be a coupon in your Sunday newspaper. There are two major categories of Sales Promotion: One is **Consumer Promotion** with an objective of delivering incentives to target consumers. Second, is **Trade Promotion** with the objective of getting distribution from the trade. In some categories, like grocery products, this is a very, very big category of activity.

Public Relations: Here, the objective is to communicate to the public through non-paid media, for example, an article in a magazine, or a review in your newspaper. Perhaps a human interest story on the local news, or, victory of victories, an appearance on a national televions program.

Direct Marketing: This type of marketing takes the message direct to the consumer, often without paid media. Telemarketers, direct mail, e-mail, and broadcast faxing are the most common methods. During political season, door-to-door leaflets and voicemail telemarketing are popular. Direct response television is a form of direct marketing – like infomercials or the home shopping networks. One thing these methods have in common is that the message usually has a call to action.

To accomplish Direct Marketing you need three key factors:

1. **The Target List** – those to whom you direct your messages;
2. **The Offer** – what you provide as incentive to stimulate response; and
3. **The Message** – a simple deliverable, interesting message that can impact your results.

Sounds easy – yeah right! Chapter 10 discusses direct marketing, public relations, and sales promotions.

New Media: This is a simple phrase for a complex and growing collection of media channels. It starts with the Internet and your computer, but it also includes mobile phones, and a whole range of services, applications, websites, and social media networks.

Other ideas: Here are some additional interesting types of marketing activity:

Cause Marketing: You can connect your brand's messaging and marketing to a range of charitable events and activities.

Event Marketing: Other events, from local street fairs to major festivals, are looking to involve brands with sponsorships, sampling events, and other ways to connect with those that attend the events.

Sports Marketing: Sports is a unique type of event marketing that can connect your brand with the "Entertainment Brand" of a local sports team.

Promotional Products: "Trinkets and trash" can actually be a very smart and effective way to get your brand into people's lives. This is a whole area of marketing activity that can provide a very effective way for you to deliver your brand's message. For example, something as simple as a refrigerator magnet can be a valuable marketing tool for a local pizza delivery.

When all of the above elements work together, we call it **"IMC"** which stands for **Integrated Marketing Communication**. IMC is typically defined to include a whole range of MarCom (marketing communication) efforts that combine to meet marketing goals and **to give one voice** to the communications.

For example, when McDonald's brings their Monopoly™ game into their restaurants, the messaging is more than a logo on a drink cup. An ad announcing the game appears on television, it is highlighted on in-store posters or window peels. There might even be an ad in magazines or your local newspaper.

What if McDonald's were to run the contest and never told anyone except for the franchised store owners? Why does McDonald's have the game and contest to start with? Does the contest fit with the lifestyle of those who eat at McDonald's?

So, we actually have multiple levels of messaging here – one to the broader audience of people who eat at McDonald's (Business to Consumer) and from McDonald's to the franchise owners (internal corporate communications). And, of course, there is messaging that goes to the McDonald's crew members, so they remember to remind you to take a Monopoly piece along with your order. You also see that by integrating this contest with their mass advertising, McDonald's adds news and excitement to their general branding message.

We might also add that this is an example of what some marketers call the "Fifth P" – People. McDonald's has to engage two internal audiences – the franchisees and the crew members – to ensure that this is a successful program.

BRAIN-BUILDER EXERCISE 1.3:
Integrating Branding Activities

The purpose of this exercise is to stretch your brain a bit and think about how one of your previously selected brands has used Integrated Marketing communications.

Instructions: Go back to Exercise 1 and select a brand for which you can find examples of how they have used various communications according to the MarCom Matrix. Using the worksheet, jot down notes in each area for which you find examples. Keep the ideas, samples, tear sheets in your folder. Store electronic files in a thumb drive.

A MarCom Matrix Worksheet.

A full-page version is available at brandbuilderworkbook.com.

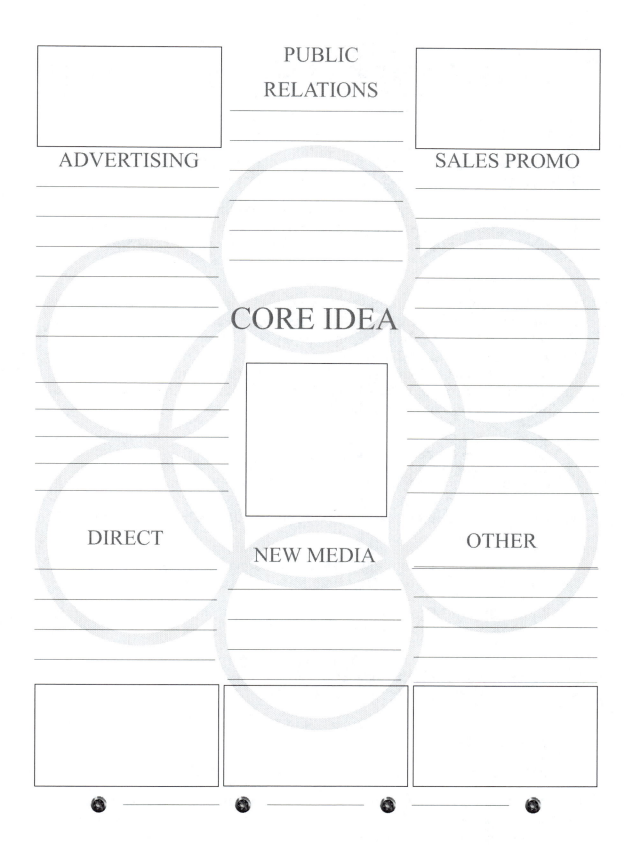

PUBLIC
RELATIONS

ADVERTISING

SALES PROMO

CORE IDEA

DIRECT

NEW MEDIA

OTHER

BRAIN-BUILDER EXERCISE 1.4: Competitive Brands

Just like getting ready for a big game, we can learn a lot by studying those with whom we'll be competing.

Instructions: Find a brand that's a competitor of one of the brands you selected. Collect communication and advertising materials for the competitive brand.

The questions you will be asked are primarily the same ones you answered in the previous assignment: target, message, message elements, message windows. I'll do an example for you first – how about smart phones?

T-Mobile HTC G1 TM

When we looked at the Apple iPhone, we had to decide which competitor to pick. At the time, I found 32 *different* manufacturers of smart phones! By now, there are probably more. Smart phones are in a very hot industry. One of the iPhone's primary competitors is HTC T-Mobile G1. Google has cobranded with HTC G1 model and T-Mobile. Brilliant! Who is the Google generation? 13–25 year olds. Who is T-Mobile targeting? Close. The 20-something's are the first to pick up the G1. Very tech savvy, hip, "pay $200 for a phone before they buy groceries" target audience.

Go to YouTube to check out their TV ads.

By the time you read this, both Apple, T-Mobile, and the smart phone industry will have matured and their marketing communications will have changed. My guess is they will still show the primary features and benefits that will attract the target to their brand.

But it also might be interesting for you to pick another, newer competitor and take a look at how things have changed – and how fast they change.

Oh wait, the DROID is in its thrid generation – see what I mean? How many phones are using the Android software?

The unique benefit for the T-Mobile G1 is Google's very recognizable brand with commonly used search applications. The Apple apps are new and gaining recognition, but might be seen a copycat or a fad.

Many of the other smart phones are look-a-likes. The primary message is about the Google applications.

By the way, the ad for T-Mobile appeared on the T-Mobile website.

How do you shop for cell phones? Probably not by sitting and watching TV, reading a magazine, or driving by a billboard. However, you probably do see it flash on TV, check with your friends, and go to the internet to see what you can find.

I would expect my students to complete this exercise by watching TV, checking on the internet, and asking their friends and relatives for ideas. I found the Apple TV spot on their own website. Now it's your turn...

1. Name your original Brand: (Select one from Exercise 1.2)

2. Name your Brand's competitor (repeat this question as often as you wish with additional competitors)

3. Describe your Target. Who is the target audience of the competitor? Is there more than one target group? Do the brands compete for the same audience? If so, how? If not, how is your brand unique?

4. What are the primary Messages of the competitor?
    Is it the same message as your brand or a different message?

5. Describe the creative delivery of the message, as well any graphic or creative elements.

6. Did the media or message window have any effect on how you understood the brand? Explain why the message window was important.

BRAIN-BUILDER BONUS – "The Big Nothing."

When we think about the Competition, we also need to remember that, in many cases, one of our biggest competitors is... nothing.

The competition for our retail brand might be staying home and doing nothing – not shopping at a competitive store. This is particularly true when the category involves discretionary spending.

Sometimes we can do something about it. Other times, we just have to accept the fact that, for some potential customers, nothing will do. Literally.

A BRAND-BUILDER CASE: The Learning Center

Here's an example of what we're talking about – a small example.

We're all familiar with big brands like McDonald's. Here's one that's a little more people-sized. It's for our local library – and it turned out nicely. Here's the story.

During one of my summer classes, a student brand-building team worked together to build a brand identity for our campus library. As you might imagine, accessibility to the client was very easy, and played a critical role in the success of this project.

Our task: to build an identity for this new brand – and a message.

Brand: For a start, the brand was changing names. The library had changed it's name to The Learning Center. The complete brand name was Hickman-Johnson-Furrow Learning Center at Morningside College. You can see why we focused on the short version – The Learning Center.

Business Goals: In addition to building awareness for our new brand name, our business goal was simple – to drive traffic to the library. We wanted to make it a preferred destination.

Our Target: It was clear – students at our school – Morningside College. But even here, we had to understand a whole new pattern of behavior – Primary Targets and Secondary Targets. The students at the college were the primary target audience. The faculty was the secondary target group. We needed to find out more. Time for some research.

Our first research goal: We needed to understand our target's decision-making process. How do people use the library? Academic libraries are facing changes across the country. They still have knowledgeable staff to help with research, writing, and the process of finding valuable information. Many of those who may need help often sit in their office, at their desk in their dorm room, or laptop on their lap and work on their own. The internet and the digital media has changed academic libraries forever. But even with Google and Wikipedia, people need help.

Message and Message Windows: The student team used the method you are about to learn in this workbook. They designed the logo and determined the visual messaging. Even here in Iowa there are a lot of competing messages. We needed to develop a clean, simple message that told our Target we had resources that were in tune with the way they study today. After a lot of discussion, we came to a simple, but meaningful message.

Here's the short version:

Brand: The Learning Center. Full Brand Name: Hickman-Johnson-Furrow Learning Center, Morningside College

Business Goals: Build brand awareness for the new name. Drive traffic to The Learning Center

Target Audience: Students (Primary), Faculty (Secondary)

Message: Connect Yourself.

Additional Messaging: We also developed a very nice visual message for the center, using the full name of the Center and a recognizable piece of architecture that helped us unify the entire name. We also added a sub-theme that reinforced the "Connect Yourself" message: Relax, Study, Get Help

Message Windows: Our campus has a number of opportunities that do a pretty good job connecting with Morningside students.

- **Advertising:** We put our message on Posters (3) and Campus Radio (:30).
- **Event Marketing:** We also did a bit of Event Marketing for Students: Frisbee Golf, Read-a-thon (with prizes), and a Research Seminar. For the Faculty, we had a Beginning of the Year Kick Off and a Faculty Appreciation event, with invitations for both.
- **Public Relations:** The local news provided additional windows. We produced Press Releases for the Collegiate Reporter and Sioux City Journal for the Faculty Appreciation and Read-a-thon events.
- **Promotional Products:** As it turned out, we also had opportunities for Promotional Products that allowed students to show our brand in appropriate places around campus. We produced "Connect Yourself" Frisbees, Pens, Coffee mugs, and T-shirts.

Inspiration for Logo   *New Logo*

Posters and Promotional Products

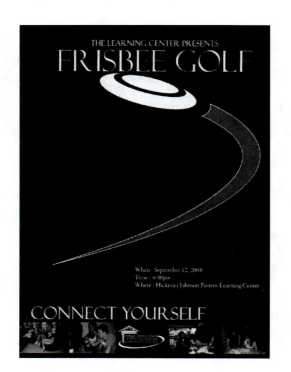

- **A Promotion with Personality:** Finally, we realized we had a new sub-theme with a bit of personality. Jim is one of the Learning Center's librarians, and was a popular "go-to" person for the students. After conducting primary research, results indicated students identified Jim as the most memorable *person* in the library. The team decided to play up his identity in the message. We developed an "Ask Jim" campaign complete with T-shirt and candy wrapper.

Joe, the artist, captured Jim's caricature with 'traditional' library tools of the trade. The caricature was used in a number of message windows. Here you see it on T-shirts.

Learning from the Learning Center

Students started the summer thinking "this is a boring project". Sometimes the word "boring" is tossed around pretty easily with students. Right? By the end of the summer semester, they realized they had made a difference.

Each time they met with a librarian, they understood the impact their work in creating a Brand identity would have. Students said, "The Library really needed our help to reach out to students and faculty." "I can't wait to see what they do with the campaign. I was really proud to work with our team."

Jim at the library was the key person to make sure we had what we needed and was the one who asked for my help at the beginning. This group was deep in talent and short on time (as all college students are), but dedicated to Jim, the library, Morningside College, and each other. And they learned something else important. *Building brands is a team sport!*

Jeremy and I critiquing one more draft of the book before The Pitch.

Last but Not Least. The Pitch.

Building Brands doesn't stay in the classroom. At some point, your student team has to present to the Brand's decision makers. It might be an owner, an advisory board, or judges at a student competition.

We call that presentation The Pitch. It's a Brand Builder's final exam.

Chapter 12 covers this critical stage in detail. As you get your team organized, you might want to skip ahead to that chapter and think about how you'll want to schedule your team's activities in the time allotted.

CAMPAIGN DEVELOPMENT STEPS

Now you're ready to start building your own campaign.

You are at the beginning of an exciting journey. You're going to build a brand. Your job is to understand your brand's Business Goals, your source of business, and the Target, and then create Messages and deliver them through the best Message Windows to persuade your Target to act favorably toward your brand.

There are a lot more details involved in getting this process right. You'll need to make good decisions every step of the way. To do that, we'll work through a process used by brands big and small.

Once you learn that process, you'll be a valuable contributor in a wide range of brands and organizations – a small to medium size enterprise, nonprofit agency, school organization, large corporation, or your own business. For all of these, the concepts and the process are the same.

The nine steps of Campaign Development (Figure 1.3) are:

1. Situation analysis
2. Research plan
3. Primary research
4. Target audience description
5. Goal Setting
6. Creative strategy
7. Extended media section
8. Creative executions, and finally
9. The Pitch

This book will guide you through all these steps as you build your brand's communication program. Business Goals, Target, Message, and Message Windows. But, first, let's take a breath and review what we've learned.

Campaign Development

Situation Analysis	Research Plan	Primary Research	Target Audience	Goal Setting	Creative Strategy	Prioritizing	Creative Executions	The Pitch
Define the Problem advertising can solve	10 Step Research Process	Brand, Purchasing Behavior, Target Audience	Target Sketch Demographics and Psychographics	SWOT	Creative Tool Chest	Marketing Services	Traditional Media: Radio, Television, Magazine, Newspaper, Outdoor, Transit	Book
Conduct Brand Audit. Use Brand Analysis. Answer the question, "Where are we?"		Quantitative and Qualitative Methodology		Marketing Objective	Big Idea	Media: Traditional and New Media	Nontraditional and New Media: Internet, Social Media, Nontraditional outlets	CD
	Literature Review of Industry, Target, Competition	Design questions		Positioning Statement	Tagline	Evaluation		Pitch
Complete Competition Analysis		Research Proposal and Report						

Figure 1.3: The Nine Steps of Campaign Development

CHAPTER REVIEW

In this first chapter, we covered:

1. The difference between marketing and advertising

2. Branding and why it is important

3. The Four P's and the marketing mix

4. Some basic definitions

5. Various types of brand.

6. The Brand-Builder Matrix – Business Goals, Target, Message, and Message Windows

7. The MarCom Matrix

8. The steps and elements of Campaign Development

REVIEW QUESTIONS

1. In your words (or ours), explain what a brand is.

2. How do branding, marketing, and advertising differ from each other? How are they similar?

3. Describe the Brand Builder Matrix.

4. Describe the MarCom Matrix.

5. What are the nine steps in Campaign Development?

READINGS AND RESOURCES

Avery, Jim (2010). *Advertising Campaign Planning.* The Copy Workshop, Chicago, Il.

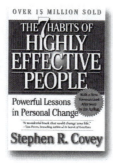

Bendinger, Bruce (2009). *Advertising the Business of Brands, 4th Edition.* The Copy Workshop, Chicago, Il.

Covey, Steven (1990). *The 7 Habits of Highly Effective People.* Free Press, New York.

Most books are available, new and used, through Amazon. Books from The Copy Workshop are available at a 20% discount from adbuzz.com in the Book Shop.

CHAPTER 2:
WHO. WHAT. WHAT.

Now let's ask some key questions we'll have to answer.

- Who is this book for? The Target Audience – which includes you.
- What's going to be involved? This will be kind of an introduction to how we're going to work.
- What are some examples? One of the best ways to learn is to see how it all works – start to finish. So we'll show you four examples of work done by teams just like yours.

As you work your way through the brand-building process, the idea of your Target Audience will be one of the most important considerations. After all, if your brand doesn't connect with its target, you won't have much of a brand.

As Peter Drucker, one of the finest marketing thinkers observed, *"the purpose of a business is to create and keep a customer."*

Sounds simple. But is it? We're all smart shoppers and we live in a world full of companies that want us to be their customer. Well, let's start by talking about who the customers might be for this book.

For a start, let's talk about you and look at some key characteristics of our target.

Someone who wants to build a brand. Makes sense. That target group probably breaks up into two important subgroups.

- **A student** who wants to learn how to build brands in general.
- **An entrepreneur or member of an organization** who wants to learn how to build a specific brand – their brand.

Now these two groups are similar, but a bit different. It's sort of like the difference between ham and eggs. Know the difference? As the pig said to the chicken, "For you, eggs is involvement. For me, ham is *commitment!*"

Our student target is involved and wants to learn – but it's not "do or die."

Our entrepreneurial target is deeply committed – in time, money, and emotion, and it is very much "do or die." There's a lot on the line.

Even though that's a big difference, both groups have a lot in common:

- **You Want to Build a Brand.** Whether you're in a class that teaches entrepreneurship, **or** rolling up your sleeves at the kitchen table, you want to do this.

- **You Want to Develop Some Skills.** You probably know that people who can build brands are in demand in the job market. Well, you're right. Even though it's a lot of hard work, just about every business wants people who can help them build that business. This book will help you develop the communications skills you need to build a brand. (P.S. Naturally, there are other necessary skills as well, like finance, manufacturing, and supply chain management. You'll probably want to team up with people who have those skills).

- **You've Got a Lot to Learn.** You know you're not there yet. And you may already be seeing a few terms that may be a little bit strange – like what's a SWOT Analysis? The good news is we're pretty good at helping you learn these things. We won't say that the things you need to learn will be easy – but we're going to be as clear as possible. Some of it may even be fun!

WHAT'S GOING TO BE INVOLVED?

We think a good way to introduce you to the Brand-Building process is to give you a few quick examples of work done by your fellow Target Audience: students, entrepreneurs, interesting non-profits, and a small start-up. And, as time goes on, you'll see more and more of those examples on our site – www.brandbuilderworkbook.com.

Along the way, we'll meet some students and look at the problems they solved and the brands they built.

In one semester, they went from slouching in their seats to running their teams. They went from hating 'group projects' to understanding how much fun playing on a winning marketing communications team can be.

The students you'll meet are real. The brands are actual. The stories are true, though they may not be big and sexy. They're slices of life from the heart of America.

The first day of class

The first day of class will probably go something like this.

You'll meet your classmates and you'll either:

- meet the marketing problem you'll have to solve – and the brand you'll have to build, or,
- your first assignment will be finding a brand to build.

Either way, this is serious, meaningful work, and some brand out there will be counting on you. Scary.

Here are a few examples of the kind of projects you might find.

- A local non-profit
- A government communications project
- A retail health clinic
- A "long tail" non-profit

That's just a beginning list. Your brand could be a local sports team, a friend's bar or restaurant, or a brand new, high-tech project. Building brands – large or small – can be a lot of fun and very satisfying. Here goes.

Example #1: A local non-profit.
"Musicians and the kids in the summer"

The Brand: Sioux City Chamber Music

The Problem: A decrease in attendance of events and membership

Eight students from the class started the project. The initial meeting was with a lead member from the Chamber Music Board.

Here's what they did for a start:

- Analyzed the situation by completing a Brand Analysis,
- Completed some secondary research (researching related articles and examples of chamber music and classical music groups),
- Conducted a focus group of board members, and
- Developed and completed a membership survey.

This was great initial learning for both the team and the brand – none of this had been completed by the Chamber Board in recent years. You may be surprised to find out how much is "assumed" and how little people know about their own businesses or brands.

You'll usually find that this is your first job – "knowing what you *know*" and "knowing what you *don't know*." Even if you're still only a student, there's often a lot you can teach yourself.

In this case, two students moderated the focus group, while other students took notes. Two students drafted and tested the survey, while others typed the envelopes and did the mailing.

Every student completed secondary research. It sure is a lot easier these days (and produces better research) with the resources of our library databases, like JSTOR, EBSCO host, Lexis Nexis, Google Scholar, and the Internet. Academic journals, trade and industry news, and websites of similar organizations also contribute to helping you analyze the situation. Every student participated in completing the Brand Analysis and tabulating the survey.

We'll tell you the results in a bit. Let's go through the whole process first.

SWOTs and Targets.

Now that we had some information based on our research, it was time to start doing some thinking.

We did two kinds of thinking. First, a far-ranging "what if" discussion of the brand's Strengths, Weaknesses, Opportunities, and Threats. Look at the first letter of each word. Strengths, Weaknesses, Opportunities, Threats. S.W.O.T.

Now you know why they call it a SWOT analysis.

It was also time to get to know our Target better. As a matter of fact, it's almost always time to get to know your Target better. In this case, the team created a primary target sketch and a secondary target sketch. The result? Now the student team knew *who* they were talking to.

Messages and Message Windows.

See how the process gets us smarter each step of the way? Now it was time to use the next set of brand-building tools we had to craft the messaging and figure out the best way to get the message to the Target Audience.

We used two new tools: the Creative Brief and the Creative Action Plan. We used these tools and our well-exercised brains to develop what we believed to be the best message for Sioux City Chamber Music.

In the beginning, the team generated six to ten average ideas. After a street test the results were the same. Our first ideas were just average – but we learned. Even when the tools and the process are in place it isn't easy. Sometimes you have to work extra hard to find the inspiration it takes for truly exceptional and effective work. Sometimes you're wrong a few times on the way to getting it right.

Going through this process the first time under a time crunch can be difficult. But you know something is starting to develop. I could see the signs of the *right* message within their work starting to emerge. But, I needed the students to discover it. As they say, sometimes it's hard to read the label when you're inside the bottle.

In this case, their positioning statement gave them the clue they needed. One reason we use a range of tools in the brand-building process is that sometimes one tool works better than others.

We started to cross off words that had little or no meaning to the brand and the target. Here is the positioning statement. It was inspired by their mission statement.

With a long-standing tradition, Sioux City Chamber Music delivers exceptional classical music in a small and intimate setting.

One of the things you need to know is simply what's important. Many things are true. What things are most important? We decided we needed the strongest three words to deliver on the Brand's promise.

We wrote down the following words and started the debate.

Tradition Exceptional Classical Music Small Intimate

If none of these words were strong enough, we could look for other words and phrases that related. But, in this case, we didn't need to.

Now we knew, because of our research, that our Target was both literate and literal. They read a lot and they wanted a clear simple message that accurately described the Brand experience.

I remember advising the group, "when you have the Logo with your Brand name and the message as your tag line, you will say everything all together." Within minutes, they found their Brand's message.

Sioux City Chamber Music...Exceptional, Classical, Intimate.

With that clear guideline, the team's lead designer developed the logo over a number of drafts, based on feedback received from the focus group.

The focus group served two purposes – to help understand the purchase behavior of those who attended Chamber Music events, and to see if they were open to updating the images of the Chamber communication pieces. (They were.)

Amber, the designer, studied classical music websites (not very common) and symphony websites (very common). The color black is often used to match and compliment the musicians and their instruments. Black depicts a certain sophistication and richness.

But we also had to communicate a somewhat updated brand image – to intrigue, to stimulate retrial by those who had stopped going, and to attract new members.

She designed neon lettering and colors to show that a more modern Chamber Music group was on the scene. She is very modest about how quickly it came to her, but her team, the Chamber, and target audience provided the inspiration she needed.

Here's how it all worked out.

Brand: Sioux City Chamber Music

Business Goals: Increase membership, and ticket sales
        Develop a future audience with a school outreach program

Target Audience:
       Primary Target: Classical Music lovers
       Secondary Target: Elementary Students and Educators

Message: Exceptional, Classical, Intimate

Time for the next stage of the process. Now that we knew what to say, we needed to figure out where to say it – and how to do so in an affordable way.

We had to find the right "windows" to deliver those messages.

In this case, we had a local classical radio station and the names and addresses of current and former supporters of the organization. We also had lists of others who had supported cultural events in Sioux City – theatrical groups, concerts, art shows.

From the SWOT Analysis, we identified one other important window – our school system. We developed an event-marketing program that brought the product to this sizable Secondary Target. And, for those who liked the experience, we made it easy for the young students to bring their parents to an upcoming concert.

We also added Public Relations and Promotional Products to our big "P" of Promotion. Here's how the program looked.

Message Windows:
Advertising:
  Radio (30 seconds): Doreen's Jazz New Orleans
    KWIT (local classical station)

Television: Donated space from local channels, slide show of logo and featured musicians

Posters: for public places

Public Relations:
Radio/TV/Newspaper public calendars
Around Siouxland – KTIV – bring artists to television talk shows

Direct:
Direct Mail: Postcards for members, educators, and school programs
Membership mailer: This was a key tactic for achieving our goal of increased membership.

Event Marketing:
School Events: Connect Chamber musicians with educators and students
Distributed tickets to kids through Big Brothers/Big Sisters

Created a new event called a 'Hall of Fame' for exceptional musicians – name of the event would need to be determined

Promotion Products:
Pens, tablets, others as budgets allow

The Pitch.

Often, particularly as a student, you have to present your plan for the Brand to someone else – often the decision-makers (and check writers) that run the Brand.

If it's your brand – and you're the entrepreneur – you may still need to present to decision-makers and check-writers – usually bankers, venture capitalists, potential investors, business partners, etc. So, either way, you'll usually need to pull your program together into a persuasive presentation.

The rest of the story

The last day of summer school was the day of The Pitch. Three board members were present to hear the students' presentation. You can imagine the excitement over the reinvention of The Chamber Music brand. It was a proud and noble moment! In this case, the board adopted our recommendation virtually in its entirety.

BRAIN-BUILDER EXERCISE 2.1:
Sioux City Chamber Music's Brand Builder Matrix

This will be pretty simple, but a review of the elements is important.

Instructions: Read through the Chamber Music case above and identify the four elements of the Brand Builder Matrix.

Business Goals: _____

Target: _____

Message: _____

Message Windows: _____

Example #2:
Human Rights Commission, a Challenge in a Municipality

It's amazing what can be considered a Brand these days. This time, it was our Human Rights Commission (HRC), an official city organization run by an office of three, handling a case load big enough for a much larger staffr. Most cities (or municipalities) in small-to-large markets have a Human Rights Commission.

The purpose of the HRC is to ensure a fair and equitable community for all and to eliminate discrimination. It is a group that can utilize college volunteers, and was an excellent candidate for a marketing project.

As we noted, many things can be brands. In this case, the Brand was an event – sort of a sub-brand for the overall Brand.

It was a project with two very different challenges.

The first challenge was to help communicate an event – The Faces of Siouxland. This was a multicultural fair for the people who live in the area we call Siouxland.

For those of you who don't live in the neighborhood, Sioux City is made up of three different Sioux Cities – including North Sioux City and South Sioux City. The locals refer to the community as Siouxland. It's located in parts of Iowa, Nebraska, and South Dakota.

The HRC Brand's second challenge was to help communicate something called the 'Rights of the Renters.' You'll find that often clients want to do too much. This was the case here. While this was a program worthy of attention, we had to limit what we could do with the time, budget, and resources available. We secured an agreement that "The Faces of Siouxland" would be the focus of the initial communication.

You can see the problem reflected in a more complex set of Business Goals.

Brand: Human Rights Commission

Business Goals:

- Long term: Build awareness, communicate mission

- Short term: Promote Event – The Faces of Siouxland,

- Secondary communication goal: Communicate, if possible, that housing discrimination violations will not be tolerated – Rights of the Renters

Target: Siouxland residents

Message: Event information – The Faces of Siouxland

In this case, we had two different student teams, and we ended up with three different Branding concepts, and, no surprise, different emphasis in the messaging.

Concept 1 – Message: Striving for Tomorrow
New Logo: This design was inspired by the Sioux City Clock Tower, a city landmark

Message Window: Poster design, easily transferable to newspaper

Concept 2 – Message: Faces of Siouxland, kids faces
We'll show you the poster for this one as it was the best-looking of the three.

New Logo can show dates and times of event

Message Window: Poster, Postcard, e-cards

Concept 3 – Message: Free Admission, Cultural fair, date, place, etc.
New Logo Design with young face image over flag (address is not shown)

Message Window: Posters, Postcards, e-cards

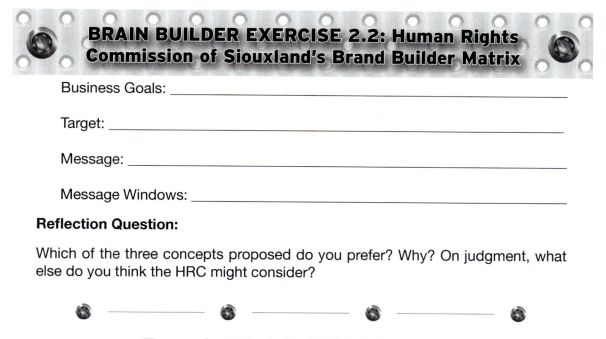

BRAIN BUILDER EXERCISE 2.2: Human Rights Commission of Siouxland's Brand Builder Matrix

Business Goals: _____

Target: _____

Message: _____

Message Windows: _____

Reflection Question:

Which of the three concepts proposed do you prefer? Why? On judgment, what else do you think the HRC might consider?

Example #3: A Retail Health Clinic

A Get Well Soon Story

Ideas for a brand or a business can come from almost anywhere – so can companies that become Brands – and each seems to have a new lesson to teach us.

Here's what happened…

One Monday afternoon I received a call from a friend who wanted to show me something. This friend is a lawyer and a partner in a radio station. He dropped enough hints over the phone to get my interest.

Perhaps we should all be careful with these kinds of phone calls because, before we know it, we find ourselves with another project. But I was *very* curious. So, I agreed. "Meet me in the library." I said, promoting a recent project, "You'll like the new coffee shop." "Great," he said, "see you Thursday."

During coffee, I found out about his new business idea, and his interest in getting help from my students.

The idea? A retail health clinic for common health care needs – flu shots, ear aches, vaccinations, school check-ups, etc. It was designed to be affordable and quick.

A business was born. What would they call their new "baby"? After much deliberation – they named it CuraQuick. Here's the logo:

Names are important. Cura is a Latin name for care and Quick because, well, the care was to be delivered quickly. Not only that, you could also get any prescriptions you might need quickly, as well.

Having the location of the clinic in a convenient retail outlet with pharmaceutical services would make it easy for the consumer – easier to find, easier to park, no waiting, no appointments. Yes. Quick!

They even had a pretty nice tag line. CuraQuick - Get Well Soon!

The clinic was staffed with Nurse Practitioners and Physician Assistants.

They already had a number of them located in HyVee Grocery Stores. At the time of our meeting, they'd been in business for almost a year.

The brand's advantages were fairly clear:

- Get diagnosed sooner
- Get your medicine sooner
- Get well sooner.

All this would happen at HyVee. Anyone could go in and pay a fixed amount and not wait, get antibiotics for their kid's ear aches, or to be checked for bronchitis – without waiting for an appointment with their doctor.

CuraQuick was becoming very big, very fast. The prospects of this business model were very exciting. It could change the way health care could be administered – or could it? It was already getting complicated.

For a start, HyVee wanted exclusive rights to the CuraQuick Brand and wanted to open more than 20 clinics. It was all pretty interesting. My friend asked if I had some students who might be interested.

I wasn't teaching a class at that time, but I did recruit three students to serve as a research team for the CuraQuick Brand.

Erin, Laura, and John had already learned the basic principles. They divided up the work and collaborated on the research. Once they delivered their reports, the client made a deal with the hospital in Sioux Falls to co-brand with them.

The Brand – CuraQuick – was growing even while we were in the coffee shop drinking coffee, and during the two-to-three months the students were completing their research. But the marketplace was already teaching us lessons.

This market segment was in a rapid growth phase, both regionally and nationally.

One big factor was a shortage of nurse practitioners and physician assistants to support the business model for the retail clinics. The demand was greater than the supply. Sometimes things look better on paper than in the real world.

The next interesting fact: our target audience was not clearly known. You can picture a certain audience, but who actually walks in the door might be different.

Was it people with insurance or people without insurance?

When you start to develop your message strategy and your pricing strategy, you will attract a certain person. The initial price was $25. Later, it changed to $49.

Would it be men who hated to go to the doctor and wait in line, or mostly moms with sick children? And then, would it be men who hated to wait in the same line with moms who had sick children, but didn't have insurance. All good questions.

The questions kept building. Would it be the business owner, self-insured organization (group plan), or someone off the street who didn't have a family doctor and couldn't afford regular health care? Who would benefit most from and pay for a CuraQuick visit?

At the time, the concept of a CuraQuick was unique to smaller markets in the Midwest. This was 2007. There were very few retail health clinics, and the concept of Urgent Care clinics was growing. Some of the models in the United States for retail health clinics were being introduced in shopping malls, stand-alone pharmacies, grocery stores, government buildings, and corporate buildings.

It truly was an entrepreneurial landscape. Very exciting.

The Minute Clinic pioneered the idea and continues to find steady growth by partnering (note co-Branding) with select CVS Pharmacies. Meanwhile, Wal-Mart partnered with RediClinic.

We had new partners, too. Mercy Hospitals and Avera-McKenna Hospitals partnered with CuraQuick. But, rapid growth is often accompanied by growing pains.

The man who hated to go to the doctor and the mom with sick children needed to know about these places, CuraQuick was a brand new Brand. Awareness and knowledge about this concept was very low.

Erin, Laura, and John completed a competitor analysis and provided on-site customer observation at CuraQuick clinics in two cities. They observed that signage in the HyVee stores seemed to be minimum. For such a new concept, this hurt. However, it was a call by HyVee, not by CuraQuick.

The results of the competitor analysis were presented in a comparison chart illustrating features and benefits of some ten different regional and national retail health clinic brands. The CuraQuick website was strong, and supported a corporate identity.

Additional secondary data was also gathered and reported to the client. After the last research report, the student's work was complete. Sometimes you'll find that providing information from the marketplace is one of the most valuable services you can provide to new entrepreneurs, who are often too busy to do this vital work.

Things can happen fast in the entrepreneurial world.

CuraQuick's life changed. Quick. By 2009, just two years later, HyVee found they could not support all the locations they originally opened.

Things changed further. Avera-McKenna Hospitals of Sioux Falls became a partner with the HyVee location in Sioux Falls. Five CuraQuick clinics serve HyVee shoppers at the time of this writing.

So where is CuraQuick today?

Two of the three original partners are still with CuraQuick. They would tell you that to build a brand in the health care industry you have to be flexible, have good resources, and be quick to recognize when to stay in and when to get out.

One of the best ways to learn is to teach. And for Erin, Laura, and John, participating in this exciting, fast-changing project was an invaluable learning experience.

Not every entrepreneurial venture is orderly – the way it may seem in a textbook. Real world experience, particularly in a growth market situation, can be an exciting and valuable lesson – one that keeps paying off in that slightly messy business environment we call the real world.

BRAIN BUILDER EXERCISE 2.3:
Growth Opportunities

CuraQuick was in a "growth category." Others with the same idea and objective were starting up. This exercise will help develop an entrepreneurial mindset.

Reflection Questions:

1. List other "growth categories" that come to mind.

2. What local growth opportunities come to mind?

3. Name two "hot" trends that are happening right now.

Example #4 – A "Long Tail" non-profit

"RESTORING A LOST PAGE IN A NATION'S HISTORY"

That was the headline in a *Chicago Sun-Times* article featuring The Czech Legion Project, a non-profit with a narrow target audience that reaches around the world.

It all started when two friends, Bruce and John, discovered a story hardly anyone knew – an amazing story about how a college professor and tens of thousands of prisoners-of-war joined together to create a country in the middle of World War One.

It was the story of Czechoslovakia – and fifty years of Communist rule had virtually erased this story from the pages of history.

They started with a big idea – and a very small target market.

"A Long Tail Project"

Know what a "long tail" is?

Take a look at this Bell Curve – it's a pretty common shape – and the thing most companies do is look for something that will appeal to the big hunk of curve in the middle. And, if they have to "ramp up" their business, they'll usually start on the left, with what we call "early adopters."

Now take a look at that little bit of the curve on the right – that's what we call the "long tail." It's a very small piece of the overall market. Well, if you give it a thought, something that has to do with a small country and something that happened almost 100 years ago, well that's a pretty small group.

And, as The Czech Legion Project planned their brand campaign, they knew that they would have a slow development process, with a small, but very interested group – people from all over the world whose fathers and grandfathers had fought in the Legion, and those who still remembered the First Republic of Czechoslovakia. Their message? *"The most amazing story you've never heard."*

A small start.

They opened for business with a Web address – www.czechlegion.com – and, sure enough, little by little, people would sign up. One person would tell  another. At each connection they collected e-mail addresses.

Some had a grandfather in the Legion. Some were just interested in history. And a few groups were more than a little interested – like Chicago's Bohemian Lawyer Association and the Sokols (Czech athletic clubs).

Slowly, they developed a support group. They connected with the Foreign Ministry of the Czech Republic – which was surprised and delighted to find a project like this in the USA. They connected with Czech-American groups in the US – and, pretty soon, they connected overseas. Step by step.

They achieved non-profit status, which made donations tax-deductible – and they learned how to fill out forms for grants from foundations. They even identified a few companies that might be interested in sponsorship.

With the website, their legal status as a 501c3 non-profit corporation, and a bit of foundation money, they took the money they raised and produced a documentary – *Accidental Army: The Amazing True Story of the Czechoslovak Legion*. They had a premiere at the Chicago History Museum, and it was standing room only.

People came to their Chicago premiere from as far away as California. It was a long tail, indeed. Then, they raised a little more money and produced a DVD – and they sold them. Not a lot, but Amazon is good for "long tail" sales.

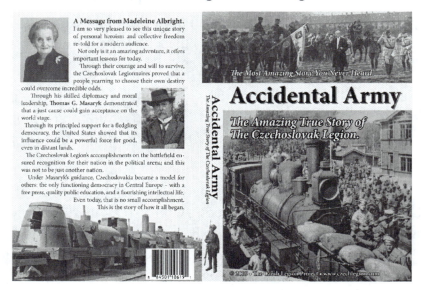

Former Secretary of State Madeleine Albright, daughter of a Czech diplomat from the First Republic, wrote some words of support. Ken Burns, the famous documentary producer called it, "a noble undertaking, a history lost; returned to its people – and the world." And, with patience, the brand grew. And the tail got longer.

Bruce at the Brno premiere with Legion re-enactors.

Then, Bruce and John visited the Czech Republic and made some new friends. The next step was adding a Czech soundtrack to their movie. They had a premiere in Brno – the second largest city in the Czech Republic. The long tail led them back to where the story began.

Today, high school students in the Czech Republic can re-discover their history because a few people in Chicago knew how to build a non-profit brand from a very small beginning – by grabbing that "long tail" and pulling themselves along.

BRAIN BUILDER EXERCISE 2.4: The Czech Legion Project's Brand Builder Matrix

How would you "fill in the blanks" for the Czech Legion Project? (If you need more information, go to their website – www.czechlegion.com.)

Business Goals: _____

Target: _____

Message: _____

Message Windows: _____

Reflection Questions:

1. How would you describe the "long tail" to a friend?

2. Do you have a special interest that might be described as "long tail?"

3. How has the Internet helped make long tail projects more possible and practical?

Building the Connection
Between Brands and Their Target Audience.

Your idea might have a bigger target, or a more local target, but the basics are still the same. Identify that Target Audience – particularly the ones who are really interested – and, as you get to know your Target, you will become smarter about how to build your brand.

The previous examples show a few ways that brands can connect with their target.

Even if you're a small brand, you'll be using some of the same techniques and principles that the bigger brands use. And, big or small, you'll find message windows everywhere. And you'll start to see that almost everything is, in some ways, a brand – the stores you shop at, the products you see on the shelves, the sports teams, rock bands, and auditoriums, theater groups and charities of every size. They're all brands.

They all look to build by connecting with a Target Audience of potential customers and meeting their needs. And they usually need someone to help them.

So if you can develop those brand-building skills, one of those brands may need you. You'll be a Target Audience they'll want to hire.

CHAPTER REVIEW

In this chapter we reviewed:

1. The target audience for this book
2. Brands that can be analyzed using the Brand Builder Matrix
   a. Musical group
   b. Public service organization
   c. Entrepreneurial venture
   d. Non-profit organization

REVIEW QUESTIONS

1. What are the distinguishing elements about the stories from this chapter that you believe helped drive the branding activity?
   a. Sioux City Chamber Music

   b. Human Rights Commission of Siouxland

   c. CuraQuick

   d. Czech Legion Project

2. Describe yourself as the target for this book. Use specific descriptors that are noted below.
   a. Demographics (age, education, gender, income, marital status)

   b. Psychographics (values, attitude, lifestyles and opinions)

   c. Interests (hobbies, memberships)

3. How do you feel this book will meet the needs of the target audience? What specific features and benefits do you think the book offers? (Use yourself here if you wish).

4. Explain how you plan to use your new-found skills in brand building.

READINGS AND RESOURCES

Fortini-Campbell, L. (1994). *Hitting the Sweet Spot*, 4th printing. The Copy Workshop, Chicago, IL. Identifying key insights to inspire and reach your target audience. Named as one of the Ten Essential Reads for marketers in 2009 by *Business Week*.

Luecke, R. (2006). *Harvard Business Essentials – Marketer's Toolkit.* Harvard Business School Publishing, Boston, MA. Written as a mentor and guide for doing business.

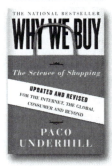

Underhill, P. (2008). *Why We Buy: The Science of Shopping – Updated, Revised Edition.* Simon & Schuster. New York.

CHAPTER 3:
ESTABLISHING YOUR BRAND

WHAT'S THE IDEA OF YOUR BRAND?

"Start your brand building with a simple, meaningfully different idea and, only after you've done this, figure out how to let people know about it."

—Allen Adamson, *Brand Simple (2006)*

We had an Introduction to Brands and Branding in Chapter 1. Then we talked about target audiences with a variety of brands in Chapter 2. Now we're going to discuss *establishing your brand*.

In the beginning, a brand is an idea, whether it's a brand you're already familiar with, or a brand-new brand idea that you want to develop. This chapter is about really understanding the Idea of your Brand.

Let's think about that. Once upon a time, a soap maker left the machine on a little too long and ended up with air bubbles in the soap. The result? Ivory Soap. "It Floats." They realized that there was an idea in the accident – a bar of soap that would float in the bathtub.

So, what's your idea? How do you describe your brand to someone else? Do you have a mission statement, or a vision statement? Maybe not. You'll want to. They are important. They help you understand what your brand is supposed to be about.

We'll spend time with you on understanding your long-term mission and vision as well as the business goals – long-term and short-term – that can help you with your day-to-day decisions. If your brand is building a team, we'll also need to be thinking about things like organizational dynamics and your brand's organizational culture. You'll learn about that, too.

Your branding efforts will be a key part of your business plan. We want you to understand where your idea is in the context of your business plan. If you are in the New Brand category, you'll have a number of concepts that are trying to become clear to you. And, even though it can be pretty confusing, this chapter should help put things in perspective for you.

And, if your branding activities are for a non-profit, you'll find a few extra tools.

LEARNING OUTCOMES

After studying this chapter you will:

1. Understand your Brand in the context of New Brand, Existing Brand, and Troubled Brand
2. Understand the concepts of Mission, Vision, and Organizational Culture
3. Explain branding in relationship to the business plan
4. Illustrate (in a general way) how an idea grows into a brand as a result of emotional appeal, differentiation, and relevancy

THREE KINDS OF BRANDS

As we discussed previously, many things are brands – products, services, sports teams, and rock bands.

But, for the purposes of this chapter, there are three basic situations:

- **New Brand**
- **Existing Brand**
- **Troubled Brand**

Each presents a different kind of challenge, particularly as it pertains to your target.

If your idea is uniquely solving a problem, if it matters to enough people, and if you can deliver it in a consistent fashion, then you are ready to start the Brand Building process. That is a big jump. Exciting? Yes! This is a **NEW BRAND.** Most often, your brand has not yet connected with its target.

What if you already have a brand and the idea is already somewhat established? Now your job will be building *equity* – giving your idea additional substance. Your brand has a history and, for better or worse, people already have an idea of what your brand is about. This is an **EXISTING BRAND**. In the main, an important part of your target will be existing customers. And they can teach you a lot about your brand – and how to make it more successful.

One last area we need to discuss is if there is an existing brand that has problems. This is yet another issue. This is a **TROUBLED BRAND**.

In this case, your target often knows who you are, and you may well have some repair work or damage control to deal with.

And, of course, it's a complicated world. What's an Existing Brand to you may be a New Brand to others. And no brand is problem free. So each of these brand types offer us important lessons to learn.

Let's think about this just a bit more. First, we have an idea that's not yet in the mind of the marketplace – a New Brand.

This may be your idea or, like CuraQuick, you'll be helping out with someone else's new idea. Or, it may be an already established idea – whether it's a small, locally established brand, like our little library, or something a whole lot bigger.

For example, car companies like GM and Toyota often have national contests to get the input of students like you on their already well-established brands.

Finally, that brand may have some problems. It could be a sports team that has had a few losing seasons – or it could be a proud piece of history that was erased by Nazis and Communists.

That was the problem the Czech Legion Project had to fight. It was as if someone had erased George Washington and the Revolutionary War from all the history books.

You'll find each and every brand has a unique set of challenges.

MISSION, VISION, ORGANIZATIONAL CULTURE

In business terms, we'll use concepts like mission, vision, and organizational culture. They're each ways to help us get at our purpose as an enterprise.

The **Mission** is why the brand exists. It's the reason for the idea of the Brand.

Some companies may be multi-brand marketers. Their company may have an overall mission and also more narrow missions for various brands and divisions. For example, a big company like Johnson & Johnson has a division that specializes in products for babies. That division has a Mission to serve its targets – babies and mothers. And, as the brand team makes its way through all the complicated day-to-day decisions in running any business, it really helps everyone there remember what their purpose is as a company and as a Brand.

Then again, Johnson and Johnson's Band-Aid brand has a very different mission, even though the company overall will be concerned with various aspects of health and medicine.

Management guru Peter Drucker notes, "The purpose of business is to create and keep a customer." So your first questions are big and simple: "Why are you in business?" and "For whom are you in business?"

Who is that customer you are going to create and keep? What is the role of your brand in their lives? It's complicated, but simple. Answer those questions in a clear and positive way and you are on the road to making a clear statement of the brand's mission and vision.

How about a few definitions?

For the purposes of this book, here's what we mean by the following words and concepts: Mission, Vision, Organizational Culture, and Beliefs and Norms.

Mission: A clear and comprehensive statement about what you are, what you do and who you do it for. Try to make your Mission Statement the kind that people can relate to and remember.

An easy-to-remember and well-written Mission Statement can provide a unifying guide for all the different decisions you make about your organization. The Mission Statement can provide direction and motivation for employees, while showing a commitment to customers. Mission statements should be no more than 40 to 50 words.

You're probably familiar with the Starbucks brand – the stores and the products. Here is their mission statement. *Our mission: to inspire and nurture the human spirit – one person, one cup and one neighborhood at a time.*

Vision: This is a broader and loftier statement, more comprehensive in nature, about the bigger picture of where you want the organization to go and its role in a larger world. A vision statement addresses key values and beliefs of the organization.

Here is Johnson and Johnson's Vision Statement: *Bringing Science to the Art of Healthy Living.*

You might be familiar with GE's tagline: *Imagination at Work.* The new "green" unit of GE is named **Ecomagination** with the environment as its focus.

"Our vision was to develop a program that was consistent with GE's mission that was to earn the best possible returns for our shareowners by solving big problems like improving energy efficiency and reducing environmental impact."

That's pretty interesting. GE combined a hard-nosed financial mission with some lofty "green marketing" goals. Done well, vision statements can help teams of people share goals. This is important because, as we'll say more than once, brand building is a team sport.

Why not visit the Internet to see how GE is leading the way. Go to http://www.ecomagination.com/

BRAND BUILDER EXERCISE 3.1:
Writing a Mission and Vision Statement

Remember our stories about the Sioux City Chamber Music Association and The Czech Legion Project? Organizations big and small use Mission and Vision Statements to organize and guide their activities.

This exercise will help you identify various parts of these statements.

Instructions: Read the following mission and vision statements. Follow the directions and answer the questions.

1. **Mission Statement: The Sioux City Chamber Music Association**. The Sioux City Chamber Music Association is an organization dedicated to providing performances of, and fostering appreciation for, Chamber Music in Siouxland, resulting in a strengthened cultural base for the community.

2. **Mission Statement: Starbucks.** To inspire and nurture the human spirit— one person, one cup, and one neighborhood at a time. (2010)

3. **Vision Statement: Masdar**. Abu Dhabi has a bold Vision for Masdar: to transform itself into a global leader in sustainable new energy technologies. It created Masdar to do that. (2010)

4. **Vision Statement: Ecomagination (a division of GE)**. "Our vision was to develop a program that was consistent with GE's mission that was to earn the best possible returns for our shareowners by solving big problems like improving energy efficiency and reducing environmental impact. (2010)

Circle the parts of the mission statements that indicate:

a. "What you are",

b. "what you do", and

c. "who you do it for" (the target).

[Hint – you may want to use different colored markers, highlighters, or pencils.]

Discussion Questions

1. How do the Sioux City Chamber Music and Starbucks mission statements guide the decisions the organizations make?

2. Do the mission statements for Sioux City Chamber Music and Starbucks provide direction or motivation for the members, performers, and the employees of these organizations? If so, how? If not, why not?

3. In your view, how do Vision Statements differ from Mission Statements?

4. Mission Statement/Vision Statement. Which do you prefer? Why?

Lofty goals are good. But sometimes we need some good guidelines on how to treat each other day to day.

Organizational Culture: Includes a number of behavioral norms, beliefs, values that are explicitly stated or implied. Components of culture could include tolerance to risk (or not), beliefs in innovation, orientation with respect towards people and communication between teams, team formations and outcomes orientation.

Zappos is another leader, not only in the shoe business, but in an economy that has seen online stores suffer. Zappos has created a culture that is about an experience – for their customers and employees.

Tony Hsieh, CEO for Zappos was recently interviewed and said he believed their mission was to "help their customers reach their full potential." He continues, "Long term, it's not even about e-commerce necessarily," he said. "I guess it's about an experiential brand that's really about making people happy, or improving their life somehow" (Jacobs, 2009).

Note: You might want to look up a retail organization – Trader Joe's. They do some very interesting things in the culture of their organization. You'll get a taste of it on their careers page. Go to www.traderjoes.com/careers.

Cultures can be complicated things – even with a small group. Different groups or functions on the team or organization can have their own pieces of that larger culture. For example, all those who answer the phone can take on the old IBM line, "every problem is an opportunity to demonstrate service."

Do you see how a thought like that can help in answering every phone call? This is the sort of thing that can help everyone pull together.

Beliefs and Norms: The leader of a company, a group, a music organization, or a not-for-profit can write the mission and vision statements. On the other hand, if an organization's culture is one that genuinely reflects its leader's values and **beliefs**, those **beliefs** then become the **norms** of the organization.

In general, a brand delivers something to the target – products for mothers and babies, a hot cup of coffee for you, shoes purchased online, a classical concert in Sioux City.

In myriad ways, large and small, those in the brand organization need to act together to deliver whatever it is the brand stands for.

These somewhat abstract concepts – missions, visions, culture, beliefs and norms – actually play a very important ongoing role in how each organization builds its brand.

When I went to the publishers with the idea for this book, they said, "Our mission is to help young men and women prepare for an industry undergoing revolutionary change. How can we say no?" They said yes.

BRAND BUILDER EXERCISE 3.2:
Vision and Culture

Here are some Exercises and Discussion Questions on the topics we've just covered.

1. **Google "Mission Statement."** Spend some time examining what you find. There's a site called MissionStatement.com. There are a few documents on "How to Write a Mission Statement." Build a folder with dome printouts and make a brief report.

2. **Vision Statements.** These tend to be more "high-minded" than Mission Statements. They are often connected. Spend some time doing a bit of Google (or Bing) research. Report back with three Vision Statements.

3. **Organizational and Corporate Culture.** We'll save you the trouble of going to Wikipedia. Here's what it has to say, *"Organizational culture is an idea in the field of organizational studies and management which describes the psychology, attitudes, experiences, beliefs and values (personal and cultural values) of an organization. It has been defined as 'the specific collection of values and norms that are shared by people and groups in an organization and that control the way they interact with each other and with stakeholders outside the organization.'"* That's all well and good. Now, let's try to say it in our own words. Write down a short definition of organizational culture in your own words – don't

worry about being complete, just try to be clear and to the point. Then write down the names of a few corporations where you think you'd like to work.

4. **Beliefs and norms.** Let's say you're building a brand – and an organization. Let's list three characteristics that you think are important for success and a productive working environment. Having trouble only writing down three? How about six?

BRANDING's RELATIONSHIP TO THE BUSINESS PLAN

Even if you're a non-profit, a brand has to think like a business.

You need customers. You need donors. You need people who like your brand for the right reasons and become involved. Whether that's buying your product, coming to a play or concert, or wearing the T-shirt.

One of the documents that will help you build your brand is a business plan.

And, while much of this workbook will focus on the communications part of building your brand, we really should spend a bit of time talking about business fundamentals. Just remember that this brief summary is not a replacement for the hard-nosed, sharp-pencil work that it takes to develop a solid business plan.

Writing a business plan and the steps you'll take in this book to build a brand communication plan have multiple elements in common. This book is about building the brand communication – not building the business plan for the brand. If you're going to a bank for financing, you'll need a lot more than a great logo and a super slogan. You'll need more than that even if you're going to rich your rich uncle for financing. Hey, how do you think he got so rich?

You can find a number of business plan books and entrepreneur books/classes that will help you develop that part of your business.

As we discussed in the previous chapter on the Target Audience for this book, we're making a few assumptions. We assume that, for the purposes of this book, you are about to start a new business or a have an idea that might become a business.

Even if it's just a class exercise, you'll do well to treat it seriously. It will give you the right kind of mindset. And, for some of you, it's certain that you'll be taking your brand new brand idea to banks, friends, a granting foundation, or maybe even The Bank of Grandma, who's nicer than the aforementioned uncle.

But before we move on, you should know that if they ask for a business plan, you will most likely have to have a document similar to the plan that is outlined below.

The purpose of this section is to help you understand how branding and the business plan are related.

TABLE 3.1: Business Plan Basics

Writing the Business Plan

Although there is no single formula for developing a business plan, some elements are common to all business plans. They are summarized in the following outline.

Elements of a Business Plan

Cover sheet

Executive Summary

Mission, Vision, Organizational Culture

Table of contents

I. The Business
    A. Description of the Business
    B. Industry and Opportunity Analysis
    C. Marketing
    D. Competition
    E. Operations
    F. Product Development and Research
    G. Human Resources
    H. Business insurance

II. Financial Data
    A. Loan applications, funding requests
    B. Capital equipment and supply list
    C. Balance sheet
    D. Breakeven analysis
    E. Pro-forma income projections (profit & loss statements)
    F. Three-year summary
    G. Detail by month, first year
    H. Detail by quarters, second and third years

I. Assumptions upon which projections were based
J. Pro-forma cash flow
K. Harvesting strategies
L. Milestones

III. Supporting Documents – as needed for investors and lenders
A. Tax returns and personal financial statements of principals for last three years (all banks have these forms)
B. Copy of franchise contract and all supporting documents provided by the franchisor (for franchised businesses)
C. Copy of proposed lease or purchase agreement for building space
D. Copy of licenses and other legal documents
E. Copy of resumes of all principals
F. Copies of letters of intent from suppliers, etc.
G. Sample of Promotional materials

Source: U. S. Small Business Administration, Write A Business Plan www.sba.org

One of these days, you may find yourself involved with a business plan, so let's briefly discuss key topic areas that are part of the Brand Development stages.

Description of business – You will need a description of the business and the idea as you develop your brand. In the next chapter, you will begin the Situation Analysis. It is typically the beginning of a marketing or advertising plan because it states 'where we are'. To begin that process, you'll describe the business.

Mission, Vision, and Organizational Culture – Earlier in this chapter we described the definitions, and now you are seeing these concepts in context of the business plan. More than likely, you'll also see it in the Situation Analysis.

Let's think through a few examples.

- A brand that is recruiting students for a new organization on campus
- An agricultural co-op that processes one of the most pristine honey products in the world for sweet consumption all around the world

Over time, you'll come to appreciate how understanding the mission, vision, and culture makes a difference from top to bottom – when you interact with the first customer of the day and when you make your presentation to the "client" (the people who need to approve your brand's communication plan).

Industry and opportunity analysis – Customers aren't just out there waiting for you. There are others serving those same customers. You will need to understand the industry or category in which your brand competes. (Note: In the next chapter there is a specific section that takes you through this step. It's the Brand Audit, section of the Situation Analysis.)

In the business plan, you are showing lenders, friends, and others that you understand the industry and the opportunity that exists for your business. In the Brand Communication plan, you will look at the business through a different lens. We will ask questions like, "what should we say or do to accomplish our business objectives?"

Marketing – Remember the 4 P's? What are they?* And which one are we usually discussing for branding activities? (*The 4 P's are: Product, Price, Place, and Promotion. Promotion is usually the P we discuss for branding activities.)

By the way, all of this should be in the business plan – it might be an excerpt in the Executive Summary, with the entire thing as an Addendum. You must tell others how you plan to communicate your brand.

The branding activities are typically much more than most young entrepreneurs (and some older ones) are prepared to do. Heck, it is more than most people are prepared to do. But if you want to be a success – or even if you just want to learn how to do it right, you really should take each of these steps at least once. After you get some experience, you may find you can skip a few steps because they're already factored in.

Competition – Your competition can teach you a lot. Even though your brand may be at the center of your thinking, you can never study your competition enough. It constantly refreshes your perspective.

If you have written a business plan, you will have most of your work completed. Additional media and message assignments are the different steps you will take.

Pro-forma Income projections – These are included in most business plans. Income projections and pro-formas can be very useful. They show trends in sales categories and projected related costs. However, their usefulness really depends on the type of organization you are working with, and the type of brand you are trying to build. (Note: Show some restraint here. Some pro-formas, in a desire to be comprehensive, merely serve to encourage a dangerous combination of naive optimism and science fiction.

Assumptions upon which projections were based – Marketing budgets are usually a part of the pro-formas. Understanding the underlying assumptions should be noted. There can be wide variance here, and pro-formas are not usually equipped ot handle this. It's a start, but be careful.

Sample of Promotional Materials – Huzzah! The mother lode just arrived. If you can show the reader of your business plan that you also have a well written Brand Builder Plan, wow! You have just impressed the President of the Bank during the board review of the loan, packages from the Bank of Grandma, are on the way. Start deciding how to use your funds wisely. Think about why and how the Czech Legion Project was able to receive its funding. The light bulb should have come on … right about … now!

A Lesson on Business Activities – Also Known As Functional Areas of Business
From Production Orientation to Market Orientation
In Chapter 1, Introduction to Branding, we gave you a short lesson on the 4 P's.

Here is a short lesson on the functions of business.

It fits nicely with the business plan above. The business plan shows you the steps outlined clearly and orderly. These two charts illustrate five functions (or departments within an organization) and their relationship to one another and the customer. As you can see, the marketing function's relationship to the customer has changed over the years.

Why is this important? You will be, or are, working with a number of individuals as well as in various industries. We want you to have as much knowledge as you can. Everyone is dealing with scarcity of resources – brain power is one.

Figure 3.1 illustrates what we call a production orientation. This means the production of goods is the driving force in the organization. In some cases, production managers will lead their people to believe that only the marketing department should

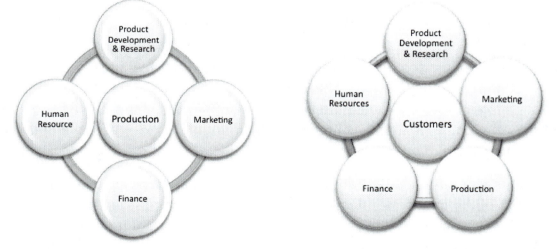

Figure 3.1 Product Orientation   *Figure 3.2 Market Orientation*

fulfill the responsibilities of communicating with the customers. This type of philosophy does very little for customer service, and we've grown past this exclusively production-centered focus (Figure 3.1 Production Orientation Chart).

Figure 3.2 shows what we call a market orientation.

With Market Orientation, all business activities or functional areas such as marketing, production, finance, human resources, and product development focus around the customer.

Let's look at that Peter Drucker quote again. "The purpose of business is to create and keep a customer." Sure, if we're already making something, we'd like people to buy that product. But, as we all know, times change and tastes change.

How many times have you said, "Been there. Done that." We all have.

But if we stay focused on the customer, we can change along with those tastes – and we're not so surprised by those changes. Often, in fact, our customers will tell us what it is they want next. That's why a Market Orientation is a better way to organize over the long term.

When it's working right, marketing will lead the efforts to develop the communications, and lead the brand building activities, but the key is that *everyone* in the organization will be oriented to serve the customer.

The previous production orientation model was developed around manufacturing industries, and still dominates in certain parts of the world. As students of the brand building process, you will be confronting both types of philosophies.

These two orientations – Product vs. Market – illustrate the relationship not only between two philosophies of business but various activities within a business.

Now, if that looks too complicated, here's a simpler way of thinking about it… differentiation.

AN IDEA BECOMES A BRAND BY DIFFERENTIATION

If I ask you to describe a friend of yours, you'll probably grab onto some aspect that's a little bit different – a nice sense of humor, red hair, freckles, an interesting hobby.

Well, that's how we remember things. We don't waste time describing all the things that are pretty much the same – we take that for granted.

If I ask you about a restaurant, chances are you won't talk about the mashed potatoes or the Thousand Island dressing. You'll probably mention some signature dish… "they're famous for…" or some other above average aspect – whether it's food, service, or décor.

See where this is going? One of the key aspects of a brand has to do with differentiation.

This difference point is very often the brand's reason for being.

It will be key to everything from your initial mission through your communication strategy to The Pitch.

By the way, if that differentiating thing is not meaningful to your customer, well, you might not be all that successful.

So let's look at this differentiating thing a little more…

A Simple Way of looking at it:

In his book, *Brand Simple*, Allen Adamson explains that you should not begin any branding activities with your idea until you have figured out what there is about it that is different (2006).

In the real world, the idea must be a *meaningfully different* idea as well.

If the difference isn't meaningful enough to create that customer, you probably need to give it some more thought. Adamson wrote as the managing director of Landor Associates, a design and branding firm, which is a division of the Young and Rubicam global marketing and communication enterprise. Y&R boasts a tool they call the BrandAsset Valuator – BAV for short.

The BAV plots brands according to five pillars:

- Differentiation
- Relevance
- Esteem
- Knowledge
- Energy

Adamson offers two primary uses for this tool: the first is for predictive and prescriptive reasons; and the second use is for the prevention of myopic thinking. Properly used, the BAV should broaden the range of thinking for major brands.

While most of the brands you will be building are not going to use the BrandAsset Valuator, think about their pillars. Let's simplify it a bit with some questions to ask, and then we'll go back and forth a bit with the concept of your idea and your brand.

These questions address the BAV pillars of differentiation and relevance.

- Is your Idea different enough from your competition?
- What problem is it solving? Does it need solving?
- Does it really matter? To whom does it matter?
- Are there enough people in that group who care? Is the group large enough to be a viable target audience?

Both Landor and Y&R have developed methods to distinguish themselves from their competitors to build their brand in order for them to aid others to become a brand that will survive and grow.

You can use the lessons of these larger brands and apply them to your situation. In fact, these are good tools to remember for later in the brand building process, as well.

ESTABLISHING THE IDEA OF YOUR BRAND

In many ways, a brand is an idea – a concept. Even though it has a very real existence – as a product, as service, we need to think about how a brand exists in the mind of our target – and in the mind of the team managing the brand.

The idea of a brand is very different for each of our three types of brands: New Brands, Existing Brands, and Troubled Brands.

Makes sense, when you think about it.

For a New Brand, people pretty much have no idea.

For an Existing Brand, you're dealing with brand equity – that's essentially the existing thoughts and history people have with the brand.

Finally, with a Troubled Brand, people have some problems with your brand, an unhappy experience, or competition that's beating your brand in the marketplace.

Let's take them one by one.

New Brand

We consider the New Brand as one that has no previous customer history. It may be a brand new idea that you have, it may be a new business that a friend or relative is starting, it may be a re-staging of a business or a piece of a business – like Domino's Pizza adding chicken, or – and here's an interesting variation – it may be what you do with a Troubled Brand.

After an airline called ValuJet had some crashes, they re-branded themselves as AirTran. In Chapter 1 you learned about the CuraQuick retail medical clinic. That was not only a new brand, but a new category of health care clinics. Sometimes a New Brand is also a New Category.

Car manufacturers are introducing new brands all the time (sub-brands, actually), but they all have differentiating brand characteristics. Sometimes, as in the case of the mini-van and the hybrid, it's a whole new kind of car. But whatever the New Brand is, you need to develop good answers to these basic questions.

Who is the brand for? Your Target.

What is it's purpose? Your Product or Service and its benefit.

How is it different? The Competition and current habits of your target.

Let's look at Facebook's description for Naked Pizza: Delicious pizza featuring an ancestral blend of seeds & grains, prebiotic Agave fiber and probiotics (good-for-you cultures) in our crust and is topped with all natural cheese, sauce, meats and veggies. No hormones, antibiotics or freaky chemicals.

Naked Pizza's corporate home is New Orleans – check out their Facebook and Website for expansions. This is a New Brand – using primarily social media to spread their 'quirky' but 'serious' brand.

It might be a product, it might be a service, it might be something brand new on the Internet. Whatever it is, you need to make it an idea that your target can understand – and one that has desirable and meaningful differentiation.

Existing Brand

An Existing Brand is one you see every day. It is the most common assignment, and, in some ways, the toughest one. You will be trying to maintain the brand's integrity, and grow the brand. You will be trying to gain new customers, and keep the old. You have to make the communications program fresh, or the brand just around the corner will have a fresh idea and steal your customers away. It's crazy out there!

But the real reason it's tough is that there's a lot at stake.

With a New Brand, well, everybody knows it might or might not go.

With a Troubled Brand, a lot of people know that it might be – as they say – "all over but the shouting." But for an Existing Brand, you've got an existing business, an existing staff, and an expectation of a continuing business. People are counting on you.

When you can bring new life and energy into a big, existing, already established brand it can be exciting. It can also make your marketing reputation. For example, consider Dove, the well-known brand of soap and beauty products. They generated a campaign based on "real beauty." The dramatic contrast between the Dove models and the typical skinny fashion model generated impact and, more important, a meaningful connection with their target.

A brand you can bank on.

A lot of brands are a combination of good news/bad news. These days, just about any bank would be a good example.

The financial industry has had a crazy branding problem. It's a national problem – and it's a local problem. You'll find this is true across many categories – it could be a story of that big auto company, or it could be the story of a local car dealer who has been part of the community for fifty years.

No, we will not get into who caused what in the banking industry – or the reason for the crisis in 2008. Our family knows all too well. We own rental property, we have two children graduating from college, and we're trying to hold on to what we believe to have been a pretty good financial plan.

Hmmmm… sounds like another great project. Existing brand that has an opportunity with a different market. Security National Bank wanted to develop a campaign for Young Professionals.

Brand: Security National Bank (SNB)

Business Goal: Add future high-value families and individuals to the bank's customer base.

Target: Young Professionals

Current Message: "Distinguished." Their current messaging highlights the bank's President Rich Waller; also used to show the bank in the billboard below. Known for 125 years of service, longest in the area.

Message Windows: As a relatively large firm in a relatively small market, SNB had a wide of range of tactics available. And don't forget those local connections. It can do a big bank good to let people know they're on the side of small business.

Print and in bank posters

Billboard

Local connection Meet Virginia's coffee shop

When dealing with existing brands, here are some things you should think about.

- **Who are the existing customers?** (Hint: you can learn a lot by talking to customers.) Find a "heavy user," someone who loves the brand – they can be a source of great insight.
- **What is the history of the brand?** Look at the graphic history (signs/logos/old ad campaigns), the business history, and the history with its customers. Get some stories.
- **What is the state of the competition?** How does this brand rate/rank in the category? What is that category? For example, there are many restaurants. Are you the destination for a deluxe dinner on the weekend or the regular spot for lunch? Each is a restaurant, but their customers and competitive categories are very different – even if it's the same person. (Think about it – even if our customer is the same person, the restaurants considered for a night on the town or an ordinary lunch are in very different categories – each can be the considered a brand in the customer's selection of "favorite restaurants.")

Troubled Brands

The last category to discuss is Troubled Brands.

It's not a perfect world. There can be lots of reasons that brands that may have been doing fine for years are now in trouble. For example, coast to coast, many newspapers, big and small, are having a tough go of it. Those classified ads that we used to read in the paper? Now a lot of that has moved over to the Internet. A cash cow moving to greener pastures.

For newspapers, although it may not be their fault, it's their problem. In just about every market, there are quite a few media properties, newspapers, radio stations, etc. that might be having a bit of rough road. As discussed in *Advertising & The Business of Brands*, the Media Revolution is changing a lot of things in our lives – globally and locally.

When you're dealing with a Troubled Brand, you can't paper over the problem. Some executives think, "let's just get a good ad campaign and we'll save our brand." If you don't fix the underlying problem, you actually may be making things worse. You're spending precious resources and, if you haven't solved the core problem, you're amplifying the problems. Those brand messages, if they actually generate some traffic, trial, and re-trial, might just take you down quicker. As ad legend Bill Bernbach noted, "Nothing kills a bad product faster than good advertising."

First, you'll want to discover why there is a problem. A product problem? A place problem?

Carnival Grocers

Here's a problem. Your location didn't change, but the neighborhood did.

When a brand is in trouble, you might want to call the problem "bad branding," but really, it could be anything.

When they tore the hospital down and built upscale condos, the world changed for Carnival Grocers. No longer were their three cash register lines busy during shift change at the hospital. And even though the neighborhood had become wealthier, it didn't make Carnival richer.

Their customer base went from families buying their weekly groceries to their new upscale neighbors needing a Pinot Noir and a bit of Brie. Perhaps your Mission or Vision or culture has changed.

You need to ask the right questions, and it might mean asking hard questions. Like "where did the customers go… and why?" If something is wrong with the brand, do people know it? You'd be surprised the degree to which customers think of brands and brand image when they make their purchase decisions.

When the brand is in trouble, something is wrong with the idea of the brand and you have to get it right to get your brand on track to solving the problem.

Information. Sometimes it helps to be lucky. Carnival was due – they became the location for some popular local commercials for the Lottery. The location fee helped pay for a scanner and new check-out lines. The scanner was key. Now the owner, Art, had real information on how things were moving. This helped Art truly see what merchandise was moving and what was just taking up shelf space. Even in a small grocery store you have thousands of items. The scanner started to tell him the story of what was really going on in the depths of his inventory.

Now he was able to start fixing one of his problems – moving out the slow items and emphasizing the types of items that were moving with his new customer base.

The Hometown Pizza Hut Story

Today, you probably know where the nearest Pizza Hut is and you don't think of it as a brand in trouble – because it's not. But quite a few years ago, they were in very serious trouble, with the whole system headed below break-even. They were headed into the red – and it wasn't from the tomato sauce.

Know what a "Rejector Base" is? Well, it's the people who have tried your product, will never try your product again, and will tell you why. Back in the late 70s, Pizza Hut had a rejector base approximately equal to the United States of America.

For years, the chain had been "getting by" with a low-quality product. A system-wide incentive had provided bonuses for managers to skimp on ingredients. That didn't help. Fortunately, two things happened. First, they developed Pan Pizza. It was the first of a number of products that had customers coming back for more (remember, the purpose of a business is to acquire and grow a customer) – in this case, they just needed to get folks to come back once and try the new product.

The second thing they had was a national campaign that talked local – the theme was "Your Hometown Pizza Hut." In developing the campaign, they discovered how people think about brands in the pizza category.

Most brands like the idea of being #1. But in different categories, that leadership position can be based on different things. So, for example, in the pizza category, they discovered that almost each one of us has a different idea of #1.

It may be the place that has your favorite crust and sausage. For someone else, it may be that special place you'd go after the basketball game. Just saying you make more pizzas than anyone else isn't really meaningful. Because favorite pizza is a *personal* choice.

So, the idea of "Your Hometown Pizza Hut" worked to establish a leadership position that was local and personal. And, along with a better-tasting product, they worked their way back into consideration with pizza eaters everywhere, particularly in the smaller markets where Pizza Hut was a bigger player. Mission accomplished.

Whether your brand is brand new, existing, or troubled, you have to ask yourself one big simple question. What's the idea?

Your Brand Building begins with answering some simple questions well and then turning those answers into the goals and guidance you'll need for the next step.

So let's ask those questions and see where we're headed.

**BRAIN BUILDER EXERCISE 3.4:
What's the Idea of Your Brand?**

We want you to start thinking about the idea of your own brand.

While you're thinking, here's an example to get you started.

CASE:
You have four ideas to begin a business. Your list looks something like the list below, mainly because you love to dance, you learned how to design websites while in college, and your grandparents are getting older. You also grew up on a family

farm and perhaps heard your parents talk about the issues of sustainability. It is a pretty typical list – all over the place.

- Buy a dance studio from your old teacher

- Start a design company that specializes in website development and the social media

- Help seniors stay at home by investing in a "Home Instead Senior Care" franchise (www.homeinstead.com)

- Use land near your neighbor's farm for an organic garden and promote local sustainability

Instructions: SELECT ONE IDEA from the list above, **or** maybe you have another idea. Given the information thus far in this chapter, jot down the steps you would need take to grow your brand.

In short, what do you believe will turn **your idea** into a **Brand**?

CHAPTER REVIEW

1. We covered some important concepts that are key to building a brand: Mission, Vision, Organizational Culture, and Beliefs and Norms.

2. We covered – in a summary fashion – what's involved in a Business Plan.

3. We discussed the difference between a Product Orientation and Market Orientation.

4. We discussed the importance of meaningful differentiation.

5. We discussed the importance of the idea of your brand and some key aspects related to New Brands, Existing Brands and Troubled Brands.

REVIEW QUESTIONS

1. To date, what's your favorite Mission Statement?

2. Name a company that, in your opinion, has an Organizational Culture that appeals to you personally.

3. Do a Google or Amazon search. List three resources that might be able to help you put together a Business Plan.

4. Provide an example of a New Brand, an Existing Brand and a Troubled Brand.

READINGS AND RESOURCES

Adamson, Allen P. and Martin Sorrel. *Brand Simple: How the Best Brands Keep it Simple and Succeed* (Aug 7, 2007)

Hsieh, T. (2010). *Delivering Happiness*. Story about Zappos and the culture that drives it.

Some sites with Missions:

AbuDhabi – Masdar. http://www.masdar.ae/en/hom/index.aspx?mnu=&MenuID=56

GE Ecomagination.
http://ge.ecomagination.com/annual-reports/letter-to-stakeholders.html

Starbucks http://www.starbucks.com/mission

CHAPTER 4:
SITUATION ANALYSIS

The Situation Analysis helps you answer the question *"Where are we?"*

It's key to helping you develop a communication plan for your brand. It will help you understand and analyze where the brand is in today's marketplace. The Situation Analysis is based on a simple but very comprehensive outline. The marketplace is far from simple; it is very complex and becoming more so, but this outline will bring some clarity to the situation. Specifically, *your* situation.

One of the tools you will use to put your Situation Analysis together is the Brand Analysis Checklist. It is also simple but comprehensive. In it, you will be guided to conduct research, evaluate the competition, and develop further perspective on the question, *"Where are we?"* This section is the foundation to lead you to a successful plan.

Once you understand where you are, you can begin to plan where you want to go. With that understanding, your goal will then be to work out the problem that the right message can address.

The basic process of building a Situation Analysis is the same no matter who you are and no matter how big or small your brand. However, depending on the business category and the information available, you may be working with dramatically different kinds of information to build your situation analysis. A major brand in a major category will have all sorts of marketing data available. For a smaller and more local brand – like our library's Learning Center – you may have to rely on marketing data such as interviews and observation.

In general, as you figure out "where are we?" you will be identifying problems to be solved and opportunities to succeed.

A key function of the Situation Analysis is *problem identification*. Everyone will start with a problem. The discussion to determine the problem is paramount. I find it very exciting for students, faculty, and entrepreneurs to engage in the process. If you are introducing a new product, or new uses for an existing product, the problem is probably that your audience is not aware of those things. If your product is out there and no one is buying it, you'll need research to determine why. It's an entirely different problem.

As the final piece of your Situation Analysis, you will evaluate the marketplace by completing a Competitive Review. The Brand Analysis Checklist provides a guide for that, as well.

LEARNING OUTCOMES

After studying this chapter you will be able to:

1. Understand the overall marketplace situation for your brand
2. Complete a brand audit using the Brand Analysis Checklist
3. Define a problem that can be effectively addressed with the right message
4. Evaluate the competitors in the marketplace

COMPLETE A BRAND AUDIT

The first question to ask is, "Where are we?" When you ask that big, simple question you are on the road to some very interesting answers.

Using a checklist to answer that very big question will help keep you on track. I like the Brand Analysis Checklist as a guide to complete the audit. It will help you establish where your brand is at this point in time. The Brand Analysis Checklist we use here was developed by Alice Kenrick of Southern Methodist University and originally featured in *Advertising & the Business of Brands*.

Each item in the checklist can serve as a topic on which you can complete additional research to supply your brand team with additional information. Not every question will be easily answered.

If you can't answer the question, you will have to determine, among other things, if you really need that answer. If you do need to answer the question, you'll have to search deeper for answers. There are multiple ways to find the answers. We'll give you tips and examples along the way.

For the first meeting with any client – in a classroom or in a business setting – it's a good idea to prepare a series of questions for an interview. Use the checklist that follows, and, if you have the luxury of a client interview, convert each of these topics into a question. If you are participating in a competition, find a franchisee or someone in the same business to interview.

If you're preparing the Brand Audit for your own brand, just start completing the information. After all, you're the client. But don't go easy on yourself. Be sure to ask those tough questions and don't avod those challenging topics.

The information needed is clear and simple, yet you may find that collecting it can become difficult. This Brand Analysis Checklist should help. (By the way, we're posting this as a .doc file on www.brandbuilderworkbook.com.)

THE BRAND ANALYSIS CHECKLIST

I. Company

- Location
- Organization and major activities, subsidiaries
- Brand History
- Financial Data
- Annual Report
- Key personnel/managers (try to arrange an interview with a few key individuals)
- Recent news (from online database sources, newspapers, etc.)

II. Category

- Category Definition
- Size of category in units, dollars, etc.
- Category history and growth
- Category growth projections
- Distribution channels/methods of distribution
- Major manufacturers/players
- Seasonal factors
- Regional factors
- Other relevant category factors
- Legal considerations
- Major trade publications
- Major trade organizations in category

III. Products Within Category

- Share of category by product
- Product-form description (size, flavor, model, etc.)
- New product introductions
- Benefits and appeals of new products
- New packages, innovations, etc.
- Recent news about product category

IV. Brand Analysis

- Top brands by dollar or unit sales
- Growth trends of top brands
- Category share by country and by region
- Pricing trends
- Recent news about brand

V. Consumer Profile
- Demographics of users
- Frequency of purchase/usage
- Place of purchase
- Heavy-user profile
- Awareness and attitudes toward brand
- Decision-makers vs. purchaser (same, different? If different, what is purchase decision like?)
- Normal purchase cycle
- Brand loyalty/switching

VI. Advertising/Marketing Communications
Messages
- Creative strategies of top brands
- Specific promises, appeals, claims, special effects
- Examples of past and current executions

Media
- Category and brand spending
- Seasonality (by quarter)
- Regionality (spot buying)
- Media employed by top brands
- Spending patterns – flighting, continuous, etc.
- Spending compared with market share

Promotions
- Promotions used in category
- Major brand promotion types and examples
- Success rates of promotions

Internet and New Media
- Website/URL
- Purpose of site
- e-commerce activities
- Social media activities

Other Pertinent Information
- Personal interviews
- Other information sources

CLIENT INTERVIEW TIP: A few quick rules: dress professionally. Get a good night's rest. Have notes and notebook in hand. First impressions are critical. Be five minutes early. Greet your contact with a firm handshake, direct eye contact, and a smile.

In 2008 my students were in a Cadillac CTS competition with other universities across the nation. The case study was written by GM Cadillac marketing executives and vetted through EdVenture Partners. To answer many of the questions on the checklist the students used the information from the case study that was provided, but there were still a lot of blanks to fill in.

The students conducted multiple interviews: the Sioux City Cadillac dealer, the Sioux Falls Cadillac dealer, and a Chicago dealer (Cadillac was the least expensive car that he sold). We also attended the Chicago Auto Show.

With each contact, our information about the brand grew. Eventually, all the blanks were filled in. This time, we were working in teams of five. Four groups competed for a class winner – and then the work of the class champion was submitted to EdVenture Partners. Did I mention they took first in the nation? Yes! Then they pitched their work in Detroit to Cadillac marketing executives! The system you are using is the same system we used.

TEAMWORK TIP: Remember, this is a team sport. Try to organize so each team has students with different skill sets. Ideally, each student team of five would have at least one designer, one marketer, and one communication student. Other skills, like research and media, are usually useful.

In the case of Stella's Barbecue, students formed teams of four, then paired off to work through the Situation Analysis/Brand Analysis and research phases independently, but shared their research findings. The first meeting took place at the restaurant itself. Students observed the workings of the restaurant as they received answers to their questions. Periodic presentations were made to share information. Each team of students would then take the information, develop a message, and pitch their plan.

Here's a good example of what we mean. It's the Cadillac National Case Study Brand Analysis.

BRAND ANALYSIS IN ACTION
Cadillac National Case Study Competition

Note: This was the first document posted before additional secondary and primary research was completed. It was posted on the team page of Blackboard after every team member reviewed each other's work. They developed this single document.

I. Company: Cadillac

Location: Headquartered in Detroit, Michigan, with dealers and distributors worldwide. Located on the web at cadillac.com.

Organization and major activities: Cadillac is a subsidiary of GM. They are a luxury car brand that is on the lower edge of the tier 1 market.

History: In the past, Cadillac served as the ultimate symbol of success in America. It symbolized bootstrap achievements that come from hard work and discipline. U.S. presidents, industry moguls, movie stars, and even royalty abroad drove or were driven in Cadillac's. This helped Cadillac become known as the pre-eminent luxury brand in the U.S.

During the 1970s the fuel crisis made American's turn to more fuel efficient cars and Cadillacs began to lose their appeal. Then in the 1980s, Cadillac lost its edge in product, technology, and design development, and, eventually, foreign imports became the new American symbol of success. Finally, in the early 21st century, the Cadillac Escalade emerged as an urban sub-segment's brand of choice and gave Cadillac a much-needed boost. However, the success of the Escalade did not serve as a halo for the brand.

The public still perceives two very different Cadillacs. They see the Escalade as edgy and urban, while the rest of the line-up is still seen as cars for "old people." Presently Cadillac is focusing on trying to make their brand become a symbol of success once again. To do this they are trying to appeal to the younger generations by redesigning their vehicles and they are also trying to change consumers' present negative perceptions of Cadillac.

Financial data: N/A at present

Annual report: N/A at present

Key Personnel: Jim Taylor is the general manager of Cadillac

Recent news from sources: Press release dated January 8, 2007: "2008 Cadillac CTS adds All-wheel Drive, New Direct-injection V-6 and Six-speed Automatic Transmission"

II. Category

Category definition: Cadillac is in the luxury vehicle market, on the lower edge of the tier 1 market. The CTS is the main focus of this campaign and it is Cadillac's entry level luxury car.

Size of category: The total recorded new US registrations in the luxury car segment in 2005, was 1,528,038; of these, 192,799 (12.6%) were Cadillacs. From Jan. to Sept. 2006, 1,119,455 luxury cars were registered, of these 140,165 (9%) were Cadillacs. These totals come from Acura, Audi, BMW, Cadillac, Infiniti, Jaguar, Land Rover, Lexus, Lincoln, Mercedes-Benz, and Volvo.

Category history and growth: Numbers of new luxury vehicle registrations have increased every year from 2001–2004 by at least 9,500 registrations. There was a slight decrease from 2004–2005, a difference of 5,131.

Category growth projections: N/A at present

Distribution channels: Dealerships and on-line

Major manufactures/players: General Motors (the maker and distributor of Cadillac). Other major manufactures are Lexus, BMW, and Mercedes-Benz, which are Cadillac's major competitors.

Seasonal factors: June and August are the best months for selling cars. January, Feburary, November, and December are the worst months.

Regional factors: Cadillac comes standard with rear-wheel drive which makes them less appealing in states that receive snowy and icy weather. If they came as all-wheel drive cars they would be more appealing in these states.

Major trade publications in category: N/A at present

III. Products within Category

Share of category by product form (For 2006): % Market Share

Lexus ES, IS	91,240	23%
BMW 3-Series	79,463	20%
Acura TL	53,087	13.5%
Infiniti G35	40,373	10%
Cadillac CTS	36,489	9%
Mercedes-Benz C-Class	33,818	8.5%
Lincoln Zephyr	29,140	7%
Audi A4	28,494	7%
	392,104	

Product form description: The new CTS is an entry luxury sedan. The 2008 CTS has all-new engineering and design advances that support the Cadillac mission behind its "Life. Liberty. And the Pursuit." Positioning. This all new model seeks to bump Cadillac back up to its former tier-one luxury status by earning both consumer respect and share of spending.

New product introductions: The 2008 CTS will be an all-new design.

Benefits and appeals of new products: The CTS is an entry level luxury vehicle. It has a direct-injection 300hp engine, all-wheel drive, a new lighting design, and new advances in electronics.

Recent news about product category: N/A at present

IV. Brand Analysis

Top brands by dollar or unit sales: The case is only focusing on the CTS, of which Cadillac sold 36,489 from Jan–Sept 2006.

Growth trends of top brands: The CTS has had an increase in sales since 2001, but the 2008 CTS model is going to be different than the past years' model so the growth in sales could increase even more or possibly decrease.

Category share nationally and by region: N/A at present

Pricing trends: N/A at present

V. Consumer profile

Demographics of users:

1. Move-Ups: Younger men and women, more male (60%) than female, at least 4-years of college (many with graduate degrees), largely single or recently married, $75,000+ income.

2. Busy Moms: Females 30–45 with at least one child, $75,000+ income, most employed part-time.

3. Alphas: Men and women, but primarily men, age 34–54, who are equally likely to be self-employed as they are to be running the whole show as CEO/President, $125,000+ income, mix of single/divorced/married.

4. Boomers: Men and women, age 50-63, relatively equal split between men (52%) and women (48%), $75,000+ income, most are married.

5. Loyalists: Primarily male (64%), average age 50+, primarily retired men with a college education and a 100k+ income.

Frequency of purchase: Consumers usually update to a new car every 5 years or less, around the time their warranty runs out.

Place of purchase: Dealerships

Heavy-user profile: Loyalists: People who have always bought Cadillac. They have achieved the American Dream and have always believed that Cadillac is the symbol of success rewarded.

Awareness and attitudes towards brand: Even though Cadillac is a luxury car and was perceived as the American symbol of success, some people now perceive it as a car for older people. Presently there is a distinct difference in perception among the different Cadillac models. While the Escalade linked Cadillac to contemporary urban culture, experimentation, and innovation; the rest of the brand is seen as cars for old people. One third of all luxury car buyers do not shop Cadillac because of the brand's image. Cadillac is constantly trying to change people's perceptions, but it has been a slow process.

Decision-maker vs. purchaser: On average, the decision-maker is the woman and the purchaser is the man.

Normal purchase cycle: Consumers usually update to a new car every 5 years of less, around the time their warranty runs out.

Brand loyalty: Current customers are very loyal to Cadillac. Cadillac's conquest sales make up less than half of all Cadillac sales in comparison to conquest sales making up two-thirds of their competitors sales.

VI. Advertising

Messages:

- Creative strategies of top brands: Cadillac's competition uses advertising that is more sophisticated while Cadillac's advertisements try to be more edgy and upbeat.

- Specific promises, appeals, claims, special effects: N/A at present

- Examples of past and current executions: From 2002-2006 Cadillac launched the "BreakThrough" campaign which successfully announced to luxury consumers that Cadillac is, again, a credible alternative in the luxury vehicle segment. This year they just launched the "Life. Liberty. And the Pursuit." campaign which embodies Cadillac's desire to reignite America's love affair with the brand. The campaign encapsulates both the core principles of the Cadillac product and the key psychological motivations of luxury car owners.

Media:

- Category and brand spending: We have a $30 million budget to work with for this campaign.

- Seasonality: N/A at present

- Regionality: N/A at present

- Major media employed by top brands: TV, magazines, billboards

- Spending patterns: N/A at present

- Spending compared with market share: N/A at present

Promotion:

- Promotions used in category: N/A at present

- Major brand promotion types and examples: N/A at present

- Success rates of promotions: N/A at present

Creative elements we need to find to help us with our campaign:

- Stock photos

- Cadillac logos

- movie clips

- audio clips

- special Cadillac fonts

Marketing/Advertising Problem:

The current problem is that Cadillac has lost its luxury status and is no longer the American symbol of success. The challenge is to increase Cadillac's conquest rate, lower the average age of Cadillac consumers, and improve the image and reputation of the brand. Cadillac is attempting to solve these problems with the introduction of the new 2008 CTS.

As you can see, a lot of work was done. Automobiles are a category where there is quite a bit of information available. Sometimes, particularly with a smaller local brand (like Stella's, our next example), we don't have as much good information available.

However, the key is how well we do the *analysis*. Take a look at how the team identified the Marketing/Advertising Problem. From that analysis the team was able to develop what was judged to be effective messaging.

Now let's look at Stella's.

Stella's Barbecue
Making the most of the information you can get

For Cadillac and the automobile industry, there was quite a bit of data – sales figures, spending reports, and market share information – plus a client that had gone to some trouble to prepare the case for a student team.

In the case of Stella's Barbecue, it was pretty much the opposite.

There was very little in the way of organized marketing information. Yet there was still quite a bit we could do.

For example, the client was able to provide a fairly accurate "guesstimate" of when business was good and when it was not so good. They knew what their customers liked. Though, as you might expect, they didn't know that much about the non-customers.

Next, interviews with customers and non-customers generated quite a bit of useful information – though the team had to take the time to do the interviewing and organize the results in a way that seemed to make sense.

Finally, collecting some kinds of very useful data – like price comparisons – was as easy as picking up a bunch of menus and doing a little bit of basic math.

The Brand Analysis Checklist is pretty comprehensive. In a professional marketing organization, you will eventually be able to collect almost all of that data. In a small start-up, or a local student project, well, not so much. But the key is that you work to get and generate as much information as possible.

Interviews with Stella's customers and non-customers generated very useful information. Likewise, looking at the competitive menus told us a lot.

Finally, wearing out a little shoe leather and understanding the local retail area where Stella's was located – things like traffic patterns and when and where people had lunch and dinner – was also useful marketing information.

Market information doesn't organize itself. It's not necessarily located or found in one place. You have to keep looking until you find what you need.

Your next assignment will be to use the Brand Analysis Checklist to assemble the background information you need for your Situation Analysis. As you do, you will begin to answer that big question: "Where are we?" Naturally, depending on the product, service, or organization, you will need to adapt the language and understand what parts of the checklist you can fill out and what will have to wait.

Learning about the Learning Center

Students who prepared a campaign for our library interviewed five librarians. Not all five of the librarians agreed when they answered the questions, but in the process of having the checklist, baseline information was established.

**BRAIN BUILDER EXERCISE 4.1:
Completing a Brand Analysis**

BRAND ANALYSIS WORKSHEET

The following is good brain training. In the checklist below, fill in the blanks in the space provided. When you have more data than the space allows, note where you can find the information. A word document is available for this (and all worksheets in this book) at www.brandbuilderworkbook.com

Date: _____

Problem Statement _____

I. COMPANY

1. Name of Brand, Company, or Organization _____
   _____

2. Location _____

3. Contact person _____ Work phone _____

   Email _____ Cell phone _____

4. Organization and major activities; subsidiaries _____
   _____

5. Company history _____
   _____
   _____

6. Company mission _____
   _____
   _____

7. Company vision and philosophy _____
   _____
   _____

8. Corporate Objectives _____
   _____
   _____

9. Financial data relevant to marketing _____
   _____

10. Annual Report _____

11. Key personnel/managers _____
    _____

12. Recent news from online database sources, newspapers (include published news releases from the company) _____

_____

_____

II. CATEGORY

13. Category definition (check SIC codes and description) _____

_____

14. Size of category in units, dollars, etc. _____

_____

15. Category history and growth _____

_____

16. Category growth projections _____

_____

17. Distribution channels/methods of distribution _____

_____

18. Major manufacturers and players _____

_____

19. Seasonal factors _____

_____

20. Regional factors _____

_____

21. Other relevant category factors _____

_____

22. Legal considerations _____

_____

23. Major trade publications/trade organizations in category _____

_____

III. PRODUCTS WITHIN CATEGORY

24. Share of category by product _____

_____

25. Product form description (size, flavor, model, etc.) _____

_____

26. New product introduction _____

_____

27. Benefits and appeals of new products _____

_____

28. New packages, innovations in products _____

    _____

29. Recent news about product category _____

    _____

IV. BRAND DESCRIPTION

This section will focus on the collection of marketing and advertising information for a brand.

30. Top brands by dollar or unit sales in category _____

    _____

31. Growth trends and history of top brands _____

    _____

32. Share of category by country and region _____

    _____

33. Pricing trends of competitive brands _____

    _____

34. Recent news about brand _____

    _____

V. CONSUMER PROFILE

35. Demographics of users _____

    _____

36. Frequency of purchase/usage _____

    _____

37. Place of purchase _____

    _____

38. Heavy-user profile _____

    _____

39. Awareness and attitudes toward brand _____

    _____

40. Decision-maker vs. purchaser _____

    _____

41. Normal purchase cycle _____

    _____

42. Brand loyalty/switching _____

    _____

VI. ADVERTISING (BRAND AND COMPETITION)

Messages

43. Creative strategies of top brands _____

_____

44. Specific promises, appeals, claims, special effects _____

_____

45. Examples of past and current executions _____

_____

Media

46. Category and brand spending _____

_____

47. Seasonality (by quarter) _____

_____

48. Rationality (spot buying) _____

_____

49. Media employed by top brands _____

_____

50. Spending patterns – flighting, continuous, etc. _____

_____

51. Spending compared with market share or ratio of sales _____

_____

Promotion, Public Relations, Direct marketing, Event marketing

52. Promotions used in category _____

_____

53. Major brand promotion types and examples _____

_____

54. Success rates of promotions _____

_____

55. Public Relation examples _____

_____

56. Major brand PR examples _____

_____

57 Direct marketing examples _____

_____

58. Major brand direct marketing examples _____
_____

59. Event marketing and sponsorships examples _____
_____

60. Event marketing and sponsorships of major brand _____
_____

Other pertinent information

61. Personal interviews _____
_____

62. Other information sources _____
_____

VII. CREATIVE REQUIREMENTS

63. Font, color, logo requirements _____
_____

64. Disclaimers required to appear in ads _____
_____

65. Affiliations or partnerships of brand _____
_____

66. Other creative requests or requirements _____
_____

COMPETITIVE REVIEW

The final section of the Situation Analysis is the Competitive Review. You want to identify those who are competing for the same customer as you are. A competitor is any company (or group) that aims to satisfy the same consumer needs that you do.

As part of that, we'll do a few exercises that will help us think about your competitors in a number of ways. Understanding the competition will help you evaluate why, even though they may be very nice people, *they are the enemy*. Understanding the competition is critical in helping you formulate your marketing and it may even help your own organization improve.

Competitors:

Who are they? Why are they successful?

How do they maintain their competitive edge? How are you different from them? Do customers see a difference between you and them? If so, how?

How well is their sales force trained?

What products and services do they offer?

In what category within the industry do they compete? Is it the same as yours? What do they spend on advertising? What does their advertising look like? What else do they do in the marketplace?

Do they have any particularly effective marketing tactics, such as introductory offers? Are there substitute products emerging? How will you compete with them in the months and years ahead?

Differentiators:

Once you've determined who your competitors are, you'll want to see how they are the same or different than you are. You may find the following list helpful.

Generally, these are approaches companies use to differentiate themselves:

> Appealing design
> Superior performance
> Technical innovation
> Reliability and durability
> Convenience and ease of ordering
> Owner safety
> Atmosphere and ambiance
> Ordering ease
> Delivery
> Installation
> Customer training
> Maintenance and repair
> and, of course… price

You might want to rate the relative strengths by company on each of the differentiators listed above. You might even establish a rating scale, and indicate if the factor (differentiator) is getting stronger or weaker in the market.

After attending the 2007 Chicago Auto Show, the students found enough information to complete the following comparison chart for the features and attributes of the 2007 Luxury Automobiles.

2007 Models	Cadillac	Mercedes C350	BMW 328I	Lexus	di A4 quattro Sec	Lincoln MKZ AWD	Volvo S40 24i	Infiniti G35
Base Price	$ 33,430	$ 39,375	$ 32,400	$ 33,470	$ 36,440	$ 31,820	$ 24,240	$ 33,450
Engine	3.6L	3.5L	3.0 L	3.5L	3.2 L	3.5L	2.4L	3.5
Torque	252 @ 3100	258 @ 2400-5000	200 @ 2750	254 @ 4700	243 @ 3250	249 @ 4900	170 @ 4400	268 @ 4800
Horsepower	255 @ 6200	268 @ 6000	230 @ 6500	272 @ 6200	255 @ 6500	262 @ 6250	168 @ 6000	275 @ 6200
Standard Tra	Manual	Automatic	Manual	Automatic	Manual	Automatic	Manual	Automatic
MPG CITY	17	20	20	21	17	18	22	18
MPG HIGHW,	26	29	30	30	27	26	29	25
Warranty (y	4 - 50000	4 - 50000	4 - 50000	4 - 50000	4 - 50000	4 - 50000	4 - 50000	4 - 60000
Warranty-Po	5 - 100000	4 - 50000	4 - 50000	6 - 70000	4 - 50000	6 - 70000	4 - 50000	6 - 70000
Standard Dri	All-wheel 2008	Rear Wheel	Rear Wheel	Front Wheel	All wheel drive	All- Wheel	Front Wheel	Rear Wheel
Cargo Space	13	12. 2	12	15	13.4		13	7.8
Interior Fron	38.7	38.9	37.4	37.4	38.4	38.7	38.9	39.2
Interior Front	42.4	41.7	41.5	42.2	41.3	42.3	41.6	43.8
Interior Rear	36.2	33	34.6	35.9	34.3	37	34.4	31.4
Exterior - Lei	190.1	178.2	178.2	191.1	180.6	190.5	175.9	182.2
Exterior- Hei	56.7	55.1	55.9	57.3	56.2	57.1	57.2	54.8

Figure 4.1 Competitive Comparison Chart, Features and Attributes of Luxury 2007 Models

Actually, it was one student, Grant, who did most of the work. Not all students have the tenacity to finish such a task, but for those who do, good things come.

When you go into research this deep, you will find you come to know your client very well, and you will know your enemy well. Then, when it comes time to develop messages and present those messages to the client, your thorough understanding of the competition will be invaluable. In this case, Grant and company knew exactly why their ideas were right.

You may be bored by this chart, but for someone in the luxury car market, it's fascinating information. Likewise, we found menu item comparisons – particularly of barbecue items – to be very useful for our work on Stella's. It helped us understand what we were up against.

There are other ways to help your team – and your client – understand what the competitive environment looks like.

Competitive Positioning Map

Here's an approach to consider when reviewing the competition. If you can identify two criteria that distinguish a variety of brands in an industry, you can map your competitors on a grid.

For example, you might map competitors in the restaurant business. In this case we use affordability and taste (Specialty Taste vs. Broad Taste) as the two criteria. The grid might look something like this:

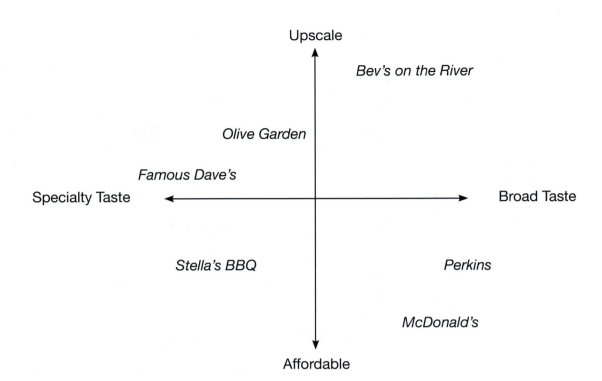

This is very helpful. We can now clearly see the position on the map where Stella's Barbecue competes – the Affordable/Specialty Taste quadrant. Other barbecue, Mexican, and Chinese restaurants would also fall in that area. Franchised groups, like Famous Dave's and Tony Roma's, also in town at that time, were a bit more expensive.

Three More Things to Consider

Here are three more categories of competitive activity that can provide additional insight.

Creative Comparison

Once you have your competitors identified, compare the creative they use in their advertising and promotion. What are the ways they show their brand? What do their ads say? Look at every place their brand comes into contact with a consumer (brand contact points) and take notes. Be a detective. Where do they advertise? Make notes.

Who is their "voice?" What is the message? Does it match other branding efforts? Are there branding efforts beyond the mass media? What are they? Do they have a website? What is the purpose of the website? Does it sell, inform, build a database, or all of the above?

Media Spending

The next area to consider in competitive analysis is media spending. *Advertising Age* publishes Advertising to Sales Ratios in many product categories. In other words, for a given category – like retail stores, or grocery stores, sweets, etc. – you can see what the industry as a whole is spending. The ratio is reported as a percentage of advertising spending to overall sales volume (A to S Ratio). In categories where advertising is a significant part of marketing activity, this can be additional useful information.

Messages and Message Windows

Naturally, big chains like McDonald's, and even smaller chains like Famous Dave's, will be able to outspend a restaurant like Stella's Barbecue. But don't let that large fact keep you from discovering small opportunities.

First, quite a few message windows are local. Even though Starbucks is a big chain, they will introduce themselves by handing out coupons on nearby street corners. And, once customers come in, there are a lot of things Starbucks can do inside the store to get the customer to come back and to buy more while they're in the store. In this case, the store itself is the Message Window.

Second, remember all the ways that a smaller operator can compete. For example, McDonald's doesn't know your name when you come back. A local operator can add that personal touch.

Finally, while it's true that McDonald's can deliver a very good product with broad acceptability, if you like barbecue, there's just no way a McRib can compete with what Stella's Barbecue can put on the plate!

So don't let the fact that you're going to be outspent by the big boys let you lose sight of all the little opportunities that can add up to nice-sized success.

BRAIN BUILDER EXERCISE 4.2: Relative Strengths Table

This exercise will stretch you to think about your competitors. The last column is a company you wish to analyze. It could be your own company, or a company or organization that you identified in Exercise 4.1.

Instructions:

1. Determine your company (see note above) and list it in the last column.

2. Determine three of the strongest competitors and list them in the top column.

3. Now determine four key factors an organization must possess in order to be successful and write them in the Key Success Factors column. Customer satisfaction is already listed for you. If you choose to analyze a student organization, membership satisfaction might be a better term.

4. Rate each of the factors on a scale of 1–10, with ten being the highest, and total the scores for each company. Answer the questions at the end.

	Competitor 1	Competitor 2	Competitor 3	Your Brand
Key Success Factors				
1.				
2.				
3.				
4.				
5. Customer Satisfaction				

1. Which company has the highest scores? Do you believe it represents the market perception? Explain your answer.

2. How can you interpret the scores overall?

3. How can you, as a marketer, use this information?

BRAIN BUILDER EXERCISE 4.3: Competitor Positioning Map

This is one more exercise to help you analyze the competition.

Here's a grid that indicates places – like restaurants – that are cheap or expensive and near or far. Close and cheap gets a lot of day-to-day breakfast and lunch business. For a special occasion, those other parts of the chart start to make sense.

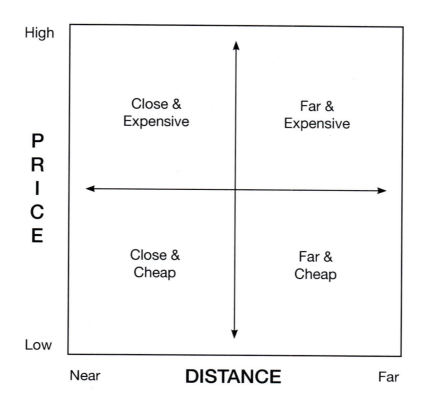

Example: For an important client lunch – close and expensive.

For an anniversary dinner – maybe farther away.

And, unless it's a real bargain, cheap and far away probably won't get your business – unless, of course, it has some special offerings, which means you might need to make a different grid. Remember, a grid only measures two factors.

Before you make your own grid, take another look at the grid the student team did for Stella's Barbecue.

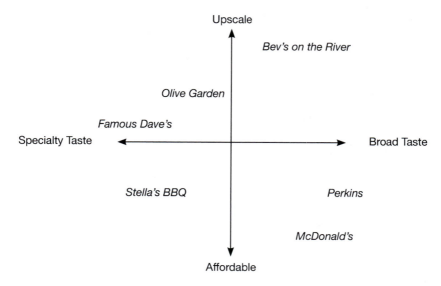

Instructions:

1. Determine two dimensions that are important to the success of the key players in the industry in which your firm competes.

2. Place all of the competitors on the grid, and answer the questions below.

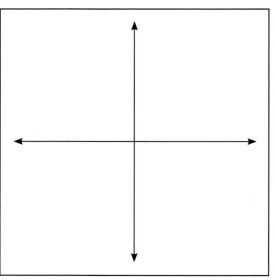

1. Are there too many firms in one quadrant for your business to be profitable or successful? Explain your answer.

2. Are there gaps or openings in the map that might indicate where a customer group is underserved? If so, explain what your firm might do to reach that group.

BRAIN BUILDER EXERCISE 4.4:
Creativity and the Competitor

Using the same exercise we did in Chapter 1, create a chart for competitors.

Instructions:

1. Find three advertisements that were in paid media (first form).

2. Find three other forms of communications (including the Internet) for your competitors.

3. Chart what you found.

4. Answer the questions at the end.

	Ad 1 _____ (Brand)	Ad 2 _____ (Brand)	Ad 3 _____ (Brand)
TARGET Describe who the ads were written for			
MESSAGE What is the primary message of the ad? Any additional message(s)?			
CREATIVE ELEMENTS Designs, illustrations, photography, logos, etc.			
MEDIA/ MESSAGE WINDOW Where did this ad appear?			

	Communication 1 ___(Brand)	Communication 2 ___(Brand)	Communication 3 ___(Brand)
TARGET			
MESSAGE			
CREATIVE ELEMENTS			
MEDIA/ MESSAGE WINDOW			

1. What are the things that are making the most impact in the marketplace?

2. What have you learned from your "enemy"? Be specific.

3. What competitive position do you believe you should hold in the market?

DEFINE THE PROBLEM TO SOLVE

As you begin the process of developing communications for a brand, you need to take time to look critically at the problem you need to solve. If you already know what it is, you're ahead of the game. Write it down and keep it in front of you, post it on your wall, in your planner, and on sticky notes on your desk. You want to keep the problem in focus.

One of the keys to unlocking communication strategy is problem identification and problem definition. Once you understand the problem, you are on the road to understanding the solution.

Here are two examples of advertising problems and how they were translated into marketing communication goals:

1. **Problem:** The problem was that the average age of a Cadillac owner was getting older. If a brand's target audience continues to grow older and a brand continues to produce the same models, market share will usually suffer. Without a model change, healthy growth could have been impossible. But with a new product line developed specifically for a younger audience, Cadillac could address the problem.
   Communication Goal: Establish the 2008 Cadillac CTS as the luxury car of choice for a younger buyer. Bring the average purchase age for that model down by at least ten years.

2. **Problem:** Stella's Barbecue had relocated to a busy intersection, but didn't experience the boost in patrons they anticipated.
   Communication Goal: Promote Stella's unique legacy barbecue to their new local market.

Each of these two examples illustrates different issues. In the case of Cadillac, a major redesign should catch the eye of younger drivers. However, Cadillac's image in the luxury car market was still older and more traditional. American-made luxury cars (including the Lincoln) have typically been purchased as a reward for someone in their later years, usually rewarding one's self. Competitors like Lexus, Mercedes, and BMW have developed an image to attract the younger affluent person in the market for a luxury automobile. The total redesign of the 2008 CTS was introduced mid-year and so was the new spokesperson – Kate Walsh from *Private Practice*. With a smart and sassy young spokeswoman and a sleek new redesign, Cadillac repositioned itself with the younger up-and-coming buyers.

For Stella's Barbecue, the project started after years of moving around. To make things just a bit more difficult, Stella herself had recurring health problems.

Nonetheless, the legacy sauce and spirit of the restaurant were very positive assets. But, often times, the restaurant was not open, or had to close because of family issues. The service was nice enough, but the atmosphere was dingy. The investment into relocation had drained all resources. Understanding the problem, it was clear that a new logo, tag line, and media buy could not solve the challenges that lie ahead.

By truly understanding problems, we often learn that communications can't solve every one of them.

But, understanding the problem can help us focus. It can also help us understand what else it might take, in addition to communication, to solve that problem – or problems, as the case may be.

For example, in this economy, there might be someone who would want to partner with Stella's family and, through "sweat equity," help re-build the business.

Moreover, the customers that did know and care about Stella's represented the kind of resource you wouldn't find at a Famous Dave's. "I'm Still With Stella" buttons, T-shirts, and coupons could start a movement combined with local pride. "Sioux City's Own Favorite Barbecue" added another bit of leverage that McDonald's couldn't achieve.

Other facts that emerge from a Brand Analysis can offer some creative marketing opportunities. For example, Mondays and Tuesdays tend to be slow for most restaurants. With limited resources, Stella's could go to a shorter week and focus – making a meal at Stella's more of a special occasion, while saving salary and energy costs for those slower days.

Finally, that little chart helped clarify the basis of competition.

Stella's was an affordable local alternative that a certain taste segment really loved. A campaign that connected with that specific loyal group of locals had a shot at getting Stella's Barbecue back on their feet, if – and it was a big if – you could get some new energy, resources, and financing into the mix.

So, there was a slightly different target and message needed. Partner Wanted.

Hey, maybe you can solve the problem with the right message.

As they say, "don't solve the wrong problem!"

BRAIN BUILDER EXERCISE 4.5:
The Problem Statement

Your assignment is to build or clarify a problem statement. Remember, for a communications plan you need to specify a problem that can be solved with the right message.

Instructions: For this assignment, ask a relative, your employer, student organization, or use a problem from your own business.

First list the organization – or a client that you are helping. State the product or service and a promotion question you need to answer. Typically, an explanation of the problem and why it has occurred is also stated here. A little historical context helps you down the line.

Client/Organization: _____

Problem Statement: _____

Product or Service targeted: _____

Rationale and explanation of problem: _____
_____
_____
_____

Remember, the purpose of a Situation Analysis is to collect enough information to analyze your situation. Simple enough, it would seem. But the purpose of your analysis is to discover the core issues – the Problem – that will lead you to developing the right message.

You may find, after doing the initial work, that you still don't know enough.

Now you know what you know – and you know what you *don't* know. Terrific.

Looks like it's time for some research.

CHAPTER REVIEW

In this chapter we covered the following topics:

1. Situation Analysis. The overall process of assembling a set of information that helps us answer the question: "Where are we?"

2. The Brand Audit and the Brand Analysis Checklist. We reviewed a wide-ranging list of the kinds of information you want to collect to understand your brand.

3. The Competitive Review. We evaluated our brand's competitors and how they communicate in the marketplace.

4. Defining the Problem to Be Solved. While this workbook focuses on problems that can be solved with communication, we need to have a complete understanding of the situation. We need to develop an accurate understanding of the challenges we face, and we need to realize that not every problem can be solved with the right message.

REVIEW QUESTIONS

1. Take a look at the brand project you are considering. In a sentence or two, how would you answer the question: "Where are we?"

2. Again, considering the brand project you are considering, what parts of The Brand Audit and the Brand Analysis Checklist seem most important? Which ones will be most difficult in acquiring good information for your brand?

3. Which of your brand's competitors are, in your estimation, doing the best job? What do you think you can learn from them?

4. At this stage of the process, how would you define the Problem to Be Solved? Is it a communication problem? What is the message that might solve this problem? Who is the target (or targets) that can truly make a difference? How sure of all this are you? What alternative problems and solutions might you want to think about?

CHAPTER 5:
RESEARCH

As Jim Avery notes in his excellent book, *Advertising Campaign Planning*, "In the Situation Analysis you learned what you know. Now you are smart enough to figure out what you don't know."

That's what research is all about – first, finding out what you don't know, then identifying the important things you need to know to grow your brand, and, finally, finding those answers.

There are a lot of reasons to do research.

Some research is for developmental purposes. Developmental research is used to do such things as observe purchasing behavior, evaluate brand images, or gain consumer insights. You may also conduct developmental research to test some of the creative and message concepts you've developed.

Overall, research is a journey that never ends, because there is always something else you want to know to grow your brand. This chapter is about putting the right tools in your toolbox and developing the right habits in your brand organization. A good brand is an ongoing learning organization. We're always learning more about our target, our product, and about ourselves.

Over the next two chapters we will discuss research. It is a serious topic, and it is also very, very meaningful. Sometimes I have to remind myself to stop having so much fun with the research stuff, and get on with the rest of the program.

LEARNING OUTCOMES

After studying this chapter, you will be able to:

1. Understand why you need to do secondary research first;
2. Have a solid initial understanding of the basics of secondary research;
3. Understand the standards of information literacy; and
4. Design a research plan to help you "know what you don't know."

In the next chapter, we'll show you how to put that Research Plan into action.

DO SECONDARY RESEARCH FIRST

Secondary research basically consists of digging up information that is already available. After all, why go to the trouble of doing a survey to find out who buys what car if that information is availabe and has already been gathered more comprehensively than we could?

You may be surprised at how much information is out there. Particularly with the Internet, Google, Bing and other search engines, as well as additional online resources – some free, others available for a small fee. You can really dig up a lot.

So – before you go asking everyone you know what car they bought, let's simply dig up automobile sales information. And, as you review the Brand Analysis checklist, you will see that, in many cases, there is a lot of information – like annual reports and industry summaries in trade magazines – that you can acquire by doing a thorough job on secondary research first.

OK, now we know why we do secondary research first. Let's get started.

SECONDARY RESEARCH

You will conduct secondary research during the developmental research phase as well as the planning phase. On some levels, this kind of learning never stops. The planning phase includes the work you completed with the Brand Analysis Checklist. A lot of that is secondary research you've already done. Now you have to figure out what else you can do.

How long does it take to complete this stage? Naturally, it depends. Student teams generally go through this stage in about two-to-three weeks.

If you are working in a small team, everyone on your team should dedicate themselves to reading at least 15–20 relevant articles. That's *relevant* articles. To find 15–20 relevant ones, you'll have to sort through a lot more than that.

Experienced agency executives or other business professionals who read marketing communications news daily may not need to do this because they're already familiar with the content. You, on the other hand, are walking into unfamiliar territory.

The good news: If you have an inquiring mind, it's usually a fascinating journey, and you can become a mini-expert in an area that was previously little known to you. Sometimes the results can be pretty interesting. For example, the students working on the community bank project found compelling evidence that mobile banking would not yield a return on the investment in the first year of the proposed ad campaign.

Their secondary research uncovered some additional interesting information.

They discovered that similar sized banks offered a number of new services and online banking features that were not being offered by our bank. One of the banks in the literature was within 75 miles, not a direct competitor of our bank. They had a like-minded target audience, similar to the one we were trying to reach. Guess what we did?

We took a field trip and were received with welcoming professionalism. Four students took a tour of the bank and conducted depth interviews. The new knowledge from the field trip added to the customer preference knowledge found in the literature, and really helped us to prepare an agenda and questions for multiple focus groups with young professionals in the Sioux City market. Once the facts were gathered, recommendations about other banking services emerged and became the focus of the creative strategy.

During The Pitch, it was very exciting to see the executives' faces as they heard the new ideas. They questioned the students diligently – especially about the mobile banking concepts – and they received solid answers. The students had done their homework. It all started with thorough secondary research, then the primary research that came from meeting many customers and non-customers. Evidence from both secondary and primary research supported all of the creative strategy.

We repeat. Secondary research is always completed first.

TIP: In your research plan, add a budget feature to cover the costs of doing all the research necessary – for example, immersion through field trips and study tours.

SOURCES TO HELP YOU

Don't just depend on Google. Here are some resources we've found to be particularly helpful.

Small Business and Entrepreneurship Groups

We've used a number of documents produced by the Small Business Administration (SBA). The material is available free of charge. Owners will answer the questions for the purpose of applying for SBA funding (see www.sba.gov). If really interested, you can find a free training course and a number of templates online.

Additionally, local SBA agencies have consultants who can help with various stages of business planning and growth such as:

- The Small Business Development Center (SBDC)
- SCORE – Counselors to America's Small Business (http://www.score.org/index.html)
- Small Business Development Training Network (http://www.sba.gov/services/training/onlinecourses/index.html),
- Women's Business Centers (http://www.sba.gov/aboutsba/sbaprograms/onlinewbc/index.html).
- The Kauffman Foundation in Kansas City also offers free online resources (www.kauffman.org).

Two other organizations have also been very strong supporters of entrepreneurship education. The Coleman Foundation funded the Morningside College Entrepreneurship Center and has a website where you can find links to other colleges with programs (http://www.colemanfoundation.org). The United States Association for Small Business and Entrepreneurship is another excellent resource for college educators of entrepreneurship (http://usasbe.org).

Next, Take a Look at Online Periodical Databases

- LexisNexis is a database that includes commercially prepared Company Profiles, SEC filings, accounting and tax publications and a collection of over 300 law journals.

- PsychINFO is a database that contains citations and abstracts of journal articles, book chapters, books, dissertations, and technical reports from over 1800 journals. It is produced by the American Psychological Association.

- JSTOR: The JSTOR collection focuses on public policy and administration as well as law, business, and education – with over 100 titles.

- Communication and Mass Media Complete includes indices of 690 titles for the fields of mass communication, psychology, marketing, negotiation. Sample journals are Information Communication & Society, Journal of Broadcasting & Electronic Media, and MediaWeek.

- EBSCOhost serves as a clearing house for a number of databases, as well as those of third parties, some of which are listed above. Many universities have this service, which also includes an Academic Source Premiere and Business Source Premiere.

- Hoovers and Bloomberg are proprietary databases that may be available through your libraries, or specialized departments on campus.

- InfoTrac One File, ABI/Inform Global are also excellent databases.

TIP: Once you find an article in one of the EBSCOhost databases that is "right on" topic – check the Subject Headings describing that article. Use these headings together with the SU Subject tag to do another search. When you find another "right on" article, check the Subject Headings again. Keep doing this, and your Subject Headings and search terms will lead you to a much stronger literature review.

Additional Resources

Here are some of my favorites – specific journals and sites that can help you complete the background information you need:

- Scholarly – Peer-Reviewed Journals that are rich with information relevant to marketing research and advertising: *Journal of Consumer Marketing, Journal of Marketing, Journal of Retailing, Journal of Marketing Services* (especially good to review for like studies and methodology);

- *Consumer Reports* is in a field all its own for independent research;

- J.D. Power online research reports rating customer satisfaction;

- *Advertising Age, Fortune, Forbes, Wall Street Journal, Economist, Harvard Business Review* offer well written and reliable articles.

- Trade magazines are specific to an industry, and can be found by asking someone in the business you are researching (*e.g.* restaurants, banks, radio stations would have their own trade magazines).

TIP: Check The Encyclopedia of Associations – a reference guide to thousands of associations and how to get in touch with them.

Some Observations on Websites, Blogs, and Social Media

Take special care when using websites that seem to be self-proclaimed experts. They may be selling something that's not reliable. I've seen a number of Blogs written by some extremists. It's pretty easy to doubt their opinion.

However, I've also read Blogs by 'experts' who spark a new area of thought. In that case, write down the new thoughts, and go back into EBSCOhost and use the new search terms you've identified.

Professional organizations and news feed groups (newspapers and journals) will have their lead journalists use Blogs to recruit readers to their sites. Journalists' opinions are often accurate and insightful, just take care in betting your business on them.

Proprietary Data

Proprietary databases are available for a fee. Many agencies and some universities may already subscribe. If you know the right people, you can ask them to share old copies of these reports to help you with your student project, or as you launch and grow your business. Here are some of the better ones.

- Simmons (SMRB) and Mediamark Research, Inc. (MRI) sell their studies about demographic information, product use, and media habits.

- Roper, Yankelovich, and Gallup public opinion surveys are available. *The Roper Report, The Yankelovich Monitor,* and *Gallup Management Journal* as well as other publications may be available from these groups:

- http://www.gallup.com
- http://www.gfkamerica.com
- http://www.yankelovich.com

- *American Demographics.* Their archived issues are part of *Advertising Age*

- VALS – Values and Lifestyles published by SRI International

  - http://www.sric-bi.com/VALS

- PRIZM – lifestyle segmentations based on neighborhood http://www.claritas. com/MyBestSegments/Default.jsp?ID=0&SubID=&pageName=Home (actually offers some free segmentation information)

Government Sources

The Federal Government offers information that can often be useful in the research process. Here are some good sites to check out.

- United States Government Manual, http://usgovernmentmanual.gov/

- Statistical Abstract of the United States (Most reference desks at libraries have these) http://www.census.gov/compendia/statab/

- U. S. Census Bureau, http://www.census.gov/

ON INFORMATION LITERACY

Electronic resources and databases can be rich in supplying you with the knowledge you need. Librarians can be very helpful to locate reliable resources for you, but, you need to develop your own skills. You need to learn how to sort through sources, evaluate their relevance, and determine the most effective use of the information. This skill is called Information Literacy. With the information explosion on the web, it has become a big issue.

The Academic College Research Libraries division of the American Library Association developed five information literacy competencies and standards for the information literate student. They are as follows:

1. Determine the nature and extent of the information needed.

2. Access needed information effectively and efficiently.

3. Evaluate information and its sources critically and incorporate selected information into his or her knowledge base and value system.

4. Individually or as a member of a group, use information effectively to accomplish a specific purpose.

5. Understand many of the economic, legal, and social issues surrounding the use of information and accesses and uses information ethically and legally (ACRL, 2000).

As you work to develop these five competencies, you'll need to develop the ability to critically evaluate information. You can't put too much faith in everything you happen to find in a Google search.

In general, Google does not have much in the way of quality control to determine the reliability of the information.

Google Scholar, however, can be a good starting point. It includes scholarly and peer-reviewed literature, but you have to specifically look for it. So if you already have a good set of Research Questions developed, begin your search with the Google Scholar options.

Use the databases for Peer-Reviewed or Scholarly Journals available at an academic or public library to insure high levels of reliable sources.

There's more to secondary research than Google. As you sort through some of the premiere databases, you'll see that there's a lot you can learn – and more every day.

DESIGN A BRAND RESEARCH PLAN (aka Research Proposal)

You're learning a lot about your brand and the brand category.

You completed the Brand Analysis Checklist. Then, you did Secondary Research.

You know a lot more than you did when you started. Now, as Jim Avery indicated, *"...you are smart enough to figure out what you don't know."*

And that's what a Brand Research Plan is for.

First, identify the important things you need to know, then develop a plan to learn those things. This next stage of the research will move you deeper into knowledge that will help you determine the type of research you'll need to do. Incidentally, this research will be primary research. It may be qualitative research like in-depth interviews or focus groups, or it may be quantitative research – such as a survey with a questionnaire you designed yourself.

In the next chapter, we'll cover how to do that work.

In this section, we'll talk about developing the plan – which is figuring out what it is we need to learn, and how we're going to learn it.

Research Design Process

The research design process is a series of steps we need to take to discover what we need to know. When you think through the entire research process first, you are buying insurance, an intellectual policy. The process insures that you've done your homework, and it will give you the best shot at finding the 'jewels' of information and insight you need to develop the right message. We're always searching for that one right thing to say that can help you connect with your target and improve your business.

Recently, a student team was given the opportunity by a former student to help develop a campaign for a local community bank. (He had been on the winning Cadillac team. He now worked at a bank.) We talked over Christmas break in the lobby of the bank about a possible project together. He'd been put in charge of building a marketing and communication plan for the Young Professional. That was his target.

Confidentiality was also an issue, so we built that into the design as well.

Using the bank project as a model, let's look at the basics of brand research.

Ten Steps: A Basic Format for a Brand Research Plan

Naturally, every brand and every problem will be a little bit different.

But the bank project encompassed most of what you'd do for most projects. It might be a bigger project, it might be smaller. However, the basic elements will be pretty much the same.

First you determine what it is you need to accomplish.

What is it you need to know?

Then, step by step, you organize a program to answer those questions.

For the bank, it was a ten step process. The ten steps are as follows.

1. Review the problem statement
2. Define the research objectives
3. Review relevant literature
4. Select a research design
5. Design the research instrument
6. Determine the sample design
7. Collect and process the data
8. Analyze and interpret the data
9. Communicate the results
10. Apply the knowledge to an advertising campaign

Step 1: Review the problem statement

The decision process surrounding the problem statement can be highlighted. Clearly defining the problem once again will insure the best data collection.

Step 2: Define research objectives

Write your research objectives by asking: "What do we want to know?" Most likely you will research four areas:

- the target audience,
- factors that motivate purchase behavior,
- unique brand characteristics, and
- competitive activity.

For example, a radio station wanted to know more about their listeners and if their listeners were loyal to the station. The research question could be transformed into research objectives: To determine characteristics of the target audience and, to identify listeners and factors that influenced their loyalty to the station.

Step 3: Review relevant literature

Secondary research is conducted to find previously collected data, or review literature related to your problem. Published studies and current literature will aid you in becoming familiar with relevant practices. Topics to search and search terms should relate to six areas:

- Target audience characteristics
- Customer satisfaction
- Segmentation variables
- Demographic data
- Industry trends
- Competition practices

Your review should not be an exhaustive historical review (assume the reader of your report is knowledgeable). Cite and reference specific works to your issue (not those of general use), and highlight significant findings and methodologies.

Even though you've already done some secondary research, with a bit more focus on the exact problem to be solved you may find quite a bit more information.

Step 4: Select a research design (or methodology)

You will do two things here, identify data sources and identify a method to collect the data. The research design is the plan that describes the methods you will use to collect and analyze the data needed to meet the research objectives. Both qualitative and quantitative research tools will be used. In the case of a radio station, you might first use qualitative methods such as one-on-one interviews with listeners who have won a call-in promotion – heavy users. You could also do a focus group with current users and another with non-users (listeners and non-listeners). Now you are starting to do primary research.

For your qualitative work, you will design questions that address the research objectives. For your quantitative work, you will most likely start with a survey. Surveys are the most common quantitative method of research. It's common to alternate qualitative and quantitative techniques. Completing a focus group or interviews – qualitative work – will help you design the quantitative methods.

Primary data is collected for research specific to a current problem or opportunity and is original data. An e-mail survey (such as Survey Monkey or SPSS) of the station's database of listeners could be used as a primary research method. (Later in this chapter, you will learn more research tools – both qualitative and quantitative).

Doing the right research often costs money. If you have any costs that will be incurred for any of the research methods, provide a detailed budget projection.

Step 5: Design the research instrument

When you need to collect primary data, you will need to design a survey instrument to record the information. The questionnaire should be designed to be reliable, accurate, and able to obtain unbiased information. Each survey instrument should be pretested for errors.

Proper questionnaire design is critical to obtaining relevant data. It is a very costly and time consuming effort. Errors are not only costly, the result is inaccurate information. Check and double-check. Additional methods such as observations, depth interviews, and word associations can provide you with the insights you need to develop the right message.

For example, for the 2008 Cadillac CTS campaign, we surveyed Morningside alumni who were in the target age, using Survey Monkey. We sent letters and a follow up e-mail with the link to activate the survey.

Recall your research objectives and determine what information you need.

In the case of the bank, we wanted to know how young professionals banked, how they selected their bank, and their opinions of local banks. The economic climate made this a particularly interesting case to research. In the main, bank products and services are slow to evolve, but our bank wanted to implement mobile banking, which was a current trend in larger markets. Research questions were developed for this area.

Step 6: Determine the sample design

To begin, you need to determine who your subjects will be for each research objective. Specify the population and the sample of that population you plan to study.

For example, in the banking case, the sample included customers and non-customers invited to three focus groups (qualitative data). In addition, bank employees in the "young professional" target group were used for a fourth focus group. Key executives were interviewed to determine both the bank's mission and their views about the bank image in the public. Since mobile banking was a concern, we added Verizon and Sprint to our plan with depth interviews. In addition, the problem statement included a goal to increase retail businesses as part of the customer base. The sample plan added one-on-one interviews with a cross section of retail businesses.

Rights and Obligations of the researcher and respondents:

As a researcher, you are obligated to protect the client's information and the rights of the respondents. The respondents' confidentiality is important, and they should be informed of the study taking place. This is known as Informed Consent. In the event respondents do not wish to participate, they can exit at any time. We've provided a sample Informed Consent form later in this chapter.

Step 7: Collect and process the data

Administer the plan and process the data you have collected. The data may need to be coded or entered into documents or programs to process. Simple Excel sheets can tabulate the data. More complex SPSS programs can be used to tabulate and analyze your information.

For e-mail surveys, Survey Monkey has built in analysis tools from simple to more complex cross tabulations. Both are very informative. For the bank project, all interview and focus group information was captured in notes and tabulated for a presentation. Organizing notes from four focus groups was a tedious process, but was very insightful.

Step 8: Analyze and interpret the data

It's time to turn the raw data into useful information. The radio station had a list of 150 winners of recent promotions. Only 15 responded to the request to complete the Survey Monkey questionnaire. The data was accurate, but it was difficult to project that 15 people would represent all of their listeners. However, even though the sample was small, the data was helpful. When combined with previous literature reviews and observations at the radio station's "live" broadcasts, specific listener characteristics were determined.

For Cadillac, over 150 Morningside College alumni responded. In the proposal, we developed a description of how the data would be analyzed.

Step 9: Communicate the results

Your next step is to prepare a research report for presentation to the decision-makers. The report will be written and excerpts made part of the final Power Point, along with the creative results. It should be clear that the results connect with the research objectives that address the problem you've identified.

Step 10: Apply the results

The results from all the secondary and primary research should be applied. Informed actions based on research are a key dynamic in the brand-building process.

Informed Consent

When you interview people, you need to have their consent. For a student sample, they're usually just paid a few dollars – enough for a cup of coffee (donut optional). For more elaborate focus groups – for example, higher level executives – it's not uncommon for larger fees to be involved.

Here is the form. As you might imagine, we've also posted it on our website: www.brandbuilderworkbook.com

---

INFORMED CONSENT FORM

The study you are being asked to participate in is concerned with _____
_____. We will be asking a number of questions related to this topic.
The data collected will be used to help us _____.
Your name will not be used in any stage throughout the research and all informa-
tion will be kept confidential. Results will be gathered and used to _____
_____. If you have any questions, feel free to contact _____
_____.

Name (please print) _____   Date _____

Signature _____

A Sample Research Proposal

If you've never done a research plan, you might wonder what one looks like.

Below is our example, created for the bank – the Young Professionals project. Here is the research proposal that followed a slightly different model.

Targeting Young Professionals
Security National Bank

Current Situation

Security National Bank (SNB) opened their first branch in 1884 in Northwest Iowa, marking 2009 with their 125th anniversary. SNB currently has five branches in Sioux City and has affiliate banks in Orange City, Mapleton, Akron, and Sioux Falls. While SNB's business is still thriving, most of SNB patrons are over 50, and fewer younger clients are opening accounts. SNB is looking to the future and noticing that, without an increase in younger clientele, the bank will be facing financial difficulties over time.

SNB is a traditional, conservative bank, which their current patrons appreciate. However, SNB wants to begin a new campaign that will bring in more small business owners and young professionals. They are currently looking for the best marketing strategies to use for this target market, so that SNB can draw in younger professionals while maintaining their integrity and retaining their older patrons.

Purpose of the Research

The general purpose of the study is to determine the best possible ways for SNB to reach the market of young professionals and small business owners. The following are specific research objectives to achieve:

1. To determine what factors are most relevant and important to members of the young professional demographic when engaging in banking activities.

2. To identify what media young professionals aged 25-35 are most inclined to engage in and interact with.

3. To identify marketing strategies for SNB's existing audience and the proposed younger target audience.

4. To determine what innovations competitors are currently using to reach young professionals, new retail and small business owners.

5. To identify local and regional events that attract the target market.

6. To determine potential "cause marketing" that could relate to SNB's values.

Research Design

The research design will be a combination of focus groups and personal in-depth interviews.

The first method consists of focus groups administered to the target audience as well as the existing SNB customers and employees. In order to obtain consistent results, it will be necessary to conduct two or three customer focus group sessions. Focus groups will allow definitive generalizations about Security National Bank to emerge, thus giving student team members more insight about what tactics to recommend for the campaign effort.

Personal interviews will consist of in-depth interviews with current SNB users and non-users, a national or regional bank known for mobile banking to the young professionals such as PNC Financial Services Group, Inc., as well as SNB upper-level management. Phone interviews will also be conducted with the Sioux City Tourism Bureau and other regional event groups.

Protecting Rights and Obligations

The rights and obligations of all parties involved in the research process are an intrinsic factor to uphold. Research participants have the obligation to be truthful. Focus group sessions and interviews are highly dependent on truthfulness of participants; if they were not, results would be invalid and ineffective. The right to be informed can be achieved by describing, in detail, the purpose of the research to the participants before they begin the focus group session or in-depth interview. At any point during the focus group or interview, the respondents will have the right to forgo participation if they wish. Consent forms will be used at each session informing the participants of their rights.

Researchers must maintain confidentiality in working with the project for Security National Bank. Misrepresentation of research and dissemination of faulty conclusions can be avoided by a tactic where all group members examine each other's work for error corrections. Confidentiality of the client sponsor is vital in research. Security National Bank will protect the security of its members and restrict dispersion of strategies and tactics to competitors.

The client sponsor for the advertising campaign is Security National Bank. The client sponsors have already provided the researchers with a full and open statement of the present situation; this situation was described thoroughly in the initial meeting with the client sponsor prior to secondary research. The researchers, faculty, and department chair have signed confidentiality agreements as a condition of working on the project. There is a timeline for the research project to be completed.

Sample Design

- Four focus groups of approximately 8-10 members will be conducted. The subjects will be selected to represent the audience. Two focus groups will be SNB clientele group members from the current customer group, as well as the young professional demographic; 4-5 members will be from each group. The other consumer group will be solely of young professional customers. Eligible respondents will be between the ages of 20 and 40. SNB will provide a list of their current customers in this age range, and researchers will call and mail a request to participate. The final focus group will consist of SNB employees who come into contact with young professionals.

- Personal interview participants, which include current SNB customers, regional or national bank such as PNC Financial Services Group, Inc., Security National Bank managers, and the Sioux City Tourism Bureau and other regional groups, are chosen for interviews based on their expertise that can add to our research findings.

Data Gathering

Marketing researchers will administer the focus groups. Two moderators will lead the topics to be discussed. Additional group members can take notes as the focus group proceeds. Qualitative data will be gathered on site of the focus groups.

Personal in-depth interviews will be administered by individual team members. Interviewees will be current Security National Bank customers in the young professional target. Interviews of the Sioux City Tourism Bureau, PNC Financial Services Group, and SNB CEOs will also be conducted. Similar to the focus groups, data will be gathered and recorded for later analytical use.

Data Processing and Analysis

Standard editing procedures will be utilized in analyzing the data. After all data has been compiled and analyzed, the information will be condensed into a format that addresses the research objectives. Also, as part of the data processing, the researchers will look for possible interviewer/interviewee errors or biases. If any are found, corrective measures will be taken so the results are as accurate as possible. Analysis of the data will be completed to determine patterns in the responses.

Report Preparation

After processing and analyzing the data, significant conclusions should be visible. These conclusions should comprise the bulk of the written report. Report preparation should also include struggles and difficulties group members encountered throughout the research process. Valid considerations for the improvement of Security National Bank should be stated in the written and oral report.

Research results will be presented to the clients in a PowerPoint presentation. Suggestions and promotional ideas will be made at the conclusion of the presentation.

Creative strategies and tactics will be presented to members of Security National Bank. After all the data has been presented we will open it up to any questions the client may have. Along with the presentation, the client will be given a report in book and CD format with all the information organized for easy future reference.

Budget and Time Schedule

Below is a tentative schedule of dates in which research should be started and completed. As with any schedule it is subject to change do to unexpected problems or added research methods.

Monday, February 9, 2009: Create draft focus group and interview questions. Compile a list of possible focus group members and interviewees. Obtain IRRB approval. Obtain SNB approval.

Tuesday, February 10, 2009: Finalize questions and list of possible contacts.

Thursday, February 12, 2009: Pre-planning.

Monday, February 16, 2009: Conduct focus groups and interviews.

Tuesday, February 17, 2009: Conduct focus groups and interviews.

Thursday, February 19, 2009: Conduct focus groups and interviews.

Monday, February 23, 2009: Complete focus group and interview sessions.

Tuesday, February 24, 2009: Compile and analyze data collected.

Thursday, February 26, 2009: Compile and analyze data collected.

Thursday, March 12, 2009: Finalize creative strategy.

Tuesday, March 17, 2009: Develop marketing services plan.

Friday, April 17, 2009: Present advertising campaign to campus.

Thursday, April 23, 2009: Present to client.

CHAPTER REVIEW

These are the topics covered in Chapter 5.

1. The importance of doing secondary research first.

2. The basics of secondary research – including major sources and techniques.

3. Information literacy – a growing concern.

4. Designing the research plan.

REVIEW QUESTIONS

1. How will you begin your secondary research?

2. How will you refine your search?

3. What are the ten steps to designing a research plan?

4. What is Informed Consent?

CHAPTER 6:
DEVELOPMENTAL RESEARCH

Now that you've developed a Research Plan, it's time to do the work.

If you do it right, the insights you develop will be critical in helping you develop the right message for your brand.

You will be conducting research for your brand-building campaign. This type of research is often called Developmental Research. That is, the research conducted will help you develop insights about consumers, brand images, demographic trends, and changing attitudes. You are continuing on the road to build your Brand's Messages!

You have been picking up little bits of information all along the way. Now, with a little bit of luck and a lot of hard work, more information is coming. We are looking for the right insight. We're looking for meaningful, actionable insights. Sometimes it's a psychological insight, sometimes it's a competitive advantage that leads you to meaningful differentiation, and sometimes it's as simple as the right words.

That's right, sometimes it is all words. Just words. Often, the right message for a brand is a word plus another word plus another word or two. You have to figure out the right ones. You have a very short amount of time to get someone's attention.

Constructing and creating media strategies means crafting the Message and identifying the Message Windows you need to build your Brand. Your research helps you make the right decisions.

As you gather information from consumers, it will lead to insights. It can be hard work and it can be complicated, but there are simple steps that get you there. This chapter is about taking those steps and developing meaningful, actionable insights.

LEARNING OUTCOMES

After you have completed this chapter, you will understand how to:

1. Design research objectives appropriate for your study;
2. Develop qualitative research methods; and
3. Design questions and surveys, used in quantitative research methods.

RESEARCH OBJECTIVES

In the previous chapter you learned about objectives as part of designing the overall research plan. This will be a short review of that discussion. The ten steps of the research plan begin with: (1) Review the problem statement, followed by (2) Define the research objectives. Then there are eight more steps.

As you work through the steps, you'll make a list of questions relevant to the things you want to know about your target audience, what makes your brand unique, what benefits you offer that are different, what values are reinforced by your brand, etc. Keep thinking of questions you need answered. Eventually those questions will be good questions that can be rewritten into research objectives.

For example, students in the campaigns class working for Security National Bank were challenged to build a campaign directed at the young professionals. Let's think about how to take good questions and convert them to research objectives. Take a look at the three questions that follow:

"What did young professions look for in a bank?"
"Why did young professionals choose one bank over another?"
"What services in a bank did young professionals use most often, and why?"

To find the answers, the research objective would look like this:

To determine the bank services that are most important for young professionals.

Three questions were rolled into one objective, with a broader meaning. We could keep asking questions. What age are the young professionals? What were their professions? Did it matter? Did technology drive their banking decisions? Typically, you'll keep writing questions and group them to help you write research objectives. As you become more experienced, you can write the research objectives first. But I still like writing the questions and then working back and forth. This method helps you find out what you truly want to know and helps you determine if you have anything useful.

TEN STEP RESEARCH PROCESS

The ten steps of the research process are listed below.

1. Review the problem statement
2. Define the research objectives
3. Review relevant literature
4. Select a research design
5. Design the research instrument
6. Determine the sample plan
7. Collect and process the data
8. Analyze and interpret the data
9. Communicate the results
10. Apply the knowledge

Now let's cover these steps in more detail.

1. Review the Problem Statement

Give this another look. While your problem might seem simple and straightforward, getting at what's really going on might be a bit more difficult. Also, you may well find that there are conflicting agendas, with different members of the team wanting to find out different bits of information.

As that advertising philosopher, Alvin Blick reminds us, "Don't solve the wrong problem." What's really going on? Is it an awareness problem? Maybe. But if you look at it again and realize that quite a few people have experienced the product or service over the years – so maybe it's not exactly awareness.

Has the marketplace changed? Often we have a situation where a once vibrant business is no longer vibrant. What's going on here?

Is there a new target audience in the mix? Often a business was successful serving an older generation and now it's the new generation making purchase decisions. What's changed? What's still the same?

The point – and it's an important one – is that defining The Problem is a critical task – and it's often easy to think it's an easy job.

2. Define the Research Objectives

Sometimes working harder on Point #2 can help you decide if you've done a good enough job on Point #1.

Simply put, you'll want to write your research objectives by asking "what do we want to know?"

Most likely, you will research four areas.

- Target audience
- Factors that motivate purchase behavior
- Unique brand characteristics
- Competitive activity

For example, a radio station wanted to know more about its listeners and if they were loyal to the station. That research question could be transformed into research objectives: to determine characteristics of the target audience and to identify listeners and factors that influence their loyalty to the station.

It's worth reminding you: "Factors That Motivate Purchase Behavior" are always something that you want to know.

3. Review Relevant Literature

You never stop doing secondary research. If you see a new magazine article, save it. If you suddenly come upon a new angle that gives you a whole new direction for search engine research, take another look. See what you find.

As you begin to identify the problem and focus on the things you need to discover, you'll find that you have a better focus on the secondary research you've collected. So now is a good time to take another look at all that secondary research you've done – and maybe do a bit more.

4. Select a Research Design

Once you have your objectives and have taken another look at the literature, you are ready to determine *how* you will reach the objectives and determine the best methodology to do so. This next section briefly describes the most common qualitative and quantitative data gathering methodology used in advertising and marketing research.

TIP: Start making your own survey of surveys. Save customer satisfaction surveys from hotels, restaurants, retail outlets, or unsolicited mail questionnaires, online satisfaction surveys. They are great examples to help inspire questions that might spark more questions that will help you uncover "what you want to know!"

Qualitative and Quantitative

There are essentially two types of research and data gathering methods: quantitative and qualitative.

Qualitative methods are conducted over a shorter time frame with a relatively small sample size. They are called qualitative because you get a certain quality of information, but you cannot accurately state the percentage of the marketplace that feels that way. So you may find out some very interesting information, but you really don't know whether that point of view represents the way most of the target group feels, or just these few individuals.

In general, if you're doing qualitative work, there are some "heavy users" available (i.e. people who use the product, or shop at the store, or – if it's a new product – people who are heavy users of the current leading competitor). "Heavy users" are usually deeper wells of information – they have more to say. But it's still qualitative, and those heavy users may be very different from other users. You simply don't know.

On the other hand, quantitative methods use larger and more statistically dependable sample sizes. Sample and sample size refer to the group of respondents selected to be a part of your study. The respondents should have characteristics that are similar to those of your targeted group. Here you can start to depend a bit more on the information. If you asked a thousand people the same question, an answer of 67% is useful and dependable. If you talked to three people, and two answered the question the same way, you may still have 67%, but you don't have the same kind of dependability. Both methods may yield important evidence, but the dependability of the data is dramatically different.

Both methods have strengths. When you do qualitative work, you can do longer in-depth interviews that might dig out useful insights for your messaging. As you know if you've ever answered a questionnaire, there's a limit to how many questions you can ask people before they get impatient.

Qualitative Methods You Might Consider.

Here are the most popular types of qualitative methods. You may want to use a mix of them. For example, do a few longer one-on-one interviews before you do a focus group. This can help you do a better job designing the focus group structure – the discussion guide.

We've added a few examples of research objectives and the questionnaires that went with them to help give you a feel for what's involved.

1. **Focus Groups** – These consist of 8 to 12 selected members of the target audience who are convened for a focused discussion of a brand or to test concepts. The focus group lasts from one to two hours in length led by a moderator following a prescribed list of questions and topics to achieve knowledge about the brand and consumer behavior. (See moderator agenda for SNB case below.)

2. **One-on-One Interviews** – These are conducted with members of the targeted group to obtain more in-depth knowledge or when a focus group cannot be convened (also known as depth interviews). Sometimes the topic is sensitive or upper management is not available for focus groups. Prescribed questions, much like focus group questions, are used to gather information from the targeted consumers.

3. **Personal interviews** – These can be very time consuming, but they have very low costs and give the interviewer control of who is selected. It can be a good way to get started.

4. **Telephone interviews** – These are also time consuming, with variable costs depending on the geographical coverage of the respondents. Sampling control can be strong, but it may be very difficult to get a decent response rate.

5. **Observations** – Habits of the consumer may often be determined by observation. The technique of observation was first developed and used by sociologists, anthropologists, and ethnographers in the field of social sciences. In marketing and advertising, observations will last for a week or two at most.

6. **Projective techniques** – These may allow the participant to view or be involved in expressing certain characteristics or attributes of a brand. The following are examples of projective techniques.

   a. **Brand Collage** – contains multiple images related to a brand. Respondents are asked to select the images that best represent the brand and explain why they selected those images.

   b. **Storytelling** – is a method in which the respondents will write a story about their experience with a brand. The researcher can use specific prompts to help start the story.

   c. **Word Association** – is used to get to the best word or words that represent a brand. The researcher would typically ask for the first word that comes to mind when a brand is mentioned. The researcher might also offer a list of words with the respondent selecting those words that best fit the brand. Word association is also good to test ads or concepts.

   d. **Drawing** – allows respondents to draw their impressions about the brand. This can be particularly useful with children who might not be able to express themselves verbally.

7. **Study tours** – field trips can be used to immerse the researcher in the market – where the brand is located or where like-minded users are located. When my students participated in the "Visit Florida" AAF competition, they did exactly that. They first used most of the methods listed above – visiting two trade shows, testing a questionnaire, conducting word association and storytelling, running two focus groups on campus, and conducting one-on-one interviews and observations. In addition, students sent a mail questionnaire to selected alumni. Of course this was after a complete review of the literature related to the case. Oh yes, and as many as possible visited Florida.

   The study tours were conducted in two areas of Florida – Miami and Orlando. The trade shows were in Chicago and DesMoines, Iowa.

   Each trip allowed students to become immersed in some aspect of the brand and allowed the students to generate creative strategies that would have never been possible otherwise.

Just as total immersion can be the best way to learn a language, a study tour can be a very effective way to get your team immersed in the topic.

Quantitative Methods

The advantage of quantitative research is that the results are usually reliable, although, of course, the results are only as good as the questions (and how well the survey is implemented). And the questions typically follow the research objectives. Communication research is not as in-depth as marketing research and, through it all, you need to keep your end goals in mind. If you are an owner/operator, or in a non-profit, and have not conducted research for your organization before, spend your time wisely. Gather as much information as you can with the resources you have at hand. In general, we never have enough good information.

There are four types of quantitative methods that are most commonly used.

1. **Sample Surveys** – surveys conducted with a sample of a population in order to estimate the characteristics of an entire group.

2. **Online questionnaires** – offer a very inexpensive method to survey selected individuals over the internet.

3. **Mail questionnaires** – are more expensive, take more time to obtain returns, and often have a very low projected return rate. Additional follow-up cards, letters, envelopes, and return postage quickly increase the research budget.

   Both questionnaire methods rely on the respondent to self-administer the questionnaire and return (or click through) the answers. (See below for questionnaire design.)

4. **Experiments** – are highly choreographed research methods to study the effects of one or more independent variables (such as ad spending levels) on one or more dependent variables (such as ad awareness, brand attitude, or sales).

   Experiments can also be conducted during the research phase to study the effect of placement of a product (independent variable) and the target audience usage or attitude (dependent variable).

   There is also a type of experiment commonly referred to as "deprivation research." Instead of measuring the object, we measure the hole it leaves. What do we mean by that?

   A classic example of this kind of research helped inspired the "Got Milk?" campaign. Respondents were asked to do without milk for a week or two. The results were dramatic. There were things where you just had to have milk. This was much more dramatic than the generic "good for you" response that came from having a carton of milk in the refrigerator.

In many product categories, this is an easy-to-implement type of experiment.

An Environmental Experiment

My marketing research students conducted research for the Environmental Sustainability Committee on campus. An experiment was conducted to determine the effect of the placement of bins on the level of recycling participation. Recycle bins were placed in various classrooms in three different buildings.

Over a two week period, observations were conducted and recycled material was counted. The experiment tracked the activity by Morningsiders with the new recycle bins, as well as with existing recycle bins in the library, the business building, and the student commons. In addition, the students observed the maintenance personnel treatment of the recycling bins in those buildings.

The results proved, first, that students and faculty will recycle if it is made convenient with bins closely located to the decision points, and, second, that maintenance personnel frequently ignored full recycling bins. After the experiment, a campus-wide survey was administered, and depth interviews of the maintenance personnel and campus executives were conducted.

I frequently encourage this type of marketing research to help understand consumer behavior.

Surveys and Questionnaires

In certain circumstances, experiments can be very informative and generate unique insights.

But, in general, the quantitative work we do will be in the form of surveys and questionnaires.

Designing questions and questionnaires follows a specific process. If this task is before you , this next section will help you through this phase.

5. Design the Research Instrument

Now you've moved from Defining The Problem and setting the Research Objectives through the qualitative and quantitative options available to you.

It's time to do some research. And, if you do a smart job designing the research you're going to do, you've got a pretty good chance of finding out what you're looking for.

Here, we'll cover two basic types of Research Instruments: the Focus Group and the Questionnaire. You'll use similar techniques in one-on-one interviewing and in the Focus Group Agenda. In fact, you'll often do a few one-on-ones as you develop that Focus Group tool.

Then, we'll go over some of the basics of questionnaire design.

Designing the Focus Group Agenda.

Here are Focus Group Agenda notes for the "Young Professionals" project for our bank client. You can see the agenda is set to determine the purchase behavior of non-members of the Security National Bank (SNB) bank. Those who were invited were our target – young professionals. The focus group was held during lunch time, so lunch was served. The response level was average, even with good follow up and high respect for the students conducting the study. SNB customers and non-customers were determined by the respondents who replied to the invitation to participate.

Young professionals, by the bank's definition, were aged 18–35, but skewed more to the college educated. While you would not ask someone's age before inviting them to a focus group, you can predetermine age by using other methods. The students used a number of methods when inviting campus faculty, staff, friends and family to the four focus groups. The agenda you see below was very useful.

Two focus groups were with non-SNB customers, one was with SNB customers, and one was with SNB young professional employees.

FOCUS GROUP Agenda Notes – Non-SNB Members

Moderators introduce the purpose of the focus group

Introduce yourself and how you chose your bank

1. Why do you bank?

2. Why did you choose your current bank?

    a. What features does your bank offer that you like?

    b. Which features do you most frequently use?

    c. What would you like to change about your bank?

---

3. What would make you change banks?

   a. What makes you stay at a bank?

4. Is quality service important to you?

   a. How does your bank provide quality service?

5. Do you know what mobile banking is?

   a. Would you/do you use mobile banking?

6. How do you feel about non-traditional virtual banking? (Online banking, mobile banking, account transfers, bill pay, etc.)

   a. Do you feel it takes away from the personalized experience of physical banking?

7. Do you pay much attention to advertising and if so, what media?

   a. What catches your eye in bank advertising?

   b. What makes a bank advertisement memorable?

      i. What catches your eye on the following local and national web-sites? (Bring up each of the following and ask a series of questions: Wells Fargo, SNB, Central, Vantus, PNC)

         a. Are the colors good or bad?

         b. Are the graphics/images good or bad?

         c. Is the organization of the website clear?

         d. Is the type/copy readable?

         e. What do you think of the tagline of this one?

         f. What would you change?

8. Is a retirement plan (401K, IRA, etc.) important to you?

9. Do you have any views concerning Security National Bank? If so, what are they? (Positive or negative are both fine!)

10. Any other comments/questions regarding banking?

Thank you for your time.

Designing Questions And Questionnaires

You will need to recall the problem statement and the research objectives to design questions for your research. You can use basic questions for your focus groups, one-on-one interviews, and surveys. You will build and design the questions to gain information to meet your research objectives. Measuring this information will be key to building your report and your strategy.

The question design process should follow the path below.

1. **Specify what information is needed**. Once you have the research objectives, the information needed for the objectives are determined. Be as specific as you can. For example, do you need to determine customer satisfaction in terms of comfort of an automobile? How do you define the information needed for the comfort of an automobile: headroom, legroom, seats, temperature? Checking JDPower or Consumer Reports will provide measurements in a number of categories.

2. **Determine the type of questionnaire and method of administration.** Decide if questions will be used online, in a mail questionnaire, in personal or telephone interviews, or in a focus group.

3. **Determine the content of individual questions**. Ask yourself two tough questions. Are the questions you're asking needed? Are additional questions needed to explore the content more deeply? Return to your research objectives and audit the two lists for relevancy.

4. **Determine the form of response to each question**. What will you use? A Likert scale, a rating scale, a "check all that apply," or semantic differential (e.g. seven point scale for "pleased me" to "displeased me").

5. **Determine the wording of each question**. Decide the best words to reach the objectives; include only one concept per question. Avoid ambiguous words.

6. **Determine the question sequence**. The first question should be simple. Use a logical order. Try to go from broad to narrow. Ask sensitive questions later. Demographic and socioeconomic classifications should be asked last (age range, education, gender, income range, geographic area, etc.). Allow respondents to skip questions that are irrelevant. Make sure the skip pattern is obvious.

7. **Design the layout**. Pay attention to the appearance of the questionnaire: carefully edit for grammar and spelling; group items by topic or scaling technique (or both); and provide an effective introduction.

8. **Reexamine and revise**. Review your research objectives. See if there are opportunities to revise your questionnaire to optimize results.

9. **Pretest and revise if necessary**. Pretest the questions or questionnaire on the target audience, or with faculty members, for clarity and ease of administering. Revise and retest if necessary.

Three sections of questioning

In any form of questioning you have three sections – the introduction or instructions section, the content section, and the characteristics of the respondent section. This is even true for focus groups.

- Introduction or instructions
- Content
- Respondent characteristics

In the introduction at a focus group, use ice breakers or stories related to the general industry being researched. In the introduction section of a survey, provide instructions for completion and return of the form, along with the purpose of the survey.

In the content section, carefully organize questions related to the research objectives. Design the questions to meet the objectives.

The respondent characteristics are typically the final section of the survey. Ask demographic, geographic, psychographic questions pertinent to the study at the end of the survey.

6. Determine the Sample Plan

When you are implementing well-funded market research or message research, there will usually be trained researchers involved who can provide the mathematical basis for sample size and sample selection. If someone like that is available to you, take advantage of their expertise, because the better your sample, the better your research.

But for the rest of us, we may not have that option.

In general, more is better. It is also a good idea to try to make the sample as representative of your target group as possible.

If you're doing a survey, here are a few of the things most commonly measured.

12 Areas of Information to Measure
- Brand awareness
- Advertising awareness

- Customer satisfaction determinants
- Market segmentation variables
- Brand knowledge or information
- Advertising knowledge or information
- Attitude toward the brand
- Attitude toward the advertising
- Purchase decision process – conviction, intention, purchase (influencers and retail or secondary environment)
- Packaging or Creative concept testing
- Demographic/socioeconomic data of the respondents
- Psychographic data of the respondents

Here are examples of how we did this.

Brand and Advertising Awareness

Research Objective: To measure awareness of a radio station and any advertising the radio station has produced.

Question for recall:

List (or name) the top three radio stations that you listen to.

1._____ 2. _____ 3. _____

Question for advertising recognition – both aided and unaided recognition:

Unaided: *Do you remember hearing or seeing any radio station advertisements? If so please name the station(s).*

1._____ 2. _____ 3. _____

Aided: *Which of the following radio stations do you recall seeing on the buses in Sioux City?* Please check all that you recall seeing.

_____ *KSUX*

_____ *Kool 99.5*

_____ *102.3 Jack FM*

_____ *1360 am*

_____ *Other, please list* _____

Customer satisfaction determinants

Research Objective: Measure customer satisfaction of cleanliness of Stella's Barbecue

(A five point Likert-type scale)

Very Clean	Clean	Not Clean/ Not Dirty	Dirty	Very Dirty

1--------------------2--------------------3--------------------4--------------------5

1. Stella's outside appearance

2. Stella's tables and floors

3. Stella's bathrooms

Market segmentation variables

Research Objective: To determine if Sue Bee Honey should segment its new product, *Buzz*, by customer characteristics (geographic, demographic, or psychographic) or product usage. (This research objective is packed with information needed to be measured.)

How likely would you be to buy Sue Bee Honey Buzz for the following uses? (check all that apply)

_____1. An energy drink before I workout
_____2. An energy drink after I workout
_____3. An energy snack before I workout
_____4. An energy snack after I workout
_____5. As a breakfast treat on my toast in the morning
_____6. An energy drink during my workout
_____7. Other uses _____
_____8. Sorry, I would not buy it at all

How often do you workout:

_____ Less than 30 minutes a week
_____ 30 minutes 1 – 3 times per week
_____ 60 minutes 1 - 3 times per week
_____ More than 60 minutes 3 times per week

Brand or Advertising knowledge or information

Research Objective: To measure the faculty knowledge of and perception about the name change from the HJF Library to the HJF Learning Center

Indicate which name you prefer:

_____ HJF Learning Center

_____ HJF Library

Please explain why you prefer one over the other.

Attitude toward the brand or advertising

Research Objective: To determine the preferred way Morningside College students find reliable online sources for their research

Which online source do you use most often to find reliable information for your secondary research? (Check your first two sources)

_____ EBSCOhost through my library site
_____ Lexis Nexis
_____ Hoover's financial and company information
_____ Yahoo financial and company information
_____ Google
_____ Google Scholar
_____ Bing
_____ Other, please list _____

Purchase decision process
conviction, intention, purchase (including those who influence purchase decisions as well as the retail or secondary environment)

Research Objective: To determine location, price, quality of food, and service influence on decision to purchase Stella's Barbecue

(A six point Likert-type scale)

Strongly Disagree   Disagree   Slightly Disagree   Slightly Agree   Agree   Strongly Agree

1-----------------2-----------------3--------------------4--------------5---------------6

1. I am likely to drive to Stella's at the corner of Morningside Avenue and Transit Avenue

2. I feel Stella's location is worth the drive.

3. I feel Stella's offers very high quality food for the price.

4. I feel Stella's Barbeque is overpriced.

5. I feel the quality of food is unique and I love the down-home flavor of the sauce.

7. I feel the service is excellent.

Research Objective: To determine how/why young professionals change banks.

How likely would you be to change banks if they offered free cookware to open new accounts?

_____ None, I love my current bank
_____ Maybe if it was Rachel Ray cookware
_____ Not if it was the cookware I saw on the billboard
_____ I'd rather have a different gift or incentive to open a new account, and here is a suggestion_____

Questions to be used for focus group or depth interview:

How do you make the decision to open a bank account?

What would cause you to change banks?

Are there sources or other influencers that you use to make the decision? (Probe to find out details.)

Packaging or Creative elements

Research Objective: To test concepts for a new logo, membership packages, and creative design elements for Siouxland Chamber Music

Question to be used for focus group or depth interview:

Show logos, membership packages, and design elements on advertisements and ask for feedback. Probe and take time to review items in detail.

Demographic/socioeconomic data

Research Objective: To measure age, income, education, gender, profession, marital status, and number of children of 102.3 Jack fm listeners

Please check the following that describe you:

_____Male _____Female
_____ Income is below $30,000
_____ $30,001 to $50,000
_____$50,001 to $75,000
_____Income is above $75,001

Psychographic data

Research Objective: To measure interest and hobbies of people who travel to Florida

Please list your top three interests and hobbies:

1._____ 2. _____ 3. _____

---

7. Collect and process the data
8. Analyze and interpret the data

For these two steps, you've got a lot of work to do.

Completing the survey, sending out questionnaires, implementing focus groups – whatever research you've decided to do, now you've got to do it.

Then you have to figure out what it is you've got. It may be collating questionnaires, or going over recordings of focus groups.

The key in analyzing and interpreting the data will be actionable insights.

Early research on mobile phones was an example. A local cellular re-seller did a survey of 250 recent sign-ups. Here were the actionable insights.

Insight #1: 30% of sign-ups were referrals from other users. The recommended action: continue a high-value "Refer a Friend" referral program.

Insight #2: Initial sign-ups were often related to a "mobile phone moment." It might have been a scary incident in a parking lot late at night, or being stuck in traffic and unable to call. Whatever it was, something happened in their lives to tell them "we need a cell phone." At that moment, they started to price shop. The recommended action: have an introductory offer as low as the competition. Since this re-seller had good distribution of retail outlets and a satisfactory local reputation, it knew it would get its share if it maintained a competitive price.

9. Communicate the Results

First you have to find it out. Then you have to figure it out.

Then you have to tell your client what it means and what should be done.

The good news for the cell phone retailer was "You're doing the right things, keep doing them." This was actually more profound than it might seem. There was a lot of pressure to spend more to "expand the market." What the research said was that the market was expanding very nicely based on "mobile phone moments." And that current programs were performing well. There was no need for extra spending or a change in messaging.

Naturally, not every bit of research will have that comfortable a result.

Often, you will find that something in the product or service is causing a problem.

And, hopefully, you will have identified those "factors that motivate purchase behavior" and be able to make them an important part of your messaging. In the case of the cell phone re-seller, it was communicating a "best price" introductory offer.

10. Apply the knowledge

Once you've communicated what you've learned, it's time for your team to get to that important next step.

Take what you've learned and work it up into a Message that builds your brand.

And, as always, easier said than done.

BRAIN BUILDER EXERCISE 6.1:
Research Design and Proposal

Use the steps in Chapter 5 and Chapter 6 for this assignment. It will take you some time to do it right.

Instructions:

1. Write a research design or proposal for the brand on which you have been working. The ten steps are pretty standard.

2. Review each step and describe the research process in writing.

3. Once you have written the proposal, do three things.

    a. Submit your work to your school's Institutional Research Review Board. They will have a few additional questions for you to insure that the subjects involved in your study are protected.

    b. While your proposal is being approved by the IRRB, continue to develop your survey and obtain approval form clients.

    c. Submit or post your documents to a common digital place for your team to review. (NOTE: I use Turnitin.com for almost all of my student's major assignments. I also use a CMS – Blackboard or Moodle – for assignments where students need access to each other's work. I prefer the Grademark and Peer Review features that Turnitin.com offers. Google Docs and Dropbox are also good for a common place to host documents.)

Research Proposal

Using the 10 Step Brand Research Design process, prepare a research proposal. You will most likely wish to refer back to Chapter 5 for the research plan details.

1. Review the problem statement.

    Restate the problem (if needed) as one the program can solve.

2. Define the research objectives.

    Ask a series of questions that are related to the problem. The questions will relate to four areas. Develop questions for each area if necessary.

    a. Questions for the target audience

    b. Questions related to factors that motivate purchase behavior

    c. Questions related to determining unique brand characteristics

    d. Questions related to the activity of the competition

    Convert the questions to a research objective or objectives. The objectives are generally broad statements. (Generally, your proposal will not have both questions and objectives – it will just have the objectives. Asking more questions now will give you a jump start on developing your research instruments.)

3. Review relevant literature and write an essay or annotated bibliography.

    Identify the topics you will search in current literature and previously conducted studies. Look at the questions above for search terms. Getting up to speed with the industry and market will provide additional insight for the project.

    Research Question:

Search Terms:

- _____

- _____

- _____

- _____

Annotated Bibliography or Synthesis Essay

You have one of two choices for this part of your assignment. Both require proper citations.

Annotated Bibliography

Read and review the literature to be used in the final report. Determine a format to use (such as MLA, APA, etc.) and complete an annotated bibliography (for each entry, include a paragraph on how the reading is relevant to your study).

Or

Synthesis Essay

A synthesis essay is one that brings all of the material together. An argumentative essay's thesis statement will argue a particular side of an issue. The issue in the synthesis essay is to become knowledgeable about the company, the customers, and the competition. Make the essay concise so as to keep the reader engage; a 500-word essay is ideal. I recommend Diana Hacker's _Rules for Writers_ for your desk (right beside a dictionary and thesaurus). It's an excellent guide. You can also check out dianahacker.com/rules.

4. Select and describe a research design (include any ethical and consent issues necessary for your design).

5. Design and give sample questions for the research instrument.

6. Determine who will be in your research plan and describe the sample selection.

7. Describe how you plan to collect and process the data.

8. Describe how you plan to analyze and interpret the data.

9. Describe how you plan to communicate the results.

10. Explain how you can apply the knowledge to your brand campaign.

TIP: Make sure to revise your résumé to show that you have completed building a proposal. In the grant writing world, the ability to write proposals and Requests for Proposal (commonly called RFP) is a skill worth paying for.

BRAIN BUILDER EXERCISE 6.2: Your Brand Research

Complete the research you proposed. Write the report and present it to the parties who will have the most interest. Here is a common report outline.

Title Page

Letter of transmittal

Letter of authorization

Table of contents

List of tables

List of graphs

List of appendices

List of exhibits

Executive summary
    a. Major findings
    b. Conclusions
    c. Recommendations

Problem definition
    a. Background to the problem
    b. Statement of the problem

Approach to the problem

Research design (Follow the Research Proposal format)
    a. Type of research design
    b. Information needs
    c. Data collection from secondary sources

    d. Scaling techniques
    e. Questionnaire development and pretesting
    f.   Sampling techniques
    g. Field work

Methodology & Results
    a. Focus Group
    b. Taste Tests
    c. Home Trial
    d. Observations
    e. Online Survey

Limitations and caveats

Conclusions and recommendations

Exhibits
    a. Questionnaires and forms
    b. Statistical output
    c. Lists
    d. Bibliography

CHAPTER REVIEW

These topics were covered in this chapter.

1. Developing research objectives
2. A review of the ten-step research process
3. The basics of qualitative methods
4. The basics of quantitative research methods
5. Research examples for 12 common information areas

REVIEW QUESTIONS

1. What are your research objectives?

2. What qualitative methods are you considering?

3. What quantitative method will you consider?

4. List the core information you would like to acquire for your brand.

CHAPTER 7:
TARGET AUDIENCE

Now you are ready for the next stage in building your brand. It's time to really understand your audience. You're already well along in knowing your target. You studied them as you developed your Situation Analysis and implemented your Research. You already know a lot. Now it's time to get that knowledge focused. Specifically, we need to know what moves them to make choices and what influences them to purchase…vote…enroll…select…click…agree with your side and your brand.

The first thing we'll do in this chapter is expand your vocabulary a bit. We'll provide you with some important words and concepts for understanding your Target Audience. Then we'll review a little classic psychology. It's called the Lavidge-Steiner Learning Model. It illustrates the steps people take as they move from no awareness of a brand to walking up to the cash register.

Next, we'll show you a tool we call the Current User Profile. You may be surprised at all the different things we like to know about our target. Certainly, some things will be more important than others. But it's a simple truth that the more we understand who we're talking to, the better we'll be able to develop our Message.

When we understand our current user, we have a deeper understanding of our brand's relationship with them and those all-important "factors that influence purchasing behavior." We also see "touch points" with the brand.

Based on the research you completed, you should be on your way to developing the insight you will need to understand where your brand is currently positioned in the mind of the consumer. And, you'll determine if that position is one that will allow your brand to thrive in the market.

In addition to the Current User Profile, you will write a Target Sketch. This is another tool that can help you understand your target more effectively. The Target Sketch is a fictional description of a person who would fit your current user profile. Even though it's fiction, it can really help make your target real. Target Sketches are great tools to provide a visual focus and, often, they can inspire creative messages.

You will also determine if you have primary and secondary target audiences.

LEARNING OUTCOMES

After studying this chapter, you will be able to:

1. Understand how to "Talk Target." We'll cover some important words and concepts related to developing a better understanding of your Target Audience.

2. Understand the Lavidge-Steiner learning model

3. Define the target audience further with a Current Users Profile that contains:
   a. Demographics
   b. Psychographic characteristics
   c. Affiliations
   d. Heavy users and lead users
   e. Buying habits
   f. Seasonality of the purchase cycle
   g. Geographic emphasis

4. Identify Factors that Influence Purchasing Behavior using:
   a. Laddering
   b. an understanding of The Importance of What's Important

5. Understand Brand Contact Points
   a. Identify the Value chain

6. Write a Target Sketch

7. Identify Primary and Secondary Target (Audiences)

If it looks like there's a lot to cover, you're right. So let's get started.

TARGET TALK

Here are definitions that will help you understand your target audience more clearly.

Awareness, Attitude, and Usage – A survey of consumers to determine their attitude and awareness of a brand as well as their usage of a brand.

Brand Contact Points – The specific places your brand touches the consumer (e.g., store fronts, signage, websites, packaging, etc). Also referred to as Touch Points.

Competitive Advantage – The unique activities within a firm that will produce a sustainable position in the market over the competition.

Demographics – Statistical data about target consumers, i.e., age, income, family size, ages of children, gender, marital status, home owner, apartment renter, etc.

Like-minded users – Those connections that are made between people who have certain things in common.

Market segmentation – Viewing a larger market of people with different demands as many smaller homogeneous markets. The large market of toothpaste has segments of whiteners added, or mouth wash added, or flavors and textures.

Primary Target – The person (consumer) who is the main source of business for your brand or the primary decision maker (buyer) for your product, service, idea or entity.

Product Life Cycle – four phases of the life of a product: introduction, growth, maturity, and decline. Consider the life of the brand in the same terms as the life cycle of the product in the industry. By the way, product life cycles can last a very long time – and they can stay vibrant by being refreshed. For example, Tide is refreshed with continual product improvements. Coca-Cola, on the other hand, is refreshed with new package designs and advertising. Some brands, like automobiles and software, are continually upgraded.

Figure 7.1 Product or Brand Life Cycle

We put a double arrow between Growth and Maturity to indicate where we can refresh and revitalize. Once the brand is in decline, the task is still possible, but much more difficult.

Psychographics – The description of target consumers' psychological interests and behaviors, i.e., nurturing, adventurous, biker, walker, swimmer, mother, etc.

Secondary Target – The influential person or group responsible for getting your product to the end user (primary). Examples of a secondary target market would be wholesalers, dealers, retail chains.

Segments – Smaller groups within a larger market group with similar characteristics and demands. (See Market Segmentation)

Target Audience – The audience at whom you are aiming your message

Target Market – The group of people in the marketplace who are the best prospects for your product, service, and idea (you get it). Also called "target," "target customer," or "target consumer."

Unique Selling Proposition – A concept developed by Rosser Reeves. Find the unique benefit in your product and hammer it home, repeatedly.

1. Each advertisement must make a proposition to the consumer – "Buy this product and you will get this specific benefit".
2. The proposition must be one that the competition either cannot, or does not offer – thus unique in the brand or in the advertising message.
3. The proposition must be so strong that it can move the masses.

Usage – How often and how much does a consumer use a brand? To find the answer, you may need to refer to Awareness, Attitude, and Usage studies.

Value Chain – A set of related activities in the operation of a firm; a decision process and usage of a brand. For example, a person who uses a washer and dryer starts with dirty clothes, needs water, detergent, (maybe) maintenance. A company that sells or manufactures laundry detergents and washers and dryers understands the chain of activities related to doing the laundry.

You might want to review these words and their definitions one more time. These are the concepts we'll be dealing with as we think about, and learn more about, the target audience for our brand. Sometimes we will have piles of data – particularly for big brands with a long history. Other times, we will have fragments of information from interviews and small surveys we conduct ourselves.

Now, whether we have a lot of target audience information or just a little, let's think about how that target audience processes new information.

LAVIDGE-STEINER LEARNING MODEL

The next topic in discussing the target audience is to discuss the stages of learning as they relate to messages – particularly advertising. This can also include other forms of communication. For example, a restaurant review in a local newspaper (PR), a free sample at a street fair (Event Marketing), a special display in a store (Sales Promotion), or a visit to a website. Each of these is something we referred to earlier – a Brand Contact Point.

Lavidge and Steiner developed a model to help us understand the effects of cumulative communication. While the primary purpose of a communication like advertising is persuasive in nature, sales are not the only measurement. This model illustrates the various stages consumers go through. After Lavidge and Steiner defined the functions of each stage, then each functional area could be measured.

Now while this model was developed for advertising, we should understand that it really applies to pretty much all brand-related information. So, also consider a newspaper article, or a flyer under our windshieldw wiper, or comments from a friend (word of mouth); each is a bit of input that helps to build our brand awareness.

Brand communications have a building effect. A single ad message may not have an immediate return. But, if the message is right, the results will build.

Start at the beginning – in this case, the bottom of our chart – and think about where the person is in relationship to your brand. The person is who you are targeting – not just anyone. That target is someone who actually has a need for your brand.

If they are on the outside of our chart, they are completely unaware. How many are out there, how many are aware but haven't purchased yet? How many are on step five, convinced your brand is a good choice, but haven't purchased yet? Awareness progresses up the ladder. This model offers a number of ways to think about where your brand is with the customer.

Lavidge Steiner Learning Model
From no awareness (at the bottom) to purchase (at the top)

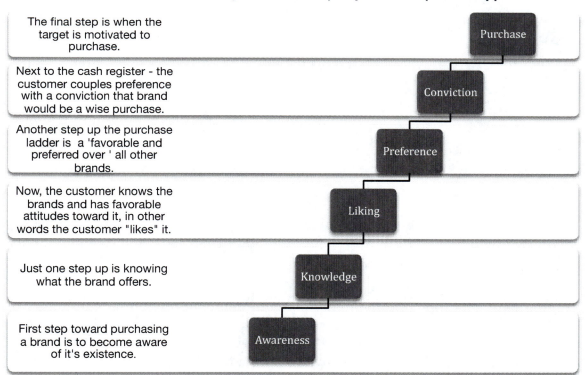

As you might imagine, people are distributed up and down the Learning Model.

In the beginning, virtually everyone is clustered at the bottom or off the chart – unaware of your brand. Then, as your messaging program builds – assuming you're delivering an effective message – more and more people move up the ladder.

This simple model helps us focus on the process, though we know the world is a more complicated place. For example, competition has its own messages and, cumulatively, each of us has to deal with a blizzard of messages – each wanting to move us up its own particular ladder.

Two more factors play a role in how we move slowly or quickly up and down that ladder. Those two factors are the degree of psychological impact and the degree of economic impact on the decision. As customers, we can make an impulse purchases – like all those things at the end of the aisles, at the cash register, during infomercials, or on a home shopping channel. We become aware of something, grab it, and find ourselves in the checkout line with the item in our shopping cart. The time it took to get through the steps from learning to purchase went very quickly.

Both factors – psychological and economic – can be powerful. If we find just the right message – one that really connects with how people feel, we can see strong results. But we will see even stronger results if we can not only increase the psychological strength of our message, but also reduce the economic barrier.

For example, if we can offer a FREE SAMPLE, that virtually eliminates barriers. Make the most of the persuasive power of your message, but don't forget the persuasion that comes about when you reduce the economic barriers – particularly for that all-important first time usage.

Oh, and one more thing.

Your brand needs to deliver on the promise you make in your messaging. Your message needs to show your brand in a meaningful and persuasive manner. Your message should be able to help close the deal, not lose a customer.

So, for example, if you overpromise, there's a good chance you will disappoint customers – and getting them to try you again will be either difficult or impossible. After all, lots of brands want your customers.

For each of us, our need state is a constantly moving target. For example, you might have the need for a new computer. Your laptop is still working, but after four years you've noticed it is slowing down, it gets hot, and the screen is a bit small. You start researching different models. Maybe it's time for a desk top. It might be time to switch from a PC to an Apple. Or, maybe your Apple hasn't been the same since you spilled your Mountain Dew across the keyboard.

In every product category, our target audience is packed with people just like you and me, making all kinds of variable purchase decisions. And, for most of us, our "wish list" always seems to be a bit bigger than our budget.

In many ways, we already understand our target, because we're a target audience, too – and we know how that feels. Hold onto that feeling, because the better you understand your target – the people you're trying to reach – the better you'll do.

Your job as you build your brand is to understand what actions need to be taken to connect with the people who will benefit most from having your brand – and not the competition.

The Lavidge-Steiner model reminds us that messaging and building our brand's reputation are cumulative. Consumers will step in and out of their decisions as they move up and down the Lavidge-Steiner Learning Ladder for all the brands competing for attention. That's why you have to keep at it.

BRAIN-BUILDER EXERCISE 7.1:
Your Brand and the Steps to Purchase

The purpose of this assignment is to have you think about your brand. We want you to start thinking like a consultant or a manager/owner. The sooner you get yourself inside the brand, the company, the industry – the sooner, this thing called Branding will become real.

Instructions:

Identify a brand you wish to use in this exercise – you might just continue with brands you have been using previously.

Think about your brand and where your customers are in the steps toward committing to your brand. Check appropriate answers.

1. Does your brand involve a psychological decision _____Yes _____No

   If yes, what are the emotions involved? (check all that apply)

   _____ Loving care

   _____ Personal gratification

   _____ Health appeal

   _____ Romance and sex

   _____ Express individuality

   _____ Demonstrate belongingness

   _____ Newness

   _____ "It's good"

_____ Natural

_____ Traditional

_____ Other appeals to emotions _____

2. Does your brand require the purchaser involved to make an economic decision? _____ Yes _____ No

On a scale of 1 – 10, is it a high level of economic involvement (10) or low level of economic involvement (1)? (Circle the appropriate answer)

Low involvement   High involvement

1   2   3   4   5   6   7   8   9   10

3. Describe the person who will most likely make the economic decision to purchase your brand and how often they will make the purchase.

Age _____

Income_____

Education level _____

Frequency of purchase _____

4. Make notes in each step of the Lavidge Steiner Learning model where you believe your target audience currently is located – and how many of your target is located in the step. This should reveal where the branding message should focus.

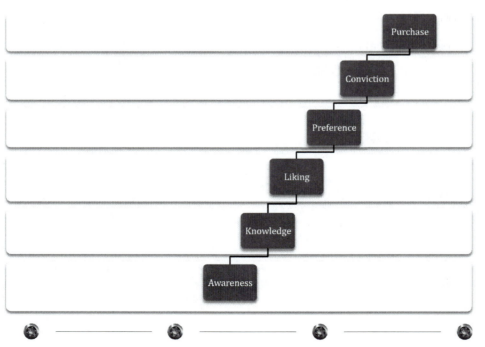

DEFINE THE TARGET AUDIENCE

In this section, you will involve yourself with the target audience in three interesting ways. Each is a tool that provides additional insight into your Target. One of them might provide the key insight that helps you shape your Message, or you might find yourself using them in combination.

You will learn how to:

1) Create a profile of the current user,
2) Explain consumer factors that influence purchasing behavior, and
3) Consider the points at which the brand touches the consumer.

Let's take them one by one.

Current User Profile

A Current User Profile has seven elements. Once these elements are defined for your current user or your competitor's current user, you will have the information you need to help you buy media, design messages, and find additional windows of opportunity. The seven elements are demographics, psychographics, affiliations, heavy and lead users, buying habits, seasonality, and geographic emphasis.

Demographic information is that which can be statistically measured. Most often demographic data includes age, income, gender, education, ethnic group, marital status, or children. You can collect this data in your survey, as we discussed in the earlier chapter, or your client may have collected it over time.

Psychographic Characteristics are those qualities about the individual that indicate their interests, beliefs, and values. Psychographic examples may include interest in sports, travel, pets, or hobbies. A person who loves organic foods may also like to garden; they might also be interested in other "green" activities or green products.

TIP: When conducting primary research, think forward about how you plan to use the demographic and psychographic data before you develop questions.

Affiliations with professional or interests groups. Involvement with groups that are dense with your Target Audience can also be helpful, particularly for narrow targets. The person you are targeting may be in a specific industry or profession, or affiliated with an organization that will benefit most from your brand. Affiliations include teachers, farmers, political parties, members of the armed forces, college students, unions, truck drivers, Corvette owners, or Harley Owners, etc. Understanding the affiliation may give you the opportunity to immerse yourself in that culture and gain insights into its buying habits and purchasing decisions.

For example, our friends with The Czech Legion Project (remember, the "long tail" project?) found that Czech-American organizations were a key connection for grabbing onto that "long tail."

Heavy Users and Lead Users. These are a special group within the current users group. Heavy users are very loyal users of your brand. Lead users are those companies or individuals who take an existing product and adapt it to their needs. Under Armor was discovered by a football player who wanted to keep warm during games and found a sleek new material that he could sew. Marketers and firms can learn from lead and heavy users. And, as we mentioned, when you're doing research, one of the richest places to explore is with your Heavy Users.

Buying Habits of the target group should be studied. Buying habits of a freshman entering college would include all of the dorm room gear needed, study gear needed, plus bank accounts set up to handle finances away from home. Understanding the buying habits related to your brand can be very useful.

Seasonality. Your purchase cycle may peak during a particular time of year, or it may be flat across the year. Ice cream sales start to increase in the summer and peak the first week in July. Make sense? Other products may have a fairly constant rate of consumption – like lunch every weekday. Understanding your brand's purchase cycle will help you reach the target at the right time.

Geographic Emphasis. This is the last factor of the Current User Profile. Is your product useful to a specific geographic region? Is there, perhaps, a longer and deeper history with the brand? Are there regional characteristics that might influence one brand's preference over another?

The organic and all natural market did very well on the West coast of the US. The Sue Bee Honey Buzz drink was introduced as an all natural energy product. Where to begin? Research indicated the Midwest, where the product was being produced, was very slow to purchase all natural products, while the West was more advanced.

Before you write your Target Sketch, you'll want to write down something in pretty much every one of these categories. Don't worry about being too specific. If the Target is a teen who enjoys comic books and superhero movies, it doesn't really matter which is his favorite. But you should develop examples that represent the spirit and the general area of taste and preference.

You should probably grab a pad of paper and write down some thoughts based on this outline.

BRAIN-BUILDER EXERCISE 7.2: Current User Profile

You will need to think about the information you gathered about your target audience in previous exercises (in this chapter and previous chapters).

Instructions:

Using the research you gained in the previous chapter, build a profile for your current user. Use either statistical measurement or descriptors to build your profile by completing information for each topic below.

Demographic	
Psychographic	
Affiliations	
Heavy users and lead users	
Buying habits	
Seasonality of the purchase cycle	
Geographic emphasis	

FACTORS THAT INFLUENCE PURCHASING BEHAVIOR

Okay, now it's time for a Big Simple Question. Why is a purchase made in your brand's product category? While many things are true, only a few will be important.

For example, taking a plane trip. The first factor will, of course, be whether or not the airline flies to your destination. Next, there will be a number of other factors. Price will most likely be the second, followed by convenience factors (time of departure, number of stops, etc.). And then, perhaps something like the airline that honors your Frequent Flier Miles.

There you have it. You're not going to decide based on the snack it serves, or the color of the logo. The clever commercial may help, but not if the ticket costs an extra $100 and you are charged an additional fee for luggage.

Now you understand the BSQ – the Big Simple Question. *What is it that you must have* to be considered for purchase? If your pricing is competitive, that clever commercial might help, but you need to have a tough-minded attitude here.

What do you need to be considered for purchase? Not every factor should be in your Message, but the important factors absolutely must be part of what your brand delivers and what you deliver in your messaging.

For example, when Southwest Airlines was making great progress in building market share, a competitor with beautiful commercials and much higher prices was described as having "*the world's best irrelevant advertising.*" Beautiful ads that are off message are ugly.

Make a list. What does your brand need to compete in the category? Are there any important factors where your brand is dramatically superior? Are there any where you're operating at a big disadvantage? In fact, let's take a look at that right now.

**BRAIN-BUILDER EXERCISE 7.3
Factors that Influence Purchase Behavior**

Instructions: List the factors for your brand. Then, rate your brand against competitors.

Factor:	Our Brand	Competition
1.		
2.		
3.		
4.		
5.		

Five factors should be plenty.

Now, which factor or factors, are, in your judgment most important? Which factor or factors, are, in your judgment, strongest for your brand?

LADDERING: Attributes, Features, Product Benefits, Consumer Benefits, and Values.

You can read about this in more detail in one of our favorite books, *Hitting The Sweet Spot* (available at adbuzz.com). But, for now we'll give you the short version. Looks like it's time for a few more definitions.

Virtually every product or service contains a ladder – going from Attributes and Features at the bottom, to Values at the top. Here's what we mean by each of these concepts.

Attributes. These are things inherent in your product or service. An oatmeal cookie is made with oatmeal. Applesauce is made with apples. A cup of coffee consists of coffee and a cup.

Features. These are things that are added onto your product or service – sometimes manufactured, sometimes added in another way. Applesauce is put into some sort of easy-to-serve container. Coffee may be made fresh with steamed milk added and served with a smile. Each, in its own way, is a feature.

Product Benefit. OK, now we're climbing the ladder. These attributes and features combine to deliver some sort of benefit unique to that product or service. The applesauce in the container makes it easy to serve delicious applesauce. The coffee creates a pleasant aroma, a rich taste, and a nice wake-me-up.

Consumer Benefit. The Consumer benefit is the flip side of the Product Benefit. The Product Benefit is inside the product – the Consumer Benefit is inside the Consumer. So the product benefit may be tires that are resistant to blow-outs; the consumer benefit is family safety. See what we're talking about? With the apple sauce, now my family gets a nice serving of fruit – and it's easy. With the coffee, I get a pleasurable experience early in the morning.

Values. Time to put on your thinking hat. What larger values do these Benefits represent? Serving fruit to your family might mean you're a good mother and smart homemaker. Having that cup of coffee might mean you're a go-getter who wants to make the most of the day, or you might be a sophisticated thinker, who likes that indulgent moment as you sip your coffee and page through the *New York Times*.

In each case, there may be more than one benefit delivered and more than one value contained in the product experience. As David Ogilvy noted, "Strategy is about choice." But, with Laddering, now you can be clearer and more precise about the choices you are making.

As we work our way through the creative tools, you will find that understanding the Features, Benefits, and Values contained in your product or service will be invaluable in working your way through the thinking process.

Specific vs. Generic.

One quick cautionary note. Don't feel obliged to end up at the top of your ladder. In general, the higher up the ladder you go, the more generic you are in your descriptions, whereas the more you are dealing with things like Features, the more specific you are to your product. And, as you might imagine, sometimes you build something with a few rungs of the ladder.

For example, my editor, Bruce Bendinger, did a famous campaign years ago for Archway Cookies – The Good Food Cookie. As he notes, the whole thing was built on the *attribute* of oatmeal cookies being made from oatmeal (Archway was the #1 oatmeal cookie). There was also some good news about the cholesterol-lowering effects of oatmeal, which made the message more powerful.

But it may be more complicated. The Mac computer is sold to you based on the Feature of their unique software and GUI (Graphic User Interface) with the Consumer Benefits of Productivity and Ease of Use seasoned with some Values – that nifty Apple/Mac personality.

Here's a quick worksheet for your brand.

BRAIN BUILDER EXERCISE 7.4: Laddering

Instructions: Make a list using the different stages of the ladder.

Brand: _____

Attributes: _____

_____

Features: _____

_____

Product Benefits (delivered by the product): _____

_____

_____

Consumer Benefits (experienced by the consumer): _____

_____

_____

Values associated with experiencing the product or service: _____

_____

_____

The Importance of What's Important.

Many things are true. Your newspaper has a lot of different sections; a car has tires, batteries, a motor, a sound system, and brand new styling on a regular basis. There are lots of different programs on your television.

That said, why do you pick up a newspaper, buy a car, or turn on your television?

Good question.

You need to answer that question for your brand. You've already covered this topic twice. First, you addressed these issues in Factors that Influence Purchase Behavior, and then, again, in Laddering. Well, let's do it a third time. What's important?

As we noted, many things are true and there's lots of news in newspaper – but you want the sports scores and the movie times on Friday night. What are the most important reasons for selecting your brand in preference to other options – which can be everything from a close competitor to pretty much doing nothing at all.

As you work your way through those factors and the Ladder, and all those different attributes, features, benefits, and values, you need to get to a clean, clear answer to what might be a complicated question. What's important? What will truly motivate purchase behavior?

Try to put those things in rank order and realize that you may end up with a combination of factors that feed into the purchase decision; things like price and convenience, as well as product quality and good service.

If you think you're familiar with the factors, let's list them all one at a time – and then let's rank them in order. By the way, there are some kinds of sorting research that can involve your target – ask them what's most important. In most cases, they'll give you a pretty good read on what's important to them.

**BRAIN BUILDER 7.5:
The Importance of What's Important**

Take everything you've thought of to date – Factors, Laddering, etc. – and list the three most important things related to your brand.

1.

2.

3.

Brand Contact Points / "Touch Points"

Now let's go back to that other ladder – the Lavidge-Steiner Learning Model.

In some ways, almost every brand-related moment helps "sell" the brand. Lots of packages on the shelf tell the consumer you're popular – unless they're dusty. A billboard on the side of a delivery truck, or a package in a shopping cart can do the same. Each, in a small way, feeds to the larger message.

Naturally, some contact points are more powerful than others. A commercial during the Super Bowl is probably a more powerful contact point than a newspaper coupon. Still, a coupon offers something that the TV can't. Let's think about this.

Each of these is a "touch point," or, more accurately, a "Brand Contact Point." In understanding your target audience, you'll want to know the points at which they make contact with your brand, and why. This thinking is going to become particularly important when you address Message Windows – the places where you will deliver your message.

For example, Nike realized that one of the most important "touch points" in athletic equipment came as you were watching your favorite team – or your favorite athlete. And being a "winning brand" was one of the major Factors That Influenced Purchase Behavior. See what's going on?

Try to get inside the skin of your Target and walk in their shoes. How are they experiencing your brand? Is it personal contact or a brochure on a shelf? Whether it's a person representing your brand or a brochure with a high value coupon, each is a contact point with the potential to turn your target into your customer.

Brand Contact Points are important. Make the most of them.

The Value Chain

Using the brand's touch points throughout the organization's value chain will shed additional light on your target.

What's a Value Chain? It's the road a product takes on the way to you. In some cases, it's not very relevant, and in others it's very important indeed.

Let's think about the Value Chain of something you're probably familiar with – McDonald's French Fries. Now while they're growing as potatoes, this important process is pretty far removed from that bag you picked up at the drive-thru. Still, in terms of price and whatever quality it is that makes a potato a potato, it's important. And we can be fairly certain that McDonald's is paying attention all the way through this value chain.

Next, our potatoes get prepared, and here, as it happens, McDonald's has a process that adds some features to their potatoes so they have that certain texture we're all familiar with. But unless you've seen a truck carrying those potatoes along the highway, there still hasn't been much in the way of contact along The Value Chain. But now it's about to show up on your radar screen.

It's up on the Menu Board, probably with a nice, appetizing photograph, and maybe with a McDonald's crew person asking you "would you like Large Fries?" You're starting to connect with their Value Chain. Do you add a little cup of ketchup for dipping? It's free, and it adds a little more value.

Now let's look at a completely different Value Chain. Let's discuss an entrepreneurial twist on a familiar young pastime – a cross between a skateboard and a surfboard. It's called a "longboard." This is a project we were involved with.

A longboard is a happy medium between a skateboard and a surfboard. The whole idea is to 'surf' the pavement rather than do a bunch of tricks as you might do on a skateboard. A student or young person looking for an alternative way to get around, someone just interested in spending some time outside, or someone looking to get into downhill skating will choose a longboard over a skateboard.

They are similar to skateboards, only longer and with a more flexible board over the wheels. They are designed for cruising and travel. They are for twenty something's and younger who enjoy the outdoors. You'll see more young men on boards than young women, and you are likely to see them in city parks rather than skate parks.

To get better insight into the target, I interviewed John, who recently purchased his first longboard.

Here is what John had to say.

Loaded caught my eye because they had a different kind of board. The drop through "truck" (the part that hooks the wheels to the wood) is revolutionary in the industry and lowers the board an extra couple inches...making for a much more stable ride and more cool stuff you can do with handling the board. But other companies do unique things too, so it wasn't this that sold me on Loaded. It came down to Loaded and another company called Original. Both had very positive reviews (the Loaded Dervish getting the best of them) and seemed to be extremely responsive to their fan base.

Both feature awesome YouTube channels featuring their boards just skating the park, taking on scenic routes all over the country, and just flat out how to perform everything from the easiest tricks to the wildest moves. Loaded won out on the reviews.

Here's a YouTube video. http://www.youtube.com/watch?v=JMLFZcONQAs

As an added caveat, something messed up with my online order. When I didn't receive a tracking number, I e-mailed Loaded asking what was up. To my surprise, the owner of the company (and legendary longboard designer) e-mailed me back within hours saying thanks for letting him know, that he saw what happened and would get the board out right away. Sure enough, a couple days later my board was waiting for me when I got home from work.

Now, if you are the manufacturer of a longboard, like Loaded, what are the parts of the Value Chain that make a difference to your target audience – like John?

The following chart shows a Value Chain of someone who manufactures longboards. The Value Chain shows a number of points in which the buyer comes into contact with the brand.

Longboards → Website for sales and demonstrations → Sporting goods stores → Designers and artists → Wood, wheels, polish, maintenance

Figure 7.7 Value Chain of a Long Board

See how it all comes together? Knowing a brand's touch points (or contact points) further helps you understand the target audience. It also helps you determine message placement and message design that will be discussed in later chapters. John used word of mouth, YouTube, magazines, company website, and sporting good stores as his brand contact points. He also considered the design and performance, and liked the personal response from the owner with the delivery. My guess is that John will have good "word of mouth" to pass along.

BRAIN-BUILDER EXERCISE 7.6:
Value Chain & Touch Points

The purpose of this assignment is to walk you through an analysis of the Value Chain for your brand and then determine the most important touch points.

Instructions:

Design a value chain to illustrate the touch points for your brand or your competitor's brand. You may require more or fewer links than are drawn here. The value chain shown above for the Longboard example is a good model for you to use.

Answer the following questions:

1. Are you currently reaching your target audience at all of the touch points? If not, which ones have the most opportunity for you?

2. Are your competitors reaching all of the touch points? If so, how?

3. What links in the chain are you reaching best? Will those tactics be useful for the other touch points?

THE TARGET SKETCH

The next activity in analyzing your target audience is to create a brief literary sketch of *your* consumer. The Target Sketch gives those who develop your message a clear understanding of the person for whom the message is written.

The Target Sketch is a tool discussed by Dennis Altman, an Associate Professor at the University of Kentucky. Dennis worked at top ad agencies – Doyle, Dane, Bernbach, JWT, D'Arcy, Y&R, and also started his own agency. The Target Sketch is featured in his chapter on Creativity and Communication in *Advertising & the Business of Brands*. This classic example was written for the Air Force while he was Creative Director on the account.

The Target Sketch is a fictional character who represents your target audience. You may have determined a number of segments of your target to better reach them. If that is the case, you may want to draft a sketch for each of those segments. You write it as a day in the life or slice of life story for a specific person. The more details related to your brand the better.

Patricia Greenwald, a researcher who worked with Dennis, used VALS (Values and Life Styles) to help the agency creative group understand what motivated Air Force recruits. VALS offers a number of personality profiles. Greenwald explained that the typical Air Force recruit falls somewhere between the VALS Belonger type person and the Achiever type.

This is the Target Sketch they developed for the Air Force. Once you read it, you will feel much more in touch with the person their Brand Message needed to reach. Then, you'll want to do the same for your brand. Here goes…

Kenny Johnson was a pretty good center fielder, but the game he really liked was soccer. Trouble was, not enough of the guys in town wanted to play soccer.

It was just another of those things that made Kenny feel the guys he ran with were behind the times. Kenny never thought of himself as a "brain," but he wasn't one of those guys that could only think about girls and cars.

When he got out of Centerville High, Kenny was going to do something with his life. Unfortunately, he didn't know what. He never thought of himself as the type who could be a doctor or some kind of professional. Anyway, that stuff cost big bucks, and he knew he came from a long in of plain working folks.

He liked computers, though. In fact, it was really cool how he just sort of picked it up when his dad got that "Spec Your Truck" CD from the Chevy dealer. He must've spent three hours fooling around with that CD. When they said he could come back, he camped out in the back room of Colson Chevy for the next month.

But that sure wasn't a way to make a living.

Or that's what he thought until the end of his senior year. Then he started listening to some of the guys talking about maybe the Army or the Navy. One of them said, "They use a lot of great stuff, and you get to shoot with a night scope." That started Kenny thinking about how things were changing all around him.

But the Army was out. He was no Rambo. And the thought of marching or swabbing a deck was a definite downer.

But the idea of those new electronic things really turned him on. He wondered if he could qualify… (This was the end of the original sketch, after the tagline had been used for over a year they added one more line to the Target Sketch.)

….and then he saw a sign. It said, "Aim High."

Dennis recommends that you include the following Factors in your Target Sketch:

- Age
- Gender
- Habits, ideas
- Standards
- Educational level
- Economic status (be specific – use dollar amounts plus a little imagination to illustrate your point, e.g., a significant purchase)
- Occupation
- Hobbies/interests

- Likes/dislikes
- Views (if applicable, e.g. politics or social issues)
- Taste (if applicable, e.g. style of clothes, décor)
- Media and lifestyle (describe your target's car, home, family situation, pets, the books, favorite music, films, TV shows, magazines, and the social media he or she likes)
- Personality features
- An everyday occurrence in his or her life (create an incident that illustrates your target's nature)

Visualize Your Target

Now that you have a profile of the current user and you understand the purchasing behavior and factors associated with their purchase decision, you are ready to search for images of the person who you think mirrors your user.

A picture truly can be worth a thousand words. After you put together the words for your target sketch, see if you can dig up visual examples. They may be in magazines, head shots from modeling agencies, or books and websites with "stock photography."

Later on, you may even find you'll want to purchase some of those stock photos for your messaging. But, for the moment, what you want to do is collect as much input as possible to help you connect to your all-important Target Audience.

It is usually very helpful to the creative team, and later when you present to the client, to create an actual picture of your targets – and use real people in your target sketches. Here are three we prepared for a museum project we have worked on.

Primary Target:
Students

Secondary Target:
Tour Guides

Secondary Target:
School Teachers

Figure 7.8: Primary and secondary targets for the Mid-America Museum of Aviation and Transportation

Primary and Secondary Targets

Primary Target Sketch and Secondary Target Sketch

Now that you've had a chance to focus on your Target, let's broaden our perspective.

Some people purchase. Some people influence purchase (for example, with many married couples, it may look like the man buys the car, but the woman is a powerful influence). Who helped you buy your first computer? Your parents? Or, perhaps, a computer "expert" at your school?

All along The Value Chain, there are Secondary Targets – sales people, purchasing agents, "influencers," and family members.

Your Primary Target Sketch will be a description of the fictional characters most like the ones at whom you are aiming your brand.

When researching and creating advertising for the launch of Sue Bee Honey Buzz, eight different target sketches were part of our case study. The primary targets for Sue Bee Honey were families and adults over the age of 50. So, in other words, there were two primary target groups for the traditional honey products Sue Bee Honey sold.

The new kid on their block was a drink (actually more like a gel) similar to its honey base texture. The natural ingredients (product feature) offered high energy (benefit) that was easily digested (benefit). The energy was produced quickly and did not leave a crash after-effect like many energy drinks (benefits). Plus, the natural energy of honey made a larger statement about that person and their commitment to a "natural" choice (value).

The traditional users of Sue Bee Honey were not necessarily going to use this product. A new market would need to be defined (as well as a new value chain for the organization). Sue Bee Honey is the largest honey cooperative in the world (company feature) and was known for having the highest standards in harvesting and processing the honey from the hives (added value and benefit). But still, this was far removed from the energy drink and energy food market, which was growing fast. Who drinks energy drinks and why? Who eats energy food snacks and why?

Here are two examples of the Sue Bee Honey Buzz Target Sketches. Having these sketches helped the team develop subsequent activities by turning the profile into a person or persons.

Primary Target Sketch 1

Tracie Track Star

Tracie is a 22-year-old college senior half-mile and mile runner who competes on the university's track and field team. In order to stay on top of her game, she trains for several hours every day. She likes to wake up early in the morning before her classes to take a three-mile jog. She then retreats to the campus common room for breakfast.

At breakfast, she has her usual meal consisting of a bowl of cereal, a couple pieces of wheat toast topped with a flavored spread, some bacon if it is available and three drinks including, low fat milk, apple juice, and water.

After her morning meal, Tracie has to rush back to her off-campus apartment to shower before her first class. Even though she is a senior, she has made a conscious decision to schedule classes early in the day to do homework and be able to train in the afternoon.

Throughout the day, Tracie carries two bottles with her. One is filled with ice water, which she can refill at any fountain on campus; the other usually contains Glacier Freeze Gatorade (her favorite flavor). Although Tracie likes having the Gatorade because it provides her with get-up-and-go throughout his day, she wishes she could find a product that would be easier to carry around with her.

Being an athlete she rarely drinks any soda, unless it's during the off-season but even then it would be unlikely.

Tracie has seen other runners use energy gels, but she does not know enough to try one yet. She has heard about a new Sue Bee Honey product, Buzz, that energizes. It is an all-natural product.

The **Secondary Target Audience** is that group who contributes to the sale or purchase of your brand to the end user. Again, you'll write a sketch about the secondary target audience.

The secondary target sketch for the Sue Bee Honey Buzz product had to do with key distribution points – a critical part of our new Value Chain.

They were convenience retail stores and athletic supply stores, which also included fitness centers.

Here is the sketch for the secondary target.

Secondary Target Sketch

Peak Performance Pru

Peak Performance is a Midwest athletic store that sells high performance running shoes, running wear, and running accessories, and is also known for customer service. The employees at Peak Performance are avid runners who are very informed. The employees have tried and tested the products available to customers and are quick to sell those products they believe in.

Peak Performance Employee of the Month, Prudence, is a 21-year-old college student who loves athletics and is always selling new and upcoming accessories and gear to friends. She likes PowerBars but thinks they are hard on the digestive system, so she's tried Honey Stinger, but doesn't like the taste.

Her primary customers are serious runners but Peak Performance also has a heavy flow of recreational joggers.

Along with attending classes, Pru (as her friends call her) is a competitive marathon runner and triathlete. She is very up to date with her store's inventory and believes in offering the best products to her customers. She is always looking for the runners' edge and is looking for a better-tasting, high quality energy product to promote to their customers.

Sue Bee Buzz was just introduced to all the employees during a recent "Street Crawl" event. The "street team" told a story about the pristine quality of the honey from Sioux Honey Association, and the development of the gel. It is convenient to carry, easy to drink, good flavor, and good for you.

BRAIN-BUILDER EXERCISE 7.7: Writing A Target Sketch

The purpose of this assignment is to develop a target sketch that best matches the person who is most likely to walk in your door or who is most likely to select your brand.

Instructions:

Create a primary and secondary target sketch for your brand. If your brand has a number of segments to target (e.g., primary target and secondary target), create a separate target sketch for each of those segments.

Find an image of the person you think looks like your character and place it with each sketch. Getty images or Yahoo images are good places to start your search. You might ask for permission to take a picture of one of your customers, as well.

CHAPTER REVIEW

In this chapter, we learned a lot about our Target Audience and how that Target interacts with our brand. We discussed:

1. Key definitions related to the Target Audience
2. The Lavidge-Steiner Learning Model
3. How to build a Current Users Profile
4. Factors That Influence Purchase Behavior
5. Laddering – a useful way of analyzing the various levels of attributes, features, benefits, and values delivered by every brand
6. The Importance of What's Important – the need to prioritize and focus on the most important factors in purchase decisions
7. Brand Touch Points – all the different ways a brand can touch our Target
8. The Value Chain – all the stages a brand goes through to reach the target.
9. The Target Sketch – a useful way of describing our target
10. Primary and Secondary Targets – the fact that there may be more than one target in the process. For example, the person who buys a product at the store (primary) and the retailer who sells it (secondary). In some cases, Secondary targets can be just as important in the overall process.

REVIEW QUESTIONS

1. Which Target Audience definition did you find most helpful?
2. Which definition was either least helpful or hardest to determine?
3. At this stage, what do you think you will have to do to move your Target up the Lavidge-Steiner Learning Model ladder?
4. How would you describe your ideal Current Users?
5. At this stage, what are the key Factors That Influence Purchase Behavior?
6. What did you find to be the most critical piece of your brand's Ladder?
7. What does your Target think is most important in your product category?
8. Are there other alternatives? For example, is one brand a price brand and another a deluxe high-quality brand?
9. Did you discover any unusual Brand Touch Point opportunities?
10. Where on the Value Chain do you see the most messaging opportunities?
11. Did you develop any new insights into your target based on the Target Sketch?
12. Where did you find the best visualizations of your Target?
13. Is there a critical Secondary Target?

CHAPTER 8 - Goal Setting
SWOT, Marketing Objective, Positioning Statement

After you've completed the research for your Situation Analysis and Target Audience, you're ready to start coming to some conclusions. This section may seem a bit shorter in length than the previous chapters, but you'll find it's mostly a shift to a different kind of work. Now you're going to take the things you've learned and apply them in five key ways:

1. You'll develop a SWOT Analysis
2. You'll identify Problems and Opportunities
3. You'll determine an initial Marketing Objective
4. You'll write a Positioning Statement
5. You'll establish your Business Goals

First, the SWOT Analysis. This is an analysis of the strengths and weaknesses internal to your brand or organization as well as opportunities and threats external to the organization. The SWOT (strength, weaknesses, opportunities and threats) analyses should address the overall Brand, and not only the marketing or communication function in the organization.

Then, narrow that list down to a set of Problems and Opportunities. These will help you focus on what, on judgment, seem the most effective ways to build your brand. Among them, identify the problem your communication must solve. You should start to see the light bulb come on now.

Next, you'll determine your Marketing Objective (MO), which is typically a sales objective or a number. The objective will be a financial goal that will help define where you are headed and what you plan to accomplish. You will set a specific goal in terms of measurable units – a sales number, a share number, a volume number. Your marketing objective will be that number. Clearly stating the marketing objective will help everyone know what the brand is aiming for.

The Positioning Statement is the next area. This will take us from the specifics of a marketing objective to something much less specific – the conceptual position you will occupy in the mind of your target consumer. Positioning goals are much more general statements. Interesting discussions will dance around the table. You will examine positioning issues such as:

- Where should your New Brand aim its efforts?
- What position do you want to achieve?

- Does your Existing Brand currently have the right position? Or does your brand need to be *re-positioned*?
- What are the issues your Troubled Brand is facing? What position or re-positioning might help resolve these issues?

Finally, after three very different types of goal-setting, you will focus on your brand's overall Goal or Business Goal. (If you are a non-profit or government service, you will simply set your Goal.) Each of the preceding three activities will help you establish a firm vision of where your brand needs to go. Let's see how you'll get there.

LEARNING OUTCOMES

After studying this chapter, you will be able to do the following.

1. Complete a SWOT Analysis
   a. Strengths and weaknesses are internal to the organization
   b. Opportunities and threats are external to the organization

2. You will identify Problems and Opportunities
   a. This will further narrow the focus
   b. You will identify the Problem the Communication Must Solve

3. Write a Marketing Objective
   a. Define areas of the organization to measure
   b. Assign a specific measurement
   c. Define the time frame for the objective to be completed

4. Write a Positioning Statement
   a. Define where the brand resides in the mind of the consumer
   b. Define how the brand compares to competitive offerings

5. Set your brand's Business Goal (or Goals)

Your Business Goal is what you're aiming for – it will be based on an understanding of your brand's Opportunities and the Problems that it will have to overcome. You will have a firm grasp on the specifics of that goal in terms of sales and business results. And you will have insight into the place you want to occupy with your position in the the mind of your Target Consumer.

So even though it's a fairly short chapter, we've got a lot to do!

COMPLETE A SWOT ANALYSIS

It's time to put on our thinking caps. You might want to look for a quiet place – the place where you work best and are able to sift through all of the research you have gathered so far. Grab a great cup of coffee, a cold soda, or hot chocolate, along with a highlighter, pad, pens, and maybe some Post-Its.

SWOT stands for strengths, weaknesses, opportunities and threats. It is a business tool used to analyze an industry, a company, or a brand. We are going to use it as a marketing tool. If this is your first marketing, entrepreneurship, or campaigns class, you probably haven't had an opportunity to complete a SWOT analysis yet. Though, if you've had a few business classes, you may have done one before. We think you're going to like it. Most people find their first SWOT exciting and eye-opening. Even though it's an important business document, preparing a SWOT is really very stimulating mentally, as you examine a whole range of "what ifs" for your brand.

Okay, once again, it's time for a few definitions.

Strength – when a company or brand excels in critical resources and programs that lead to a competitive advantage

Weakness – when a company or brand does not accomplish its goals or fails in resources and programs needed to be competitive

Opportunity – an external condition in the marketplace that, if acted upon in time, could lead to an advantage for the brand or company

Threat – an external condition in the marketplace that, if not addressed or resolved, over time could harm or lead to a negative impact for the brand or company.

SWOT Guidelines
Now here are some guidelines to help you develop a SWOT for your brand.

Strengths and Weaknesses are internal to the organization or brand. They include the following key areas:

- **Marketing** – the product or service, price, distribution, placement, promotions, quality, customer service

- **Management** – information systems and expertise and quality of executives, management, and staff, training and development, recruiting, compensation

- **Manufacturing or Operations** – efficiencies, cost structure, capacity, productivity, labor, speed of response

- **Finance** – profitability (income and expenses), stability, capital, inventory turnover, loans, assets

- **Organization** – leadership, strategy, innovation, employees

- **MIS** – state of the art, user friendly, efficient for internal and external users

Naturally, a SWOT will be different for a large organization that's been in business for a while compared to a brand new venture. That's OK. In each case there will be Strengths and Weaknesses.

Since our main tasks will be in the areas of marketing and marketing communications, it stands to reason that the concerns we raise will be in these areas. As you might imagine, engineers and operational executives, financial executives, and even those who run a restaurant kitchen can do a SWOT. You might even want to do one for the student organization you belong to.

Be as complete as possible, but realize that your concerns will, for the most part, be limited to your brand's marketing and marketing communications. But not always.

For example, with Stella's Barbecue, some of the operational and financial concerns were so severe that they affected virtually every other part of the restaurant's business. Later, we'll narrow them down to the few most important – that's when we'll get to our Problems and Opportunities.

Opportunities and Threats. These are factors in the external environment in which the company or brand operates and will include the following:

- **Competition** – rival companies and brands

- **Industry** – trends in the marketplace

- **Political** – laws, regulations, or other political factors

- **Economic** – economic climate (interest rates, unemployment, stock market)

- **Social** – impact of trends and social changes

- **Technology** – processing or core efficiencies

Again, depending on the size and scope of your business, these may be different as well – only not quite as much – since these are the external factors. In theory, these will be the same whether your company is brand new or well-established.

One cautionary note, though. Remember our story with the in-store clinic CuraQuick? As we discovered, this was a fast-changing and fast-growing category. So if your brand is diving into brand new waters, you might want to dial up your radar to see what else is going on out there. Realize that in a fast-changing marketplace, you may need to keep updating your SWOT as new factors emerge.

TIP: Think of the brand or company as a box. What is inside the box is internal, and you have controls over the inside. Outside the box is the external environment in which it exists; you must react and be aware of those elements so you can make decisions, but your control of these factors is severely limited.

To begin your SWOT analysis, have your research on hand. I prefer printed copies of the material, even if you're operating in a digital environment. Review all of your information and determine which of that information qualifies as a strength or a weakness within the organization, or if it is an opportunity or threat in the external environment.

Here are some examples of what to have on hand:

1. **Literature reviews** (secondary research) – either your essays, articles, or the annotated bibliography

2. **Competitive analysis** – charts or one sheets of competitive brands with the following information noted (if possible):

   Competitive position, sources of profits, degree of vertical integration, cost structure, product differentiation, resources, and historical response to industry trends

3. **Quantitative research results** (secondary or primary research) – experimental (or test market) data, statistical results from surveys (questionnaires)

4. **Qualitative research results** (secondary or primary research) – focus group notes, observation details, one on one interviews, depth interviews

5. **Brand Analysis Checklist** (brand audit) – here is where you add information that is not already included in the above

6. **Other information** – Statistical Abstract data from the Census Bureau, Industry data such as the RMA Annual Statement Studies: Financial Ratio Benchmarks

Remember Stella's Barbecue? We had a one-semester class that revolved around the development of an ad campaign for Stella's. The restaurant had been in the city for many years, but had recently moved to a location near our Morningside campus. Here is one group's SWOT analysis; note their focus on marketing and the brand. Also note my comments in the bubbles.

SWOT Analysis
Brand: Stella's BBQ
Problem: Low awareness and low profits

Strengths:

- BBQ sauce is "home-made" or "Original taste"
- Free pool while waiting on food
- Daily and weekly specials – Combo's and Picnic specials
- Family owned business, serving Siouxland for over 25 years
- Only BBQ restaurant in the area

These are already listed as strengths and are really not an opportunity. Delete it from the section.

Opportunities:

- Promote Stella's through print ads (The Shopper and The Weekender), billboards, pamphlets, banners, posters, shirts and other promotional paraphernalia this could reach more of the target audience and create awareness, too
- Using radio, newspapers, KTIV, KCAU (major mass media) to create awareness and reach more of the Target Audience.
- Create a tagline to give consumers a name with a product (they will remember the product better if they have a tagline or something catchy)
- Has a pool hall and can attract customers looking for entertainment with their meal
- Is family owned; does not need to conform to franchise policies

Weaknesses:

- Limited parking, not many convenient parking spots
- Located on Morningside Avenue, which is a busy street
- No set Advertising budget: "Whenever they feel like it."
- No mission statement
- No business plan, no known goals, no Unique Selling proposition
- No tag lines, no slogan (Lack of brand preference and awareness)

Threats:

- Famous Dave's is Stella's main competitor
- It's all Good BBQ is Stella's second main competitor
- Places that cater such as HyVee, Convention center, Marina Inn are definitely a threat to Stella's Catering
- Well established franchises and businesses have a well known tagline or slogan
- If business does not increase, Stella's could go bankrupt
- Stella's has negative opinions on their ribs (too much bone, not enough meat)

These are weaknesses. Just move them over and delete them here.

Figure 8.1 SWOT Analysis for Stella's BBQ (with a my notes)

Overall, nice work. I like your focus, and I think you have found the key areas that advertising can address. I would only suggest that you now prioritize the list to help you focus.

The original SWOT had quite a few more details. After editing and prioritizing, the students developed a SWOT that was manageable.

However, this SWOT had a few "blind spots."

In Strengths, Stella's relatively low price and the existence of some loyal customers were missing. Each was a strength with significant potential.

In Weaknesses, the very real management issues, including Stella's health and the lack of working capital were either glossed over or placed in the wrong section.

As a result of the non-recognition of low working capital in Opportunities, there was too much focus on paid media and too little on low-cost "guerrilla" media.

The negative opinion of the ribs (too much bone, not enough meat) was also placed in the wrong quadrant. Moreover, these could have inspired some product development opportunities (either meat-only barbecue – or some other reason for re-trial.) Complaints about the product were a sign that there may have been a "rejector base" problem that needed addressing.

TIP: At least some of the time your SWOT will deliver bad news. When delivering bad news, keep to the facts and don't mince words. Be sensitive to the listener's views, but stand by your research.

Now you're ready to build your own SWOT. Grab your highlighters and pens + all of the documents you have prepared so far.

A SWOT.doc – When you begin, you may want to be in a room with a wall and plenty of Post-Its. Then, you'll start to build a text file – probably a .doc file in Word. You might want to use columns or boxes to help keep each category in its place. The template we've included in the following Brain-Builder Exercise is available to download at www.brandbuilderworkbook.com.

BRAIN-BUILDER EXERCISE 8.1: SWOT Analysis

The purpose of this exercise is to apply the information from your research to a SWOT analysis.

Instructions:

1. Continue using the brand you've been working with.

2. Assemble all the data and resources you have thus far collected, highlight and make column notes on the documents you have. Your information should be

rich with ideas. Be patient here and work through all of the extras. Think about panning for gold – sifting out all of the junk and dirt. Some start with big pads or whiteboards, others input things into a growing document – be sure to make it a system that allows all members of the team to add their input.

3. Sort your notes into Strengths by writing an S in the column, Weaknesses with a W, Opportunities with an O, and Threats with a T.

4. Once all of the material is reviewed, start building your SWOT on a grid similar to the one that follows.

5. Make one more pass to prioritize the list that *you* believe are elements that you can address with advertising.

This is just like in the real world, there's no multiple choice, or True/False. Do your best to identify areas you think should be considered a strength, a weakness, an opportunity or a threat. Review the definitions above.

If you place something in two categories, or place it in the wrong category, you have time to rethink its placement. Sometimes you will identify factors that have a good news/bad news aspect. For example, a restaurant may have good personnel and not-so-good personnel, some menu items that are terrific and others that aren't. In that case, similar factors may show up on opposite sides of your SWOT. That's okay.

SWOT Analysis

Brand:

S	O
1.	1.
2.	2.
3.	3.
4.	4.
5.	5.
6.	6.
7.	7.
8.	8.
9.	9.
10.	10.

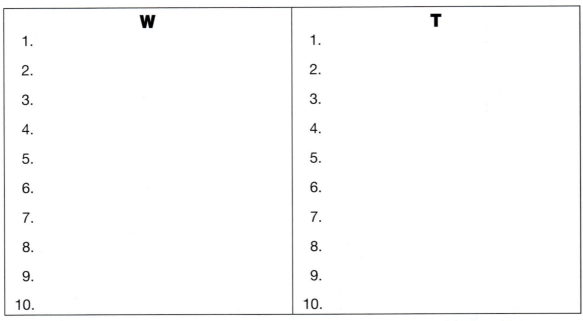

W	T
1.	1.
2.	2.
3.	3.
4.	4.
5.	5.
6.	6.
7.	7.
8.	8.
9.	9.
10.	10.

In the beginning, you may exceed 10 items. Certainly, you can add more. But you might also examine whether that might be too many. Perhaps some minor points on individual items might be handled by a larger point encompassing the minor points. You don't want to ignore things, but you don't want to pack too much stuff into your SWOT. Now you can see why you might need to go through your SWOT a few times to work it into manageable proportions.

PROBLEMS and OPPORTUNITIES

For some campaigns, the SWOT may be all you need, but usually you need to find a bit more focus. A Problems and Opportunities section can provide that. This is like turning a lemon into lemonade. The key is taking all this information and condensing it down into a few actionable items.

Some of those actionable items may have to do with operations. That's important, but these operational concerns, which may be important but not specifically related to marketing, may need to be organized into a different sort of document – perhaps an internal memo on the need to improve the barbecue product at Stella's. Then again, that's the big Product "P" in our Four P's. Not every aspect will be in the Promotional "P." In fact, the new location (Place) was a big part of Stella's situation.

That's the thing about problems. Once you identify them, you feel you have to solve them. However, for the most part, the problems we get to solve have a marketing communication focus. We will be working this information into Problems and Opportunities that can be addressed by communications.

For example, the lack of awareness of Stella's new location is a problem that can be addressed with communications that make people aware of the new address.

Prioritize your Strengths and Opportunities: see if you can align them. Review Weaknesses and Threats. Decide if you can narrow them down into two or three bullets that represent significant areas advertising can address.

Most likely, you have been able to identify the most important factors – major opportunities and key problems that need to be addressed. Some of them may surprise you. It is quite common to discover through the literature and research, that the industry or competition have successes in areas that were not initially apparent with your brand. Keep looking. You'll start seeing the important Opportunities as well as the Problems your brand will have to overcome.

With Stella's, the SWOT brought solid insights. Next, the students selected key areas they believed would be applicable to their campaign and the original statement of their challenge or problem.

As you might imagine from our previous discussion, there were other issues with Stella's that could be "make or break" for the survival of the business. However, in our class, we needed to focus on what could be done short-term.

So, issues such as new products and additional new management were not part of this document. In this case, the team set aside some of those larger issues and focused on things that communication could do to address the short-term problems. As you can see, some of the larger issues were addressed (i.e. no business plan, no known goals.) Opportunity #3 "Promote specific specials or products" could, hopefully, lead us into "meatier" issues. One thing about a restaurant, it's pretty easy to add or introduce a new product.

Here's how the team ended up.

PROBLEMS AND OPPORTUNITIES BRAND: Stella's BBQ	
Problems	**Opportunities**
• No set advertising budget: "Whenever they feel like it." • No business plan, no known goals • Lack of brand preference (lack of brand recognition)	• Expanding current advertising • Creating a business plan with specific goals • Promoting specific specials or products

Consider changing "business plan" to "advertising plan" and you are right on! Consider their 25 year history and homemade legacy recipes in your opportunities – rather than "specials or products". Nice Job!

177

The Problem the Communication Must Solve.

Many things are true. Most businesses have both many problems and many opportunities. But this stage of goal-setting demands that you narrow your focus.

Let's take another look at Stella's. The Problems are common to many small struggling businesses and the Opportunities are not necessarily earth-shaking. But now let's look at them again through a consumer's eyes.

The fact is Stella's can deliver a delicious dish at a very reasonable price. How is this a Consumer Problem that Stella's can solve? Hmmm. Let's think. Try this? The Problem is Consumers are not aware of the delicious barbecue items available at Stella's for a very reasonable price. In fact, it may be the best taste value in town!

So, the Problem the Communication Must Solve is this: Consumers are not aware of Stella's delicious barbecue values. Once we frame it in that context we start to know what we have to do. Other Problems may remain, but if we solve this problem, business will improve. And, as Peter Drucker observes, "volume solves a host of problems."

This is the first step in our goal-setting process. We now have a fairly clear idea of our Communications Goal.

Now it's your turn. Wrap your minds around all the factors in your SWOT and distill them to the key Problems and Opportunities you must address to build your brand. And then move to the Problem the Communication Must Solve.

BRAIN-BUILDER EXERCISE 8.2:
Problems and Opportunities

The challenge in this exercise will be to narrow your SWOT into a workable list of Problems and Opportunities, and then distill that short list into a consumer problem that the Brand can solve.

In the beginning, you will no doubt have more than three of each. However, you'll need to tighten up that list.

If you have a wide range of problems that range into some of the other Four P's, you may even want to develop two sheets. One sheet would focus on communication-related problems and opportunities and the other might focus on other important factors, such as operations or product-related issues.

There may be quite a few other issues, and they may be quite important. Chances are, they are the beginnings of a report to management. However, we also need to focus on problems that can be addressed with communications. And, if it's communications-related with other implications (i.e. a campaign to communicate a new meatier barbecue special), that's fine.

Try to focus on problems and opportunities the brand can address within a reasonable time frame. With luck, you'll get that list down to three or four important items. Again, you may need to develop a short-term and long-term list. That way, without ignoring the longer-term problems, you won't be prevented from getting to work on the problems and opportunities you can address short-term.

Problems and Opportunities	
Brand:	
Problems	**Opportunities**
1.	1.
2.	2.
3.	3.

Finally, take all those Problems and all those Opportunities and work them into one big Problem the Communications Must Solve. That Big Problem may combine some of what you've just outlined, for example the Problem of Stella's lack of awareness and the Opportunity of her tasty special items. Together, we had a Problem we could solve – and, in solving it, the result will be an improvement in Stella's business and awareness. Got it?

The Problem the Communications Must Solve

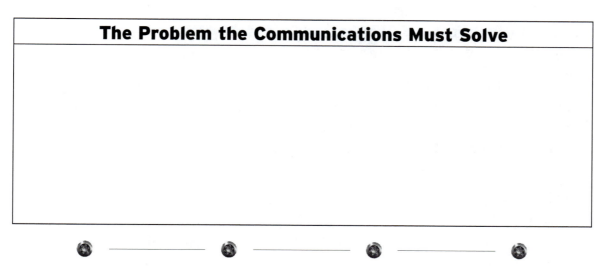

MARKETING OBJECTIVE

This is a process full of conjecture, analysis, informed insight, data extrapolation, qualitative and quantitative research, and a wide-ranging collection of almost every-thing that can go right and wrong. But, eventually, we have to make a decision and take a stand. Even if we're not exactly correct, we have to set a specific goal.

The Marketing Objective is a specific number related to the marketing function that you will measure. It will usually be something you hope to accomplish with an organized program of marketing communications activity. So, for example, we developed an increased audience marketing objective for our Sioux City Chamber Music group. This gave us a goal to aim at as we developed our programs.

This goal-setting is related to the previous goal – solving the Problem. While it may be conjecture – a best guess – it's still pretty clear. If we Solve The Problem, what will the business result be in terms of volume, or increased membership, etc.?

Now, with that focus, you write the objective that you plan on reaching with your plan. You have a lot of resources and information to help you set that number. For example, you often have hard numbers from the previous year's results. In this case, the Chamber Music group had figures for current membership and average atten-dance. You also have a lot of subjective measurement guides – the Lavidge-Steiner Learning Model, those Problems and Opportunities, the Situation Analysis, and the Competitive Analysis.

You should have a feel from these for what is possible. It's time to put your you-know-what on the line and state a specific goal. If your problem is to increase sales, or increase brand preference, or build awareness, then state your objective with those verbs. How are you measuring it – in units, percentage points, dollars? State the factor that will be measured. Finally, state how much you expect it to change. You should also indicate the time period in which you think you will reach your objective.

Be clear. Be aggressive. And be realistic. You should also realize that if you ac-complish only 60% of your first year's goals, that may still be pretty good. It's a tough marketplace out there. A friend recently noted that he'd finally accomplished his "five year plan." It had taken him ten years. Sometimes you just have to keep pushing. Like the old NW Ayer agency slogan – "Keeping Everlastingly At It."

The marketing objective format is simple and straightforward. "To (verb) (mea-surement) (value) (time)." So, for example, your marketing objective might be "*To increase paid membership by 20% within the first year.*" You might even go further "*and to increase attendance at performances (current average 120) by 25% for an average attendance of 150.*" You now have a Marketing Objective.

Formula for Marketing and Advertising Objectives

To + Verb + Measurement + Value + Time

Examples of word choices for:

Verbs: increase, build, expand, develop, grow, construct

Measurements: awareness, preference, conviction, knowledge, likeness, purchase, units, sales, online ticket sales, takeout orders, Christmas sales, votes, membership, donations

Value: dollars, percentage points, general number

Time: 4th quarter, annually, end of 2012, monthly

So even though it was a difficult business situation, the marketing objective for Stella's Barbecue looked something like this:

To increase lunch and dinner sales by 30% during the 4th quarter.

This looked very aggressive, but sales and location awareness were quite low. A steady program of flyers and coupons made this an accomplishable goal – if Stella's health held up. If not, all bets were off.

It's good to have a goal. Now I'm reminded of another ad agency slogan. This one is for the very successful Leo Burnett Agency. *"When you reach for the stars, you may not get one. But you won't come up with a handful of mud either."* Let's set that objective – and then reach it.

BRAIN-BUILDER EXERCISE 8.3:
Marketing Objective

This assignment is complex, but simple.

Write the objectives for your brand's campaign – probably for the next year.

To + Verb + Measurement + Value + Time

To (verb)_____

(what you will measure)_____

by (amount/value)_____

(timeframe)_____

● ——————— ● ——————— ● ——————— ●

POSITIONING STATEMENT

Understand the Problem. State your Marketing Objective. Establish your Position. This is the next part of your brand's goal-setting process.

Positioning is a concept that we haven't discussed yet. Simply put, Positioning is managing the place you hold in the customer's mind.

When I coach someone to develop a positioning statement, I have them start with "in the mind of the consumer, _____ will be…." It is a goal, but much broader and more qualitative than the objectives you just wrote. In general, your position will connect with the single most persuasive benefit your brand offers.

Briefly, there are four core types of Positioning: #1, Against, Niche, and New Category. And, as we'll mention in a bit, there are a few books that can help you get smarter in this area. There are even a few resources parked in our BrandBuilder website. OK, here are the Four Basics.

#1 Position. Here you claim category leadership. This can be national leadership, like McDonald's in fast food restaurants, or some sort of local leadership, such as "#1 in Siouxland."

Against Position. Here you position yourself against some larger competitor and communicate a meaningful dimension of superiority. A recent example that was both well done and successful was the "I'm a Mac. I'm a PC." TV campaign developed by Apple Computer.

Niche Position. This involves positioning yourself as a leader in some meaningful aspect of the category. Volvo has done this well with a safety position. Cheer detergent positioned itself as a leader in color protection. Popeye's Fried Chicken promotes its unique spicy flavor and New Orleans/Louisiana heritage. These all play to a meaningful product characteristic for at least a segment of the Target Audience. Not everyone wants spicy fried chicken, but for those who do, Popeyes has captured the "more flavor" position.

New Category. Here you establish a brand new category, and then claim leadership of that category – a #1 position. In our fast-moving marketplace, there are new categories emerging all the time. And it's a brand new opportunity to take that #1 position for your brand!

If you'd like to know more, we have two things to recommend.

First, we've posted a pdf on Positioning from *The Copy Workshop Workbook* on our website. You can download it and learn a little more.

Second, you really should go to the source and read the little book *Positioning: The Battle For Your Mind* by Jack Trout and Al Ries. You can get it new, used, or in an electronic format. It's worth reading.

**BRAIN-BUILDER EXERCISE 8.4:
Positioning Statement**

You will be thinking about the best position for your brand in the mind of your audience. Simply put, think what they might say about your brand.

Instructions:

1. Review the strengths and any statements made by your target audience.

2. Review the mission statement or values statement for the organization.

3. Use the following formula to help you develop a statement that describes the **position or place** you wish your brand to hold in the market place.

In the mind of the consumer, \<brand\> will be positioned as the .....

Your Business Goal

You've just been through a wide-ranging set of goal-setting exercises. Now it's time to do one more: The core goal for your brand. It will be compatible with everything you've just been through.

- The Core Goal will address **The Problem The Communication Must Solve** – though it may not solve everything listed in your Problems and Opportunities, or swat everything in your SWOT, it will focus on solving that One Big Problem. So for Stella's, which had many many problems, we knew we needed to build awareness of those delicious high-value specials and, as customers enjoyed the unique taste experience, we would be able to establish Stella's as "the value choice," which, just incidentally, was part of the Position we wanted to establish.

- Next, the Core Goal will be compatible with your **Marketing Objective**. The Sioux City Chamber Music group wanted to increase membership 20%. With Stella's, we just hoped to improve the dismal sales numbers. Things were so low that 30% was reasonable. Be specific. Be realistic.

- Finally, the Core Goal will relate to your **Positioning Statement**. In addition to your specific Marketing Objective, you want to have a general sense of the conceptual space you want to occupy in your Target's mind. Positions are, in their essence, pretty simple. Volvo/Safety, Apple/Hip and Easy, Dodge/Performance (with a bit of hot rod), DiGiorno's/Good as Delivery Pizza, Wal-Mart/Low Price. Pretty simple. Yet, you can feel it as a goal. As you develop your messages over time, you'll find that it can really help.

Now it's your turn. You know your brand – perhaps better than anyone. It's time to set a goal for your business. And, if you happen to be working with a non-profit or a governmental effort – like our Siouxland Conservation Project, take away that "business" word and simply state them as "Goals." But don't throw that "business" word away too soon. You'll find that even non-profits have to take in money.

One Goal or more than one Goal? Just as we sometimes have Secondary Target Consumers, we may have more than one Goal or Business Goal. Just as breakfast, lunch, and dinner are very different businesses within the same restaurant, you may find that achieving that single Marketing Objective, which is usually some sort of sales increase, may actually involve achieving a combination of Goals.

Short-term, the Chamber Music group wanted to maximize existing classical music fans. Long-term, having an outreach to schools made a lot of sense.

Sioux City Chamber Music Business Goals:
Increase membership and ticket sales.
Develop a future audience with a school outreach program.

Got it? OK, now it's your turn.

BRAIN-BUILDER EXERCISE 8.5: Business Goals

State your brand's Business Goals.

CHAPTER REVIEW

In this chapter we learned how to:

1. Put together a SWOT Analysis
2. Condense your SWOT into Problems and Opportunities and then further focus on The Problem the Communication Must Solve
3. Write a Marketing Objective
4. Formulate a Positioning Statement
5. State your Brand's Goals or Business Goals

It's a short list, but if you become a Brand Builder, these are tasks you will do over and over and over as you build successful brands.

REVIEW QUESTIONS

1. Which aspects of the SWOT Analysis did you find easiest to determine? Which were the most difficult?

2. Did you find anything surprising as you developed your Problems and Opportunities? Which problems, on judgment, seemed to be most easily solved with communications? Which were going to be the most difficult?

3. Which opportunities seemed to stimulate easy and exciting solutions? Which of these seemed to be most challenging?

4. What, after all your thinking, is The Problem the Communication Must Solve? Are you already thinking of messages that might solve this problem?

4. For your brand, how did you choose to develop a Marketing Objective? Were there some alternative types of objectives you considered? If not, why not do that now?

5. What type of Positioning did you choose for your brand? #1, Against, Niche, or New Category? Or is there some other variation you chose?

6. Do you have Goals or Business Goals?
   Do you have one Goal? Or two? Or three?

CHAPTER 9:
MESSAGING: BUILDING A CREATIVE STRATEGY

The last chapter was a relatively short one. If, based on the Goals you established and The Problem the Communication Must Solve, you have a fairly clear idea of the Message you need to send, this chapter may go fairly smoothly. You'll see how to frame that Message in a number of Communication Strategy Formats. With luck, it will go smoothly, and your message will be clear and effective.

If, however, it's not clear at all, this chapter may be quite complicated.

Let's review what we know up to this point. You understand your brand's Business Goals. You know your Target. During your goal-setting, you established The Problem the Communication Must Solve, a specific Marketing Objective, and a sense of your Brand's desired Position. So far so good.

Based on this information, you have the knowledge needed to write the strategy behind your core Message. Remember, objectives are *what* you hope to accomplish. Strategy is *how* you plan to accomplish those objectives.

In this case, we will be writing a Communication Strategy. Our objective will be to develop a message to motivate our Target in a direction that will help us achieve our objective. Now we're going to try to figure out how to do that. Hmmm.

Our Strategy will be the underlying architecture of our message. Once you figure that out, we'll need to mobilize the additional skills like creative writing and graphic design. But underneath it all will be our strategy. Got it? Good.

Message is the third part of our brand building matrix.

Sometimes, if what you want to say is not yet clear, this stage of the plan can be daunting – both for students and for clients – particularly if it's your first time. To help you get the job done, we'll use some tools we have found to be most helpful to work our way through the process.

We have some excellent tools in this chapter – a whole toolbox full.

They'll help build your strategy in a smart, sensible way and put you on the path to developing that persuasive message. They're tools to help you work through all the information and figure out what you want to say to your Target.

Before opening the Creative Toolbox, let's refresh your thoughts with what you know about the Factors That Influence Purchase Behavior. What moves your Target to buy, choose, attend, judge, enroll, donate, or vote for your brand?

After developing your Message Strategy, you should be ready to brainstorm a bit and look for that Big Idea or concept that will make your message come alive.

As we move along, you'll find we have a lot of words for what is all pretty much the same thing – you might call it a Selling Theme or Tag Line – for your brand. Others might call it a Slogan, or a Selling Idea, or maybe The Big Idea. Some call it a Proposition (or a Unique Selling Proposition) and some call it a Concept. We call it all those things, though mostly we're going to call it your Message.

Whatever you call it, it's the idea or line that will emphasize or dramatize a point and differentiate you from your competitors in a meaningful way.

One more thing. This doesn't happen in a vacuum. If you have an Established Brand, or even a Troubled Brand, you will also be dealing with your brand's history, which will, for better or worse, provide additional context for your Messaging.

Okay, here we go.

LEARNING OUTCOMES

After completing this chapter, you will be able to:

1. Understand the Factors that Influence Purchasing Behavior and their relationship to developing your Message Strategy. This will include a Laddering review, which will cover:
   a. Attributes
   b. Features
   c. Product Benefit
   d. Customer Benefits
   e. Values associated with your brand
   f. Identifying those attributes, features, benefits, and values through Laddering.

2. Understand the concept of "Hitting the Sweet Spot."

3. The Creative Toolbox. Develop the Message Strategy a number of different ways using a dozen different formats:

   a. GE Focus System
   b. Target Sketch
   c. Creative Brief
   d. Creative Action Plan
   e. Who, What, What
   f. Copy Platform
   g. Headlines, Taglines, Concepts: the Thinking About It Worksheet
   h. Brand Character Capsule and the Brand Character Statement
   i. Learn/Feel/Do Circle
   j. Left brain/Right brain – the FCB Grid
   k. Strategy Selection Grid
   l. Six Stages of Ideation

4. Decide on your Message Strategy.

5. Determine and develop your Core Message.

FACTORS THAT INFLUENCE PURCHASING BEHAVIOR

Before starting on the strategy discussion, let's review the Factors That Influence Purchase Behavior. You identified them in Chapter 7. They need to be clear in your mind.

If it's not crystal clear, go back and review the information you completed for your brand. Chart those factors again. If you've learned new information since then, make the appropriate revisions or updates.

Since it has been a few chapters since you focused on those factors, make sure you take time to reflect on your responses and your customer responses. Note any factor that seems to be distinguishing from the others, and, in particular, distinguish your brand from competitors.

Laddering Review

Need a little more help? Let's review the Laddering definitions: Attribute, Features, Product Benefit, Customer Benefit, and Values. We also covered these in Chapter 7, but here's a recap.

Attribute – Characteristic of product, usually inherent or natural to the brand.

Feature – aspect of product, usually based on some manufactured or designed aspect

Product Benefit – a benefit to the consumer, usually based on a product feature or attribute

Customer Benefits (Consumer Benefit) – a benefit to the consumer, usually based on how the product benefit delivers a positive result to the consumer

Values – the human dimension reinforced by the benefit that is a stronger motivation to use a brand

Laddering – this is the process of moving through the sequence. Generally you will ask why a product feature or benefit is important. Answers will move you to the next level on the ladder

With that in mind, here are a couple of questions you should be able to answer:

Why do customers buy your brand?

Where on the ladder do you find the most important aspects for your brand? Are these the same aspects for the entire category, or is there some factor that is somewhat more unique for your brand? And that leads you to the second question.

Is it different or the same for why they buy other brands in the category?

One of your communication jobs will be *meaningful differentiation*. In some way, your message should communicate that your brand is different and better. It may be a feeling or it may be something quite real and specific.

Have you traveled lately? How did you choose an airline? Was it price, schedule, amenities, or all of the above? Have you seen ads for locations you're thinking about traveling to, or airlines that you might use? Southwest Airlines is one of the few airlines not charging you to check your luggage. Is that a feature or a benefit? It's both. It is a differentiating feature that Southwest offers, and it delivers the benefit of savings to the customer. So it's no surprise that they are advertising it very heavily. It will probably be effective as long as others charge for checked luggage.

Remember Stella's BBQ? One feature was the legacy barbecue sauce from Stella's family recipe. It's a Feature. However, the customer sees a benefit in the pleasure they will have when eating the sauce. And, the customer might find a valuable emotional connection in eating at a place that appears to have strong family ties. But the hook and the bait that's going to get the fish in the boat is that Special – a high value for a down-home barbecue meal. Then, with that taste in their mouth, customers can decide how they feel about legacy barbecue sauce and those strong family ties.

As you know, the path from product Attribute to Values is called Laddering. Moving up and down that ladder is a good example of the kind of strategic choices marketers make as they decide what to emphasize in their messaging.

Do you have those factors clearly in your mind? Let's write them down. And, at this point, it's OK if there is more than one factor, though it will be helpful if you have a sense of which one is most important. Later, we'll have to choose.

These are the factors that motivate purchase behavior for _____

1. _____

2. _____

3. _____

"HITTING THE SWEET SPOT"

This concept is from Lisa Fortini-Campbell's consumer insight classic, *Hitting the Sweet Spot*. You might want to pick up a copy.

Basically, the "sweet spot" is that connection between insight into what's important in the category (Factors that Motivate) and insight into what's important to the consumer.

For example, the current Wal-Mart campaign connects two big simple ideas. First, that they have low prices, no surprise. Second, they connect that with real people's lives and the idea that a low price means that a family can have more – and live better. So they get to the very powerful theme. Save Money. Live Better. Their message has both logic and emotion. It's clear as a bell. And, if you're a Mom working to make the most of the family budget, I'm guessing it hits that "sweet spot."

This is where the target and the brand meet with persuasive insight. Looking for that "sweet spot" can be fun – particularly when you find it.

We'd also like to mention one more of Lisa's insights. It's about the nature of "breakthrough." A lot of people think that breakthrough comes from a wild crazy noisy "creative" execution that "breaks through the clutter." We're not sure that's a good idea. Sometimes with all that noise we just add to the clutter. Lisa's point is that real breakthrough happens when our target "breaks in" to the message. They look at it and say, "Hey, that's a good idea. We should do that."

My editor, Bruce, likes to remind me why horoscopes are such a popular part of the newspaper – "it's about you." Keep that in mind as you try to find that "sweet spot." Messages that really break through happen when our customers "break in."

THE CREATIVE TOOLBOX

Your Message Strategy can be created from a number of tools. They help you "shape" your Strategy. We can't tell you which one will be most useful in any given situation, but we're pretty sure the tool you need is sitting in that Toolbox. Our Creative Toolbox is full of conceptual models and strategy systems that are agency tested. We're going to introduce you to a dozen of them that will build your skill and confidence in developing your Message Strategy.

But, another story first. When a student comes into my class, say along the time-line of Chapter 4, the Situation Analysis, they might start with a statement like "I have this idea for a TV spot, and it goes like this…" (This happens quite often.)

I start asking questions like: Who is the Target? What specific reasons lead the target to purchase the brand? What evidence was used to determine the answers? What business goals or position does the brand hold in the market or consumer's mind? What Message Windows would best fit this brand, target, message, and objectives?

After a long pause, the student realizes that those answers are really needed, smiles and steps back into the brand building process.

You do not start building TV, radio, print, or any other creative executions without having a strong strategy and a clear message. Rarely have I had a beginning student execute those early ideas in the same way they conceived them. The Selling Ideas you need to think up will be based on an understanding of your Target, your product, and the competition.

Once you've been around that track a few times, you'll be surprised at how comfortable you become at digging into your Tool Box and finding what you need to solve the problem. But in the beginning, we're going to go slow and keep the training wheels on. So, I'll repeat, at this stage, you do not start with creative ideas when beginning your branding efforts.

This section will give you lots of tools. You'll also see I am highlighting a number of other sources here. They have the expertise. Students use these with confidence in my classes. With their permission, you have a nice toolbox.

TIP: Bruce Bendinger's book (the entire book), The Copy Workshop Workbook, is devoted to creating strategy and writing the message. It has lots of excellent examples you should check out!

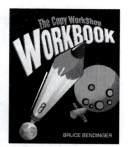

Some of the Toolbox items might seem similar, and, in a way, they are – just like there are different kinds of screwdrivers. But each offers a little different twist. Since you are new to creating messages and branding, I'm asking you to start to become familiar with each of them. Then, as you create Messages and Message Strategies more often, you'll recognize which ones work best for you, your team, and your brand.

Opening the Toolbox.

Here we go. Before you look at each individual tool – and try it out – here's a quick guide to what we've put in there. Oh, and one more thing. With one exception, there's no particular order for using any particular tool. As you become more experienced with each one and what they can do, you'll find yourself knowing which one to grab.

That exception? From Tool #2 to Tool #6, you'll find yourself sort of doing the same thing in a slightly different way. This will give you a few different angles on your Message Strategy. Eventually, you're going to choose the one you like best.

But in the beginning, you're kind of going to want to use them all – just to get familiar with what they can do and to discover which ones you like using the best.

Here's the order in which we're presenting them. This first time you might want to use them in this order – after that, it's entirely up to you.

By the way, when appropriate, we'll put the templates for each on our site.

1. **The GE Focus System.** We're going to start you with this one. A simple three-step process developed by Bob Lauterborn at General Electric.

2. **Target Sketch**. We already did this in Chapter 7. It's a great way to get thinking about your Target and how they connect with your Brand.

3. **Creative Brief**. This is the kind of document Account Planners use to "brief" the Creative Department. It's another useful way to organize your way through what you're thinking and what you want the Target to think when your messaging has been successful.

4. **Creative Action Plan**. There are a lot of different Creative Strategy Worksheets – this is a good one, developed by Dennis Altman in *Advertising & The Business of Brands*.

5. **Who, What, What.** They are three simple questions that give you another way of focusing on what you want your messaging to accomplish.

6. **Creative Strategy Template**. More tightening up. Again, these are similar tools, but by using a hammer, sandpaper, and a microscope, you see that your strategic thinking is getting better.

7. **Headlines, Taglines, Concepts – The "Thinking About It" Worksheet.** Hey, we're going to be making messages; maybe you've already thought of a few things in the back of your mind. Let's work on more of the Messages that are going through your head – and then move on to having a few more thoughts.

8. **Brand Character Capsule & The Brand Character Statement**. What if our brand was a person? This is a terrific way of focusing in on our Brand Personality with a short essay. And then focusing in further by condensing it into a simple statement.

9. **Learn/Feel/Do Circle**. There are three ways we interact with a product or service. We learn about it. We feel (or don't feel) a certain way. We use it, we do it, eat, wear, consume, enjoy… whatever. Now, as you will see – we can do that in any sequence. A fresh way of thinking about the whole process.

10. **Left Brain/Right Brain – The FCB Grid.** We're the same person – but we're different, depending on the type of purchase decision. The FCB Grid is a nice graphic way of thinking about it.

11. **Strategy Selection Grid**. Have you considered all your options for your Target Audience and Competitive framework? This grid can be particularly helpful when developing new brands or identifying secondary targets and market opportunities.

12. **Six Stages of Ideation**. Still need a few more thoughts? Maybe it's time to bring your team into a brainstorm. Here is the idea-creating process. You can do it alone or you can do it with your team.

The Twelve Tools.

OK, here goes. Each of these tools is capable of helping you solve your problem. But, depending on the problem, and depending on you, some will work better than others. You'll want to start by trying them all and then, as you discover your favorites, well, those will be the ones you use most often.

If you get stuck, go back to the Toolbox and try a different tool.

1. GE Focus System

We're not all creative geniuses. And sometimes we have to dig into a problem without as much time or as much information as we'd like. That said, the first tool we're going to give you is an approach that was developed for exactly that situation. It was developed for an internal creative department at GE, where, in any one day, they'd have to go from advertising light bulbs, to diesel engines, to posters for an appearance by Mr. Wizard – a lot of different things. Here goes…

First, focus on the Target. That's right, first think about who you're going to be talking to. We've been thinking about our brand almost all the time. Let's re-focus and think about who we're talking to.

Next, focus on the Proposition. This is a word that we don't use a lot, but it can be very helpful. Simply put, a Proposition says: Do this and you will get that. Buy this product and you will get that product performance. Adopt this behavior and expect the following result. Got it? Of course you do. Let's talk about our brand in those terms. Use our brand and get _____.

What do you get? That's your Proposition. If it's strong enough, a simple statement should be almost enough to get some people to use your brand. If it isn't, your Proposition isn't strong enough.

Dramatize your Proposition. Once you know what you're going to say – your Proposition – then it's time to say it in a special way. Naturally, some writers will say it better than others and some graphic artists may do a better job than others. But, when you think about it, if you have that Proposition clearly in mind, you know what your Message should be, and now your job is to say it as well as you know how.

2. Target Sketch

Remember Dennis Altman's Target Sketch from Chapter 7. You'll want to go back and review what you have prepared, or if you are just picking the book up at this chapter, this is what you need. A Target Sketch is a fictional character and story about your audience.

The factors to be included in a Target Sketch:

- Age
- Gender
- Habits, ideas
- Standards
- Educational level

- Economic status (be specific – use dollar amounts plus a little imagination to illustrate your point)
- Occupation
- Hobbies/interests
- Likes/dislikes
- Views, (if applicable e.g. politics or social issues)
- Taste (if applicable e.g. style of clothes, décor)
- Media and lifestyle (describe the target's car, home, family situation, pets, the books, music, films, TV, magazines, and social media he or she uses)
- Personality features
- A few of his or her everyday life occurrences (tell of an incident that illustrates the target's nature)

3. Creative Brief

A number of agencies use some sort of Creative Brief to aid the creative department through the creative process. You'll have two versions here. You will be asking questions, and providing answers. Another tool for you to use!

Some quick tips to help you in writing briefs: Make sure you have the facts. Write multiple briefs to clarify the points. Involve others – client, creative, and other key parties.

Four basic questions are:

1. What are we trying to accomplish?
2. Who are we talking to?
3. What is the single most persuasive idea we can convey?
4. Why should they believe it?

Here is one more set of questions for the creative brief:

1. Why are we advertising?
2. Who are we talking to?
3. What do they currently think?
4. What would we like them to think?
5. What is the single most persuasive idea we can convey?
6. Why should they believe it?
7. Are there any creative guidelines?

And here is what it looks like when applied to a brand.

This one is used with permission from the Richards Group.

Learjet Creative Brief

Warning, people don't like ads. People don't trust ads. People don't remember ads. How do we make sure this one will be different? (Source: Richards Group)

Why Are We Advertising?
To create excitement about the Learjet 60 as a cost-effective solution to prospects' need for a trans-continental jet and to reinforce Learjet's high performance mystique.

Who Are We Talking To?
High-level corporate executives, corporate fleet managers, and chief pilots who need a corporate jet with trans-continental capability. Learjet buyers are motivated by emotion, but must justify their decision to peers and constituents in rational, financial terms.

What Do They Currently Think?
"I'd love to own a Learjet and get that kind of high performance. But you pay a price: either in dollars, in range or in comfort. I think they have a transcon jet now, but it's probably just a longer version of their old 55."

What Would We Like Them To Think?
"Learjet does have a jet that will fly my longer missions, and it's not just a stretched version of the 55. And it's cheaper to fly than any trans-continental Hawker, Falcon, or Citation 10."

What Is The Single Most Persuasive Idea We Can Convey?
Learjet performance is a cost-effective transcontinental jet.

Why Should They Believe It?
Transcontinental range (2,750 nautical miles) is the highest of jets with comparable performance.

Seats up to eight, stand-up room for passengers, stand-up private lavatory.

Learjet allure.

Are There Any Creative Guidelines?
Call to action: "Call Ted Farid, VP Sales and Marketing."

Consider a new theme line.

4. Creative Action Plan

- **Client:**
  Name of the product, service or idea we're selling

- **Target:**
  Description of Target Audience.
  Demographics, geographic, psychographics, etc.

- **Competitive Snapshot:**
  Quick overview of the marketplace.
  Key competitors and their positions.
  Selling problems, if any.

- **Old Thought/New Thought:**
  What target thinks now/what we want them to think?

- **Main Claim:**
  The big thing to say. It could be a customer benefit, a product benefit, or a whole new way to use the product.
  Customer Benefit is "What customer derives from product (clean breath, white teeth, prestige, relief, confidence).
  Product Benefit is Actual claims the product can make (Prevents dental plaque," "gets up to highway speeds in 4 seconds," "Unbreakable, aged in oak, low in carbs").

- **Support:**
  Proof-points that justify claims: "Approved by ADA," "More power than any other car in its class," "Sugar free," "All steel construction," "All-natural."
  Any real tests, charts, facts, documentation, and research to back up claims.

- **Tone:**
  Mood of ad (informative, urgent, beautiful, entertaining, sexy, funny, warm, authoritative, professional, classy, worldly, etc.)

- **Added Tools:**
  Road map, cutaway, coupon, comparison, prices, etc.

Here's how Dennis Altman used his Creative Action Plan for Toomba, a fictitious tropical island. The Core Idea: Nothing is on the island for tourists yet – no resort hotels, golf courses, just a few good places to eat. See how Dennis uses facts to *differentiate* the brand. (From *Advertising & the Business of Brands*.)

Creative Action Plan: Toomba

Client: Toomba Island, in the Caribbean

Target: Vacation couples with more than $50k incomes

Competitive Snapshot: Preferred resorts in the category are Jamaica, Aruba, Antigua, and Barbados. All have been successfully marketed via airline promotions and travel agency packages. They are known for their luxury facilities. Toomba is still rustic.

Old Thought/New Thought: (Turn Toomba's disadvantages into customer benefits.)

Old: "NOBODY ever heard of Toomba! It's deserted. Why would anyone in his right mind want to go there?"

New: What a find! No crowds, no traffic, no V, no kids, no restaurant lines, no gift shops, and – best of all – no pushy tourists.

Main Claim: Peace and quiet

Support:

Travel:
- Last year Toomba got its first airstrip
- Today, it had one inbound flight a day
- Jeep taxi service is available along the beach road

Accommodations: Seventeen guest houses and small hotels are on the island, most on or very near the beach. Only two have locks on their guestroom doors. Most have no phones in the rooms (only in lobbies), and a few have grass-hut bars on the beach. Cellular providers are just starting to put towers on the island. There is no wireless internet service yet on the island

Dining: Four good seafood places, one diner that serves meat loaf and kiwi pie, and several native restaurants where local fruits, vegetables, and crab cocktails are served.

Tone: Serious and sophisticated. The ads must present Toomba as a heaven on earth for jaded, travel-weary vacationers who just want to rest, walk, swim, dive, read…and not deal with tourists.

And here's how the creative turned out.

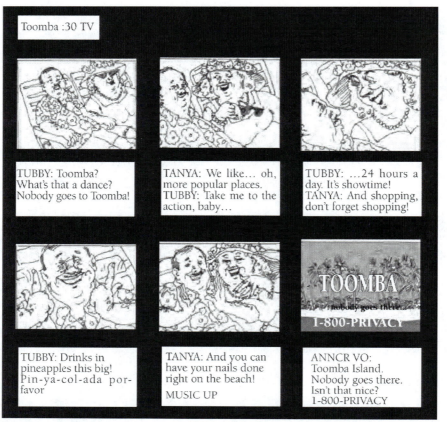

5. Who, What, What

A shorthand version of the Creative Action plan is the "Who, what, what?" As you create more and more messages, this shorthand version might be useful for you.

- Who are we talking to?
- What do they think now?
- What do we want them to think?

6. A Creative Strategy Template

The Template looks like this in a list or in as illustrated (Fig 9.2).

To convince _____

To use _____

Instead of _____

Because _____

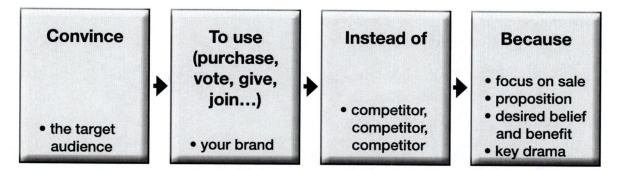

7. Headlines, Taglines, Concepts – The "Thinking about it" Worksheet

Working with others, take a look at some of the ideas and see if they don't inspire you to have other ideas. This worksheet orders the headline through the end of an ad.

- **Headline/Visual Idea**
  Ideas: arresting, involving, newsy
  Hint: Visual and headline should work as one
  Example:
  Visual – Man with a broad toothless smile
  Headline: "IGNORE YOUR TEETH, AND THEY'LL GO AWAY."

- **Opening of body copy**
  A grabber. Ideally, a short, punchy sentence that bridges the headline/visual
    with the why and how to follow. Promises a good customer benefit.
  Example "Is this your future?

- **Middle of body copy:**
  Support for claim
  Summation of benefits
  Good spot for memorable phrase
  Example: Give your teeth ten minutes a day and they'll last a lifetime.

- **End of body copy/Call to Action:**
  What the reader should do.
  Reference to headline.
  (Remember what this is about)

- **Feel good ending:**
  (With love and promise)
  Example: "Call 800-IVORIES and we'll send you everything you need to do
    all that. Then, you'll have plenty to smile about. For the rest of your life."

Headlines

Let's try for "effective surprise."

It's one thing to write a headline that's a flat declaration, but, in most classes, flat is simply not enough.

You want to create "mind stickers."

You want to state your ideas with charm or humor.

You want to provide your audience with the surprise that comes with the joy of discovery.

That calls for saying things in an unexpected fashion.

That's what effective surprise is all about.

A good headline attracts attention and suggests a customer benefit in an unexpected way.

Taglines

A tagline will come out of a headline and be used for the whole campaign. Sometimes, it might be the headline/tagline all together.

A tagline is the way a brand wants to be known. It summarizes the brand's promise or the definition of the brand's mission. It appears in the final phrase, often right next to the logo.

In a campaign, a tagline feeds the whole campaign (Altman 2000).

Concept – The Headline/Visual Idea

The **concept, idea, or selling idea** is a communication idea that helps a brand achieve the goal of persuasion. You can use a concept through the campaign. It becomes a driving force in all areas of building the message and finding the right windows to put them in. It "speaks" to the target as well.

Imaginative Divergence and Structural Connectedness are two methods that might help you develop the right concept

Imaginative divergence: takes an aspect of the problem, or the brand or the strategy and builds on it in a surprising way; that's often the surprise part.

Structural connectedness: means that the concept connects with the strategy, with target audience perceptions, and other aspects of keeping the campaign organized.

When a branding campaign has both these elements, they almost seem to organize themselves into strong, focused advertising (Altman 2000).

Visual symbiosis

The headline and visual are really symbiotic. Each does a job and they work together to become one statement. It immediately identifies an ad as a message worth noting. It has good advice, humor, and a very important implied benefit. All in a simple picture and a few words.

That's what to go for. When it works, you can make $1 + 1 = 3$.

8. The Brand Character Capsule & The Brand Character Statement

A Brand Character Capsule describes what the brand stands for in terms of customer perception.

Since the character of the brand is defined by the customer; you can use your insights and research to create this capsule. Altman provides the following capsule for Mercedes Benz.

Mercedes Benz cars are unmistakable status symbols. The name denotes class and exclusivity. These cars are made in many different sizes and types, which all bear a definite family resemblance. Mercedes Benzes are often thought of as "driver's cars," which refers to their handling qualities, precision, strength and endurance. Because of their considerable cost and unique look, they convey a high prestige image.

After you have completed your Brand Character Capsule, try to condense it into a Brand Character Statement.

The **Brand Character Statement** is a statement about the values of the brand over a long period of time.

Here are some examples from *The Copy Workshop Workbook*:

Crest is the dedicated leader in improving dental health for the family.

Coast is a product that is exhilarating to use.

Pampers – pre-eminent reputation as the leader in baby care... a warm and affectionate attitude toward babies.

Camay – the soap of beautiful women.

9. Learn/Feel/Do Circle

OK, now let's think about it another way. There are three things – and pretty much only these three things – we can do related to a product or service.

We can learn about it. We can feel a certain way about it. We can do it – eat, wear, enjoy, drive, etc. That's it. And, we can do these things in pretty much any order. You can enter at any point, but most frequently you involve the target in one of these ways.

Learn: We read about a product in an ad, look at the label, or learn about it as we experience it.

Feel: We may have feelings about products or product categories – some based on our experience, some on personal preference, and some on who knows what.

Do: We buy a product, use it, and experience it. Perhaps we get a free sample at a street fair. It's a sequence.

Three rules:
1. **You can enter at any point on the circle.** Your initial experience with a product may be learning, feeling, or doing. Sampling might be the best for foods, or some new version of toothpaste.

2. **You may go in either direction.** The sequence of experience can go in either direction, any way you wish. Think about it. Think about the way people involve themselves with your product and with your advertising.

3. **Be careful to always write in one mode.** If you always write with "learning", you are always writing that yours is better, and it might be, but there might also be another way. (Bendinger, 2009)

So, as you work on your messaging, think about how you want to approach your Target – in the "do" mode (like sampling a bit of food – a new dish at Stella's), in the "feel" mode (like the emotion you have about classical music), or in the "learn" mode (like finding out about a lost piece of history for The Czech Legion Project). This can have a big impact on your messaging.

10. Left Brain/Right Brain – The FCB Grid

Yes, we're the same person – but we're different, depending on the type of purchase decision. Is it left brain logic or right brain emotion? The FCB (Foote, Cone & Belding) Grid reveals in a graphic, tangible way how consumers approach the purchase of a particular product or service.

Here's a nice graphic representation of how it works.

The two axes are right and left – Emotion/Thinking and Involvement (meaning whether it is important to you, or not so important).

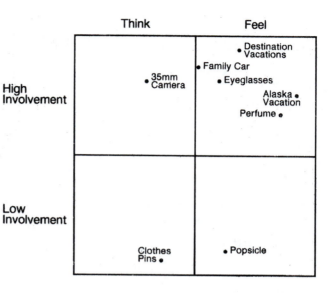

Here are some examples.

Low Think: Practical and functional products – let's say you're shopping for paper towels or cleaning products.

Low Feel: Sensate and pleasurable products – now, you're looking at the candy display – or maybe you want a beverage.

High Feel: Products that reflect on you – this is more important – say clothing for an important event.

High Think: Considered purchases – this is important too, but you're more logical – like terms for a student loan, or car payments.

First, think about where on the grid your brand's purchase decision is being made. Then, you might want to go inside out and think about how there is a bit of each aspect – left brain logic and right brain emotion – in the purchase decision.

This little grid can help you think about your Target in a very useful way.

11. Strategy Selection Grid

You may still have some important strategic questions about your brand.

Maybe there are some interesting secondary targets. Maybe there are some unique positioning opportunities. Maybe you're still debating the emphasis of your messaging.

Here's a way to get it down on paper (or up on a wall) and give it some more thought.

You can fill out every square – or you can just use the parts you are debating.

Strategy Selection Grid			
Product Class Definition			
Target Group Selection			
Message Element Selection			
Rationale – based on information and/or judgment			

There's a more complete PowerPoint on this topic on www.adbuzz.com, in the Café section.

12. Six Stages of Ideation

Still looking for that idea?

Two things. First, why not try some "ideation?"

Work at thinking up new ideas, which are, after all, "a new combination of previously existing elements." That's what James Webb Young observed in his book *A Technique for Producing Ideas*. And it's good news for you. Because it means that one or both pieces of your new idea are already parked between your ears. You just have to put 'em together.

So here's the process. Take a deep breath and give it a try.

1. **Preparation:** Collecting input and doing your homework. Information enters your left brain and flows to the right brain. The more information you have, the more connections that can be made

2. **Frustration:** If it doesn't come quickly, frustration can set in, but simple logic sometimes doesn't give you the answer. The left (creative) side doesn't quite know what to do with so much information. You go back and forth and get frustrated.

3. **Incubation:** Now the right brain looks for new combinations. Sleep on it,

mull it over, and a natural process will take place. You might consider shaking things up a bit here, stir them around as you discuss it with others, and let other brains kick it around with you. Sometimes groups of creative people can duplicate the incubation function.

4. **Illumination:** Aha! The light bulb goes on. Two previously unrelated elements connect – you've got an idea; it might not be a blind flashing light.

5. **Evaluation:** Is it good enough? Creative solutions and ideas need to be evaluated by the right (analytical) brained folks – the critical role of the Creative Director. Using both evaluation and imagination, you'll learn to evaluate your own work. Recognizing good ideas of others is another useful skill – sometimes you can make them better.

6. **Elaboration:** Work it out. Copy and layout. Translate it to TV, Radio, and unpaid media. Then it gets harder. Having ideas, even good ones, is often pretty easy – making them work, is work.

So, what's the second thing?

Go back to the top. You're already smarter – you might want to work your way through the Creative Tool Box one more time – and maybe do it in a new order.

That Selling Idea is there waiting for you.

But you might have to give your brain a little bump – to see things in a slightly new and different way.

You might need to rewrite The Problem. Often, you can find that just re-stating the Problem a new and different way can give you that extra perspective you need to develop a Message that connects with your Target in a powerful new way.

Or maybe it's a new perspective on Factors That Motivate Purchase Behavior.

This isn't like other classes, where the teacher already knows the answer. You've got to figure this one out for yourself. Not easy. But when you finally get it right – well, it's a special feeling.

So – good luck on getting the right idea.

DECIDE ON THE CREATIVE STRATEGY

You've done a lot of thinking. You may have clearly determined your strategy by now.

You may feel clear and confident about the most effective way to persuade your target audience. If so, your strategy will most likely have these characteristics:

- It will offer your Target a **persuasive reason to try** or *reason to buy* based on a Factor that Motivates Purchase Behavior.
- It will provide a reason to try or reason to buy *in preference to the competition.*
- It will *stimulate* you and your team to develop what you feel will be effective and persuasive messages.

If your Strategy has these characteristics (even though we never know for sure until after the sales results are in) then you're probably in pretty good shape.

However, if things are still not clear and you're not confident, here are some thoughts to help you work through this difficult time – in no particular order…

1. **Work Backwards**. Write Messages. Look at them. Which ones seem to be the most persuasive? On judgment, the most persuasive will be the ones based on the strongest strategy. So – back out the strategy implied by those messages. There's a good chance it's a winner.

2. **Attack The Enemy.** In politics, it's called "going negative." Since you want your strategy to demonstrate why we should want to choose your brand in preference to the competition, this is a good way to focus on it. Now, in most cases, you won't make a lot of sales – or a lot of friends – just being negative, but it will help you focus on why your Target should choose you in preference to the competition. When Taco Bell tells us to Think Beyond the Bun, they're attacking the enemy at the same time they're telling us that you're going to have a fun and tasty time at their restaurant.

3. **What's The Proposition?** This is a useful word, that doesn't get used much these days. Perhaps you remember the USP – the Unique Selling Proposition. Simply put, why should we buy or try your brand? That's your proposition. Your strategy should be compatible with your proposition. Write down your brand's proposition, such as: *Morningside students will discover that the Learning Center is the best place to connect with the knowledge they need to succeed. In school and in life.* Even though we wrapped it in fun T-shirts and much shorter and catchier slogans, that's the underlying proposition of the Morningside Learning Center's message. One more thing – see how "Connect" emerged as a key and consistent part of that strategic message? Your message will emerge from your strategy.

4. **Think like your Target.** Walk in their shoes. Try to put yourself into their place. Good messaging has a component in it that's "about me." It's why so many people read their horoscope. And it's why we all cheer for our team. It's a connection with us. Sometimes we're so busy thinking about our brand that we don't really think as much about the people we're trying to reach.

Let's face it, they're all thinking, "What's in it for me?"

So, using those four thoughts as a checklist, review the thinking about your brand. We bet you'll find a solid strategy. You may also find more than one – it's not uncommon for brands to find more than one possible strategy. It's a problem, but it's a good problem.

You may want to stay on two tracks for a little while and then do a bit of research on the messages you come up with. Ask your Target what they think. Put those messages on two sets of windshield flyers – with the same basic offer. See if one does better than the other.

DETERMINE THE CORE MESSAGE

Our focus in this book is effective communication.

Message is one of the key components of our Brand Builder Matrix. Like so many things, it's easier said than done.

Once you've settled on your Strategy, it's fairly common that you've already written a few messages – and there may be some you already like a lot. Good.

This can be a confusing time. Some say you have to keep going and working and thinking and working and thinking. And others say, that first obvious thought, chances are, it's pretty good. Well, guess what? We can't help you.

In some cases, you need to keep going and in others you need to realize you have already found it. That's just one of the frustrating and fascinating things about ideas. Not only do you have to have those ideas, you have to be able to tell the good ones from the not-quite-good-enough ones. Here are four simple ways to look at and think about your messages. They're not the only ones, but they're tried and true.

1. **Find the Best Words.** They may be adjectives. They may be verbs. But, when it comes right down to it, every brand has its own little vocabulary. Adjectives that describe its unique benefit – like Exceptional, Classical, Intimate for our little Chamber Music Group. The famous art director, George Lois always looked for *"words that bristle with visual imagery."* Isn't that in interesting word right there – *bristle*. It lets us know that George wants us to pay attention to what he's saying – and he does.

2. **Visualize the Benefit.** OK, what does your brand offer? What visual imagery related to that benefit comes to mind?

3. **Create a Brand Icon.** There may be a brand icon somewhere – the big green healthy Jolly Green Giant, the mascot or the logo of your favorite sports team,

or the way the logo of your favorite rock band reminds you of their music. And remember, these visuals can build over time. The first time that they made a double arch for the "M" in McDonald's, it didn't have the impact it does now. But your brand's message should have a memorable visual. Incidentally, some of us call a combination of slogan and logo, a "Slogo."

4. **Catch a Cultural Moment.** This one's a moving Target. Popular culture is water we all swim in. We surf the net and channels on cable, we pop the buttons on our car radio and look at who's on the cover of magazines. New brands are part of that culture, too. Whether it's national, or our cozy corner of Iowa. It's big and it's small. And teens, and parents, and kids, and college students and business people each have their own flavor preference. Your brand's message can be a part of all that. Only it will come from your heart as well as your head. If it feels right, well maybe that's a pretty good thing. After all, it's your brand.

OK, even though we haven't answered your questions exactly, we've answered them – because the real world isn't like school. Even when we're teachers, we don't have all the answers. You have to discover those answers for your brand, and for yourself.

Welcome to life on the learning curve.

BRAIN BUILDER EXERCISE 9.1: CREATIVE STRATEGY – SEARCHING FOR THE MESSAGE

The purpose of this exercise is to develop a strategy use multiple tools.

Instructions:

1. Select at least six of the twelve tools to complete for your brand. Try to use a variety of the tools. Stretch yourself a bit. List the tools you've chosen here.

   a.

   b.

   c.

   d.

   e.

   f.

2. Now, complete the writing of each of the creative strategy tools you've chosen in separate documents.

3. Share each strategy builder with others in your group, (preferably someone who uses another side of their brain more than you do). If you are a left brain (logical thinking person), you might want to seek out a right brain (more creative person).

4. Select the tools that best fit the strategy you wish to move forward with, and rewrite it based on feedback you have received from others.

5. Which tool or combination of tools led you to the Strategy for your brand? Explain and reflect on the process.

You now have twelve different tools – twelve tools to help you get it right. The next section takes you to the final decision to create the message for *your* brand.

THE CREATIVE STRATEGY

We're going to share an example with you – Siouxland Chamber Music. See how they did it, and, hopefully, that will be additional help for you doing something wonderful. Then, see you in the next chapter.

Now decide. You have to make a decision on the message that will deliver the promise you wish to make. You want the **message** that captures your brand and will connect with your Target.

Go back and forth with a number of the tools you just reviewed; use both sides of your brain AND your team's set of brains.

Let's see what this looks like in action.

Tools Used by the Siouxland Chamber Music Team

You've seen the results of Chamber Music team earlier in Chapter 2, and have followed some of their work throughout this book.

They used these tools:
- Creative Action Plan
- Creative Strategy Template
- Copy Platform
- Positioning Statement
- Target Sketch – Primary
- Target Sketch – Secondary

No one tool gave the group what it needed. They used a combined set of tools, and a combined set of discussions before the right message emerged. You should have begun to see how each 'tool' leads the writer a bit differently through the benefits, features, and values in order to create a message and rebrand the Chamber.

Here is what the work looked like before the team got to the Message.

Creative Action Plan

- **Client:** The Sioux City Chamber Music Association presents informal concerts by small groups and soloists playing great classical music of the past and present

- **Target:** Sioux City Chamber Music Association is composed of both men and women above the age of 45, who have some musical background, are educated, and who are physically active.

- **Competitive Snapshot**
  The key competitor is the Sioux City Symphony Orchestra. For over 90 years, the orchestra has been the premiere performing arts organization in the tri-state area utilizing the Orpheum theatre.

  Selling problems include a limited budget for advertising. Ticket sales are low and decreasing, along with membership packages. Performances are limited to Sundays. Brochures appear dated giving a very negative image to the organization. The schedule for the events is not internet accessible through a website.

- **Historical and Old Thought:** the Sioux City Chamber Music Associations foundation was built to foster appreciation for classical music and help strengthen families and children of Siouxland's cultural base. However, many families and individual members in the community are unaware of the Chambers qualities such as offering informal concerts meant to provide a lighthearted and informative feeling for audiences. The Sioux City Chamber goal has always been to provide a fun-filled and relaxing musical environment for all ages especially children at an inexpensive cost.

- **New Thought:** As a newly recognized addition to the musical performances offered in Sioux City, the Sioux City Chamber Music Association would like to draw in new audiences composed of all ages including families and children, along with attracting new memberships. Consumers have a new found appreciation for an organization with such quality of musical performances.

- **Main Claim: -** Consumer benefit
  Mission Statement – SCCM is an organization dedicated to providing performances of, and fostering appreciation for, chamber music in Siouxland, resulting in a strengthened cultural base for the community.

- **Tone:** The advertisements must present The Sioux City Chamber Music Association as being composed for four outstanding concerts performed by talented individuals worldwide.

- **Added Tools:** Prices of season memberships Family - $80, Individual - $40, Single Admission - $10, Students - Free

---

Creative Strategy Template

- *To convince* men and women 45 and above to attend Chamber performances

- *To use* Chamber Music events to experience classical styles of music from regional to international artists.

- *Instead of* or as an alternative to The Sioux City Symphony Orchestra and Orpheum Theatre sponsored events

- *Because* concerts put on by the Chamber are of exceptional quality and a reasonably priced entertainment in an intimate setting.

Copy Platform

- Brand: Sioux City Chamber Music Association

- Target Audience: Men and Women 45 years and older

- Objective: To inform the public about the Sioux City Chamber Music Association, their purpose and upcoming events. In turn, ticket sales and memberships would increase.

- Strategy: To convince men and women 45 years and older to attend the concerts put on by the Sioux City Chamber Music Association. We will also inform them of the variety of musical performances. The Sioux City Chamber Music Association is also an inexpensive way to hear and enjoy good quality music in a nice, easy to find facility.

- Considerations: First Presbyterian Church is easy to find. The acoustics in the church are great. First Presbyterian Church is close to downtown Tickets are reasonably priced and it is easy to buy a membership to see all of the concerts. The concerts are held on Sunday afternoons

- Support: Concerts put on by the Sioux City Chamber Music Association are good quality music that is inexpensive to listen to, and you can be comfortable for your listening pleasure. It is personal and intimate. There are international and national performers coming right to Sioux City.

- Tone: Lighthearted, somewhat elegant and informative.

Positioning Statement

With a longstanding tradition, the Sioux City Chamber Music delivers exceptional, classical music in a small and intimate setting.

(Note the positioning statement is not one of the tools in the tool chest, but it became one of the key elements in the branding and message process.)

Decision time – THE MESSAGE

Taglines and a new logo would be delivered. Each student came up with three ideas, tested them and brought the results to class. Remember – this was all going on during the summer and a 7:30 class.

Taglines were brainstormed and tested:

1. Sioux City's Best Kept Secret

2. Broadening your Musical Horizons

3. Stay Classical

4. Music for the Ears

5. A little culture for everyone

6. New Experiences lead to opportunities

7. Wet your musical appetite

8. Exceptional, classical, intimate.

Exceptional, classical intimate. This was selected as the best message to promote the brand image that the Chamber offers. It is to the point, and descriptive of the unique qualities of the Sioux City Chamber. It could serve the Chamber for years to come with widespread appeal and application.

If this seems like a complicated way to get at something very simple, you've been paying attention. That's exactly what it is. You are taking everything you know and distilling it down into the most important thing you can say to build your brand.

But, when you think about it, that's a pretty important job, isn't it?

So take a look at the Message you and your team have crafted. You should feel good about it. Mission accomplished.

CHAPTER REVIEW

This chapter covered a lot of territory.

1. Factors That Motivate Purchase Behavior.

2. Laddering – to identify important aspects of our brand: Attributes, Features, Product Benefits, Consumer Benefits, and Values.

3. The Creative Toolbox. Starting with the Target Sketch, we examined a dozen useful formats to help us create a Message Strategy.

4. When we're done, we should have what we believe is a potentially effective Strategy for our Brand Message.

REVIEW QUESTIONS

1. How confident are you that you have correctly identified the Factor that Motivates Purchase Behavior? How much of an incentive might you need to add to make that message effective? What other options did you consider?

2. One of the key aspects of laddering is understanding that interesting oscillation between Product Benefit and Consumer Benefit. How does that work for your particular brand?

3. What part – or parts – of the ladder are you using to build your message?

4. Which tools in the Toolbox did you find most useful? Which, at least at present, seem to be the least useful?

5. Take the least useful tool and try to use it again.

6. Now take the tool you like best and use it again. Did you get an additional insight or perspective?

READINGS AND RESOURCES

Collegiate Entrepreneurs Organization
http://www.c-e-o.org/

Self-Employment in the Arts
http://www.seasource.org/

The Coleman Foundation and John Hughes
http://www.colemanfoundation.org/

Altman, D. (2000). "Creativity and communications." *Advertising & the business of brands.* The Copy Workshop, Chicago, IL.

Avery, J. (2009). "Marketing and the planning process." *Advertising & the business of brands.* The Copy Workshop, Chicago, IL.

Bendinger, B. (2009). *The Copy Workshop.* The Copy Workshop, Chicago, IL.

Fortini-Campbell, L. (2001). *Hitting the Sweet Spot.* The Copy Workshop, Chicago, IL

CHAPTER 10:
MESSAGE WINDOWS 1: MARKETING COMMUNICATIONS, MEDIA, AND EVALUATION

This chapter is about identifying and evaluating the right places for your messages. Even if your budget is small, this can be a very complicated task – with an amazing range of options. Your choices cover these general areas:

- What forms of Marketing Communications (MarCom) will you use to deliver your Message? What will be your MarCom Mix in the MarCom Matix?
- What traditional media will you use as a channel for those Messages?
- What other non-traditional channels – from Social Media to local Guerrilla Media – will you choose?

Finding the right mix of marketing services and media for your brand is the focus of this chapter. Opportunities outside the traditional, mass media channels have exploded. It is literally a Media Revolution.

Now we can design and produce print more easily using computers, and the media itself – from digital outdoor boards to HD radio – is being affected. If you were media-aware in the '90s, you witnessed it. If you were born in the mid '80s and '90s, like many young entrepreneurs and many of my students, the "revolution" is business as usual.

LEARNING OUTCOMES.

After completing this chapter you will have:

1. Reviewed The MarCom Matrix.

2. Considered the range of message windows available for your brand – traditional media, new media, and what many call "guerilla media."

3. Understood the basics of social media strategy.

4. Developed a Media Flow Chart and Marketing Calendar.

5. Decided on an initial Score-Keeping System so you can begin measuring the success or failure of your programs as you move through the year.

Today, brands need to consider every part of the MarCom Matrix: advertising, public relations, sales promotion, direct marketing, event marketing, promotional products, and the growing range of activity on the Internet – like social media. They can all work together to help your branding efforts. These days, they are less and less separated from the "advertising/mass media" part of the promotional P. A number of factors, including how long your brand has been around, your budget, your location, and the best way to connect with your target audience will help you determine the best message windows.

Message Windows can be categorized a number of ways – traditional and nontraditional, paid or unpaid, and, by some, "above the line" and "below the line." Some of it is what we traditionally consider "media" and some is not. In general, you might find this kind of categorizing limiting. As you evaluate your options, your standard should be simply, "what is best for my brand?"

We think you need to start using a different type of categorizing – "what works best for my brand" and "what doesn't work so well for my brand."

It's all part of the revolution changing media. Traditionally, what we call "traditional media" is usually television, radio, magazines, and outdoor. However, the Media Revolution has created a major shift, and we're all swimming in a brand-new media world. Dealing with that world in a sensible way is the reason for using the term Message Windows as a key concept in this workbook.

Think about it. Even though a brand like Starbucks has enough money to do traditional advertising, when they open a new outlet, they look to establish a local footprint. "StarBucks" coupons are handed out. Employees hand out samples. When new customers come in, they're greeted like old friends. Starbucks uses "high-touch" moments to connect with their customers.

Starbucks' concern for the brand experience reaches into things like making sure that the delicious smell of roasting coffee wafts through their stores, and that employees stay motivated because they have good health insurance. Makes sense when you think about it, because that employee's connection with the customer and that hot cup of coffee is their brand's major "message window."

What's your brand's message window? It may be an ad, but in today's over-messaged world, you may have to do more than just running an ad.

Looking to nontraditional outlets where you have time to connect with your customer outside the normal "blizzard" of media messages can open up additional avenues for your brand to be with your customer.

The media is evolving. As we wrote this book, we watched e-books on platforms like Kindle grow in popularity, and we watched people stand in line for their brand new iPad. Our video screens keep getting bigger and our devices keep getting smaller at the same time they get more powerful. Now we have a TV in our pocket or purse on our mobile phones. And media is going to keep changing. It's pretty exciting, but it's also pretty noisy. That's why finding those message windows for our brands has become a more important challenge. The good news – it's a fun challenge. I've seen the triumph and elation in my student's as they opened Message Windows to deliver their brand's creative Message.

EVALUATING THE MARCOM MATRIX FOR YOUR BRAND.

Remember the MarCom Matrix from Chapter One? Well, it's time for another look.

We need to determine the best ways to deliver our brand messages.

Briefly, these are the MarCom disciplines we can choose from.

1. **Advertising**
2. **Public Relations**
3. **Sales Promotion**
4. **Direct Marketing**
5. **Event (and sponsorship) Marketing**
6. **Promotional Products**
7. **New Media.** This category can connect with all the previous MarCom disciplines – you can advertise, release your press kit on the Internet, use your e-mail addresses for direct marketing, and put your web address on promotional products.

We're going to add one more…

8. **"Guerrilla Media."** From Starbucks handing out their own "StarBucks" to you handing out your business card, there is a whole range of low-cost tactics available to businesses of every size.

Now, before we determine our Message Windows and your own MarCom mix, let's quickly review the strengths and weaknesses of each discipline. (This review will be very, very brief – you can find more detailed analyses in most marketing books.) There's good news and bad news for each part of the MarCom Matrix.

1. **Advertising**
   Strength – you control the message.
   Weakness – it's expensive and you can't control who pays attention.

2. **Public Relations**
   Strength – "Third party credibility." An external source, like a newspaper and magazine provides the story, it has more credibility than an ad. Very low cost – when your PR efforts are recognized.
   Weakness – you can't control whether your material is used or how it's used. Many more PR efforts are attempted than are used. Low "hit" rate.

3. **Sales Promotion**
   Strength – if your "bribe" is a good one, you'll get results.
   Weakness – it's expensive and you may have additional costs for things like display and distribution.

4. **Direct Marketing**
   Strength – if you have a good list, a good offer, and an effective message, this can work very well.
   Weakness – beginners die like flies. If any of the three things (list/offer/message) isn't good enough, you will have an expensive failure. Direct often has a very expensive learning curve.

5. **Event (and sponsorship) Marketing**
   Strength – if it's the right crowd, it's a great way to connect with your target – for example trade shows and conventions.
   Weakness – the crowd isn't necessarily there to see you. Again, it can be an expensive way to be ignored.

6. **Promotional Products**
   Strength – the right item in the right hands is a cost-effective reminder of your brand.
   Weakness – they don't call it "trinkets and trash" for nothing. Plus, if you don't have an effective way of distributing the item, all you have is a storage room full of stuff with your name on it.

7. **New Media**
   Strength – low barriers to entry. It can be extremely cost-effective. An instant way to be in business with PayPal and e-commerce.
   Weakness – you may need expensive experts to do what you want. Audiences can be small and response levels extremely low.

8. Guerrilla Media

Strength – relatively low-cost, and, if done well, reasonable results.

Weakness – small footprint, not that many opportunities, relatively high per unit cost, an ongoing need for personal attention and supervision.

Getting It Right.

The key, when you compare the strengths and weaknesses, is getting it right for you and your brand.

Sure, advertising is expensive – but there's a bus bench back just a block away from your store – affordable awareness awaits! Yes, press releases can get ignored, but you have a great story, a wonderful photo, and your sister knows one of the reporters. Hey, you might get some PR after all. In every case, you need to find a reason why it's right for you. TV might be expensive in a big city like Chicago – but here in Sioux City, we just might be able to fit it into our budget. And we can all make a video message that will fit on our website – and maybe YouTube to boot!

Guidelines and Idea Starters.

You might not be a MarCom Matrix expert, but we all have to start somewhere. So here are some thoughts to help you get started. And, as time goes by, we'll be posting more ideas from Brand Builder teams on our website.

Let's assume that you're a relatively inexperienced team in a small to medium-sized market with limited resources and a lot of enthusiasm. Okay, here goes…

Advertising.

Let's look at the traditional advertising channels. Hint: Whichever medium you choose, don't forget some sort of offer to stimulate that all-important first visit.

Broadcast/TV. Television has the benefit of sight and sound. Now, with cable, the Internet, and lower-cost video production tools, you might want to give it a try.

Broadcast/Radio. Now that everyone has their own iPod, radio might not be the powerhouse it used to be, but it can still be a good retail partner – particularly if the station is a favorite of your target audience. There are usually people at the station who can provide some assistance. Or maybe a friend's band can write a song about your brand. Record it. Put it up on YouTube. What a great excuse for a party! Who knows, you might get a bit of local TV.

Newspaper. Your local newspaper is an important part of your market's media mix – and there is a vibrant world of second-tier papers – often specializing in art and entertainment.

Magazines. Your area may have a city magazine or some sort of regional magazine – get to know them. They are also a possibility for a local story on your brand.

Outdoor/Out-of-Home. This is an exciting area, combining old-fashioned traditional billboards with the latest technology in surprising places.

Plan Ahead – Look for Added Value. Media companies have extras to offer. Maybe a radio broadcast for your store – or an appearance on the local TV show. When you do advertise, try to publicize your advertising moment – hand out reprints of your ad, and post it on your website.

Need more thought starters? Pick up a copy of *The Copy Workshop Workbook* – or, if you already have a copy, crack it open.

Public Relations

Public Relations is defined as any activity designed to generate news so as to gain a positive impact with the "public." Publicity is any free media coverage about your product, service, or idea.

Size matters. In small organizations and non-profits, a PR person might handle all marketing activities, or, you might act as the PR officer for your club. In a small business or entrepreneurial venture, the owner/operator usually wears all hats, and conducts financial, personnel, operations as well as the marketing decisions. Medium sized firms have marketing departments to manage all of the branding activities, while larger organizations often have their own PR staff separate from those who deal with the advertising, or they may hire a specialized PR agency, as well as an advertising agency. But for all of them, the job is pretty much the same – make it into the media in a good way.

There are two kinds of PR: Marketing Public Relations and Corporate Public Relations.

Marketing Public Relations (MPR) includes those activities that directly generate news and interact with the media. Here are some keys to getting it right.

1. **Planning** is needed for the MPR.
2. **Timelines** are set, with an understanding that the flexibility and responsiveness of media organizations is limited.
3. **Merchandising your own Public Relations** activities can be done by including reprinted articles in your press kits, or framing them in company hallways. Consider keeping awards and recognition posted in permanent plaques for all to see. Making t-shirts for the events will pass the word along after all is said and done – until the next event.

4. **Develop strategies and tactics**. Strategies should follow the other branding building efforts you have established. Use the messaging strategy as much as possible to keep all branding efforts as strong. Tactics to consider are:

a. **Press kits** are packets of company history and information. If you are on a company's website, check out the 'history' or 'about us' links. You should be sure to include names of key personnel, brand history, and company photographs.

b. **Press releases** are objectively written news stories about a company, its products or services, or newsworthy items about its staff. A press release is written professionally in journalist form. Requirements include readiness for publication or use by a broadcast outlet or blog. Contact information is provided in case others have questions.

   Video news releases are another method to let the media outlets know about your news. Our college has a PR department that writes and video tapes significant work by students, faculty, and staff. Most of the time the local newspapers will run the story and the story is sent to the student's hometown news.

c. **Media and press tours** are conducted in two manners. You can invite the press to your place for news announcements or to cover events, or you can escort key personnel to visit the media. If you invite members of the press, they have an opportunity to interview your people in depth and gain an understanding about technical fields. You'll want to manage these visits to show off the best you can. Planning is critical.

d. **Technical articles** are written by your office or other experts and carry your company image. You may interview someone to respond to an economic situation in the community. Dr. Sam Clovis in our department is sought after for his expertise in economic and political issues. In smaller communities, technical articles and opinions are very helpful to listeners and readers. Environmental and green activities are news. If you have expertise in this area, offer your own technical knowledge – and be sure to wear your logo while you talk. Or you might also offer "tips of the week," such as caring for aging family, "ask the doctor," or "an organic menu from the farmers market."

e. **Feature article development** is an activity where you write a lengthy article that might be considered for a feature story. You might have a series of articles that develop the story in depth. The media might run it as is, or they might call and make it a bigger story.

f. **Product publicity** promotes your product or service in a number of ways, such as:
   - **Awards** – create your own,
   - **Books** – write a book, go on tour, get on talk shows, write a history

book then release it, compile other eventful things for your company and publish them.

- **Blogs** – watch for legislation directing bloggers to identify their corporate sponsors
- Hold **Demonstrations**
- Sponsor **Youth programs**
- **Marathons, run-a-thon, bike-a-thon, walk-a-thon**
- **Product placement**
- **Events**
- **Support a worthy cause**
- **Official endorsements**
- **Grand opening – or reopening – renovation**
- **Holiday, weeklong celebrations, festivals**
- **Newsletters**
- **Museum**
- **Scholarship**

One of my former students hosts a weekly "renovation" lesson sponsored by a local hardware store one week, a heating/air conditioning place the next week, and maybe at a carpet store another week. The series runs during the spring and summer, and usually airs during the news. It will also be linked on the local paper home page. The lesson is in the format of the backyard gardener or local chef series. This person is very warm and friendly on the camera as he tackles common household problems. He will interview an expert who 'fixes' a problem.

Corporate Public Relations include those activities of the corporation not related to marketing. Examples are:

- **Investor relations**
- **Employee communications**
- **Government relations**
- **Crisis management**
- **Community relations** – contributions to local groups and cultural organizations, serving on non profit boards, sponsoring athletic teams

You want to have your 'business in order' in the event something happens, so you can be proactive in your reaction to the situation.

The next area is also a broad, sweeping type of marketing service with many opportunities for you to continue your brand building – Sales Promotions.

Sales Promotion

Sales promotions may be categorized by the two types of customers to which they are directed – Consumer and Trade.

Consumer promotions are conducted to increase consumer awareness of the products and services and stimulate sales. Trade promotions are conducted between the company and the trade that helps to distribute the goods to the consumer. Here, the key is getting distribution.

Here are types of **Consumer Promotions** you might consider. Remember, "What's the Bribe?" What are you offering to stimulate those sales?

- **Coupons**
- **Coupon redemption and fulfillment**
- **Games** – sweepstakes, scratch and win, contests
- **In store sampling and display**
- **Licensing**
- **Loyalty and continuity programs**
- **Premiums** – buy one and get something free (cosmetics do this really well) or buy one get one
- **Rebates**

The types of **Trade Promotions** you will want to consider should produce results for the end sales. Some of the types of trade promotions are:

- **B-2-B** (business to business), such as
  - Trade allowances
  - Spiffs – free items awarded for purchasing blocks of product
  - Co-operative – advertising with a partner to share expenses
- **Point of Purchase** – display allowances
- **In store marketing** – TV's in airports, Wal-Mart, Best Buy
- **Dealer contests**
- **Newsletters** to dealers, wholesalers, distributors, and retailers

Direct Marketing

This area has seen some revolutionary changes in the last ten years. Once, mail and telemarketing were king, now electronic marketing is a mainstay. Remember the three key ingredients for success: list, offer, and message. Here are current choices in Direct Marketing:

- **E-mail marketing** – through loyalty programs or
  - Building lists by driving traffic to websites
  - Mail and ping

- **Direct marketing**
- **Telemarketing** – inbound and outbound
- **List management** – using email
- **Direct Response Television** – infomercials or one minute commercials
- **Database services** – managing the lists
- **Interactive marketing**
- **Customer Relationship Management** – The Big Question: how can you maximize the relationship with youir brand?

Event Marketing and Sponsorships

Finding an event to sponsor or developing events for your organization can provide great opportunities to grow your brand. The Event is the Message Window! Get it?

You may not directly sell products, but sampling may be your purpose. For example, my students working for Sue Bee Honey planned a series of college events. The Swarm Team would handle all the events. They put together a 'street team' to travel to colleges and either host or co-host special events while distributing samples of the new Buzz products. Buzzman would come, the BuzzMobile would carry them around and generate a "buzz" about the product. Posters, coupons, social medial, and e-mail marketing would all be part of the message window package. Timing and coordination would be critical; they followed the distribution plan. The Swarm Team was a key part of a brand building program.

Of course you can consider the granddaddy of all events, the Super Bowl. Maybe we don't have a few extra million to spare, but there are plenty of local Super Bowl parties that might be pleased to have your participation – and maybe you can think up your own Super Bowl Special.

How about this one? Corvette and Harley Davidson owners meet in the streets. The event is called Hot Summer Nites. It's organized and hosted by the Downtown Association of Sioux Falls, South Dakota. Thousands of owners drive in for the event and park their Vettes along the streets (which are blocked off for blocks). Near dusk, the Harleys slowly ride in and park two deep in the middle of the street flanked by Corvettes.

The day starts with a luncheon provided by Billion Chevrolet, a feature article appears in the local paper's travel magazine as well as *Motor Market* (a specialty magazine). Remember, one of the key considerations for getting your story placed is that it's newsworthy. This one certainly was, and the paper was glad to run it. Record crowds attend each year to enjoy the street dance, sample the food vendors' booths, and of course to view some of the newest and oldest Corvettes and custom Harleys only seen in show rooms. Two of America's pride and joy icons on one street in one night. Rightfully named – a Hot Summer Night. Hot Cars, Hot Bikes, and over 30,000 people in a six-block area in the middle of July. This is a very successful event with many sponsors, including the local Corvette club, which sponsors the Black Hills Corvette Classic that kicks off in Spearfish, SD the following day.

Cause Marketing is another aspect of Event Marketing and Sponsorship.

Our Tyson Events Center and our hockey team, the Musketeers, got involved with Breast Cancer Research with "Pink in the Rink." The pink hockey puck was a good example of a unique promotional product with keepsake value.

Promotional Products

Products that feature your name or logo are referred to as promotional products. The most popular are T-shirts, followed by caps, cups, and pens. You will most likely have promotional products that tie in to another marketing strategy. For example, you can design watches, pens, jackets, rocking chairs around annual employee awards. You might have a logo for an anniversary party – and have it imprinted on a number of items that will be displayed or given away. Remember, the better looking your item, the more people will be willing to be walking billboards for your brand.

These are from the Sue Bee Honey campaign.

Don't just let your thinking cap stop at the usual for promotional products. For example, John Hall, President of Goose Island, Chicago's Craft Beer, noted that one of the lessons he learned was allowing his company's customers to be a part of the experience – seeing the brewing process. Goose Island had recently released a new Urban Wheat Ale called *312*, named after Chicago's original area code. During the summer months, the *312* promotion included contests, concerts, imprinted coolers, deck chairs, T-shirts, and other items and events that celebrated summer.

Goose Island made unique keepsake promotional products with strong local appeal a key part of their small, but very effective product promotion.

Let's pause for a moment and put our event, sponsorship, cause marketing, and promotional products hats on – yes, all at once. Let's think of an event that makes sense for your brand, and determine how we can extend it. Then, let's see if we can't bang the PR drum and make some advertising – at least a poster.

BRAIN BUILDER EXERCISE 10.1:
When in the Course of Human Events

1. First, let's make a list of possible events our brand can connect with. Here are some examples.

   a. A Holiday or Special Event – Valentine's Day, Super Bowl, etc.

   b. A Traditional Local Event – Music Fest, Food Fest, etc.

   c. A Cause (local/national) to Sponsor – Breast Cancer, Special Olympics, a local charity

   d. Something that is yours alone. It can be as simple as your brand's birthday or anniversary, or you can connect with something bigger, like our Chevy Dealer who connected with Corvettes

2. Write down your ideas and pick one. We bet you've already got a lot more than one good idea.

3. Now let's decorate our idea – here are some things you'll want to develop.

   a. A great looking logo

   b. A poster and an invitation to the event

   c. Promotional Items

   d. Events you can publicize – will there be music, food, entertainment, or maybe something cultural, like an art exhibit?

   e. Now, it's time to put your other MarCom Matrix hats on. You can use our MarCom Matrix Worksheet – or just make a list.

      i. Advertising – where can you advertise this event in a cost-effective way? And don't forget things like door hangers and flyers on windshields.

      ii. Public Relations – what media outlets will find this event newsworthy and how can you make it more newsworthy?

      iii. Sales Promotion – is there some sort of offer or context that will stimulate attendance and participation? A raffle? A free sample?

      iv. Direct Marketing – this event and an invitation to this event is a terrific opportunity to work on your database.

      v. Promotional Products – what is a memorable item from this event that people will keep? For example, how about setting up a special photo opportunity – then taking a digital photograph that people can retrieve from your website? It's low cost and many people like to have photos of themselves and their family.

Guerrilla Media

Ever hear The Legend of The Chicken Suit? As the story goes, one of the original Kentucky Fried Chicken franchisees had a chicken suit in the back of his store. Sometimes, if business was slow, he or another employee would go in back and – you guessed it – put on The Chicken Suit. They'd walk out into their local trading area with a handful – or a wing-full – of coupons and pretty soon there were people in the store.

We can't all wear chicken suits, but that's a perfect example of a guerrilla campaign – low cost, easy-to-implement, fast results.

If you do business in a certain local trading area, there are lots of these kinds of opportunities: menus on the doorknob, flyers under the windshield wiper, someone in a costume handing out coupons (not much fun on hot summer days).

Done well, they can be a big help to a small business. Done wrong or overdone, you're just contributing to litter on the street. Done without supervision, those menus could end up going directly into one big trash can, instead of on a few hundred doorknobs.

There's one other guerrilla medium you should be aware of – you! Always have those business cards, and maybe a clever little intro piece about your brand. What about a nice high-value offer on the back of the card? A good guerrilla media thinker is always looking for opportunities.

OK, there are a lot of options. Now let's see what makes sense for our brand.

MESSAGE WINDOWS – TRADITIONAL AND NONTRADITIONAL

Think about paid and unpaid message windows. Most of all, let's think about the ones that you might build for your brand that do the best job of reaching your target.

Here's what we'll do in this section:

1. Discuss your Target's Personal Media Network
2. Make some initial MarCom Matrix decisions for your brand
3. Understand some of the challenges in making a good media buy – because some of your choices may involve paid media

Personal Media Network

Each and every one of us has our own personal media network. It's that group of media outlets we've selected to use personally. If you were to follow five of your targeted customers around (you may have done this during your market research), you might have this information already. Let's think about their media habits.

Just as a reminder, this is called ethnography research. This type of study identifies what people do in their everyday lives. In this case, we want to understand their media choices, and why they make them.

If you conducted one-on-one interviews, you may have collected personal media information as well. However you obtain the data, understanding this Personal Media Network will help you optimize your Message Windows. If you collected the data during the research phase, retrieve the data now.

For an even better fix on this, try to find five customers or potential customers now. Interview them and record the media they normally use. If you can get them to participate, give them a journal and ask them to make notes.

What's unique about your target? Here are some things to look for.

1. **Location, location, and location.** At Morningside, we have our Learning Center. We have a place students get coffee. There are kiosks, bulletin boards, and a few outdoor opportunities. If your brand is location-based, these are some things to look for. You might also look for "traffic-generators." For Stella's Barbecue, our school was a traffic generator. Nearby buildings are good examples – office buildings for lunch, apartments for dinner.
2. **Habits.** Does your target look for entertainment on the weekends? Do they drink coffee? Eat pizza? Cheer the local team? What is going on in their lives on a regular basis? Are they students who need a study break or moms who need a sitter? Figure it out. See how you can connect.
3. **Values.** Sports. Music. Local pride. Those message windows will be more meaningful if your target already feels a connection.
4. **What's Special About You?** For example, if you are a carry-out restaurant, what else can you put in the bag to connect with your customer? If one of your employees was standing on the corner handing something out – what would that person be wearing (probably not a chicken suit) and what would they hand out? OK, now can you do something like that in the media?

Now combine those things with what you already know about your Target Audience's Personal Media Network. You're on your way to figuring out the best Message Windows for your brand.

Analyze. Prioritize. Optimize.

Some things are a science. Some are an art. This step will be a little bit of both. Looking at the habits and Personal Media Network of our Target, you should be able to identify a half dozen or so traditional media vehicles, plus a few location-specific opportunities.

Next, add the two or three "best bets" in the other MarCom areas. Still need help? Here's a quick list of suggestions:

Public Relations (and Event Marketing): What are your best local media opportunities? Your best event opportunities?

Sales Promotion: Introductory Offers, Coupons & Certificates, Contest with prizes, Free Samples. Unique added value?

Direct Marketing: Anything and everything you can do to build a good Target List will be a step in the right direction. What's your best offer?

Promotional Products: Is there one other thing besides your business card that seems like a good idea?

Guerrilla Media: Look at your marketing environment with an eye to making an impact.

Prioritize.

By now, you should have a pretty good list – maybe more than you can do, but that's OK. Now put those things in some sort of order, using your best judgment.

Optimize.

Now look at that list one more time. Consider cost-effectiveness, production logistics, timing, and the ability to measure results. Put them all together. You should have a pretty good list of opportunities. Now it's time to get a little bit more organized.

SOCIAL MEDIA

Social Media (SM) is an emerging opportunity, and one you should particularly consider if you are a small business and can afford to give it attention.

As of this writing, the key players in SM are Facebook, Yelp, FourSquare, Twitter, You Tube and LinkedIn. This, of course, will change with time and circumstance.

While most of the formats of Social Media are free, selecting the ones that will work for you may demand an investment in time and effort.

We've posted four resources for you to get started:

- A Thought-Starter outline – contributed by Grant Wittstruck, Creative Director of Powell Broadcast's iCast Interactive.
- 7 Essential Elements of Social Media Marketing – from copyblogger.com
- 10 Effective and Time Efficient Social Marketing Tips from Chromatic sites – Web Solutions That Work chromaticsites.com
- Finally, a nice article full of examples of successful use of Twitter. It has the clever title "Marketing Small Businesses with Twitter."

As you might imagine, all four are linked on www.brandbuilderworkbook.com

Now here are a few additional thoughts, probably based as much on common sense as experience.

1. Your Social Media usage should be appropriate. A large commercial posting saying you love your brand of automobile or your cellular phone carrier will ring false. However, if you said something nice about a local auto repair shop, or recommended an inexpensive iPhone app, well that seems appropriate. A Yelp restaurant review – that's appropriate.

2. Your Social Media Message should be appealing. If it's not entertaining or useful, or interesting, why are you wasting everyone's time? Try to maintain a standard, and try to stay interesting. Sending a Twitter that says <My Sox don't match.> seems like you're wasting our time – unless, of course, you're in Boston or Chicago and you have a bit more to say on the topic.

3. It would be nice if your Social Media Message was actionable. OK, you shared something appropriate and it was sort of interesting. That's fine as far as it goes. Is there any way we can make something happen? Get people to attend an event – come into your store – get a free Ice Cream Cone – or have a slice of the pizza that you just wrote about on Yelp and are serving at the nearby Street Fair.

4. It will be best if you become an agile user of Social Media. As you come to understand the SM options that make the most amount of sense for your brand (appropriate), and the (appealing) offers that stimulate (actionable) response, you will become more agile in your use of Social Media. This will be a good thing.

5. Set aside a consistent time and day to devote to Social Media. As agile as you are, keep in mind the learning curve and the payoff new learning will yield. Find a time of day that you can spend on SM and have a bank of interesting items to share and reflect about. For example, each day at 4:00 you can devote an hour to planning your SM, learning new features or contacting those who are experts, listening to customers, and replying to any outlets appropriate.

Here's an example. Colin runs an outdoor gear store in Chicago and he knows the business. He's also an outdoor enthusiast. Colin uses his own Twitter account.

He tweets about kayaking, the Chicago River, conservation, camping, outdoor photography, and other of his personal interests. This gets people with similar interests to start following his Twitter account.

Then, whenever he mentions a sale or event happening at his store, several hundred outdoorsy folk see that mention, and can follow the link or click on the store site or whatever hashtag he uses to get more info.

This can get tricky if the Tweeter just seems like a corporate shill, but it works because Colin is tweeting from his personal account rather than a corporate account, and he's tweeting about his interests.

Often, the real trick to Social Media marketing is getting enthusiastic members of the Target to do your work for you. Colin shows that enthusiastic marketers or employees can do the same.

CREATE A MEDIA FLOW CHART AND MARKETING CALENDAR

This next tool will help you organize all of your media into a visual calendar-type planner. You will build a matrix type of spread sheet called a Media Flow Chart. It provides a visual plan for your message windows. Across the top is a timeline – like weeks and months of the year. Down the side are message windows that you may choose from for your brand.

Steps to Create a Media Flow Chart in Microsoft Excel

I recommend using Excel because cells and rows can be manipulated easily. Save your spreadsheet as a pdf file and insert it into your planning documents.

1. Determine the message windows and media forms for your branding campaign.
2. Determine the times of year the message will most likely be heard by your target audience. If there is no seasonality to the message, determine the timing of the message and the lead time needed to produce the work.
3. Plot the months across the top of the worksheet beginning with the first month the campaign will begin. You can include a row underneath the month for weeks if you need additional detailed information.
4. Plot the media form, marketing service, blogs, and cinema along the left column of the worksheet.
5. Use a different color fill for each type of window.
6. Repeat until you have recorded the entire branding campaign.

Next is a Media Flow Chart example for the Chamber Music Association. In this case, you can see messages will be delivered primarily twice during the year – two months in the fall and three months in the spring. The media buys are timed to support the primary activity of the Chamber Music events. The membership drive is conducted in August just prior to the September concert kick off. The target audience of the Message Windows selected are aligned with the primary and secondary Targets for the Chamber Music Association.

Chamber Music Association Media Flow Chart										
	Aug	Sep	Oct	Nov	Dec	Jan	Feb	Mar	Apr	May
Radio										
KWIT, KMSC		▓	▓				▓	▓	▓	
Newspaper										
SC Journal		▓	▓				▓	▓	▓	
Weekender										
TV										
KTIV										
KMEG/KPTH										
Membership Brochure	▓									
Membership Postcard										
Internet										
Website	▓	▓	▓	▓	▓	▓	▓	▓	▓	▓
Posters		▓	▓				▓	▓		
School Events										
Hall of Fame									▓	
Around Siouxland Calendar		▓	▓							
Kids Tickets										
Big Brothers/Big Sisters		▓	▓				▓	▓	▓	
Other Youth Organizations										

Media Flow Chart and MarCom Matrix

Your Media Flow Chart can be built with a number of tiers. The illustration above shows traditional and nontraditional media. It also illustrates other MarCom programs such as the school events and the Big Brothers/Big Sisters tickets. Excel makes it easy to keep adding more details as programs develop.

Look for opportunities to add and connect other MarCom disciplines. For example, your events are also an opportunity to capture additional e-mail addresses for your direct marketing programs. And, even though not every activity may be judged newsworthy by the media, it doesn't hurt to try. Take some photos, do a press release, invite the media. Who knows, you might hit them on a slow news day.

Budget and the Media Flow Chart

The Media Flow Chart can also help you manage your MarCom budget. Add a column to the far right to keep up with the amount you spend on media, production, and related services. If you're tracking media impressions, add another row at the bottom of the chart for those totals.

Determining Your Budget.

First, it's never big enough. It will always be far easier to think of wonderful ways to spend marketing money than it will be to have the money to spend.

Second, you need to have a budget – even a small one.

Third, prioritize. Programs that connect effectively with current customers are almost always money well spent. While you're at it, if it's at all appropriate, implement some sort of referral reward program – 20–30% of new customers come through referrals (and word of mouth) from your current customers.

Finally, don't spend money you don't have. The pages of marketing history are littered with optimists who ran up sizable media bills in the hope that a big ad campaign would turn their business around overnight. Advertising works, but it works slowly. You need to, as we said, "keep everlastingly at it."

That said, you need to work hard and remember that a lot of what you add to the brand-building process is between your own two ears.

Think before you spend. And keep at it.

BRAIN BUILDER EXERCISE 10.2: Media Flow Chart

The purpose of this exercise is to build a media flow chart. It is a visual representation of 'how' you plan to get the message to the eyes, ears, and hands of your target.

Instructions:

1. In the chart below, begin to build a media plan for your brand.

2. In a separate Excel spreadsheet, add columns to allow you to customize your flow chart, and include your budget in a column at the right hand side. Project it out for three years to show what your branding campaign would look like.

Media Flow Chart												
	Aug	Sep	Oct	Nov	Dec	Jan	Feb	Mar	Apr	May	Jun	Jul

Answer the following questions:

1. Review your completed budget. What do you think the most cost effective message window is for your campaign? Why?

2. What will be your focus in Year Two?

3. What decisions are needed in Years One and Two for something that you would like to do in Year Three? What decisions are needed in January for action necessary for September?

SCOREKEEPING: CRM & CAMPAIGN EVALUATION

First, one more set of initials you need to memorize. CRM. They stand for Customer Relationship Management. Businesses depend on repeat customers. Some, like car dealers and appliance dealers, only see their customers once every few years. But even they have an ongoing relationship with the service department and, if they treat their customers right, this generates referrals and word-of-mouth references that keep building the customer base. Remember, it's not uncommon for 20–30% of new customers to come from referrals by current customers.

So, as you work hard to build your business with new customers, remember that one of the best ways to build your business is with current customers.

As restaurant marketing guru Tom Feltenstein notes, there are four ways for a restaurant to increase business. First, your current customers can come more often. Second, they can order more. Third, they can bring a friend – or recommend you to a friend. Finally, someone new can show up because of an ad or coupon. All four are good – but three out of four depend on your current customer base.

Now do you see why CRM is so important? Of course you do.

Another important aspect of knowing how well you're doing is, quite simply, knowing how well you're doing. You not only need to know how your sales are doing, but where those sales are coming from. This is critical when it comes to allocating a budget for your subsequent marketing efforts.

The most logical campaign evaluation criteria are an increase in sales, traffic coming through the door, or clicks on your website, etc. But actually, there are additional methods to determine if your branding campaign is a success.

1. The first method to evaluate your campaign success is to determine which of the activities were the most effective. Find out what is working for your Brand. Some messaging and message windows have a short-term return and some have a longer-term return. Keep track! Over time, this information will become a valuable part of your CRM.

Next, let's think about the Lavidge Steiner Learning Model Steps: awareness, preference, conviction, knowledge, likeness, and purchase

2. The next step in evaluating your campaign success is to start tracking your brand's awareness. For example, if you intended to have a certain level of awareness and knowledge of your brand by a certain date – those would be two things you need to measure. Most likely, these results would be identified in a feedback survey of your target audience – a simple survey should do it. Most evaluation programs have benchmarks and measurement systems to help guide you.

3. The final evaluation activity is to reflect on what you have learned. Based on that, rewrite and improve your plan for the next year with the marketplace knowledge that will make next year's programs smarter and more effective.

Smart marketers tend to do better every year. They pay attention to their customers and they learn from their successes as well as from their mistakes.

BRAIN BUILDER EXERCISE 10.3: Evaluation

The purpose of this exercise is to develop an evaluation plan for your campaign.

Instructions:

1. List the marketing and advertising objectives stated in Chapter 8.

2. Now think of the methods you will use to determine if you have met them.

3. If possible, check to see if you have met the objectives – will most likely be after the campaign is over.

4. Reflect on the most effective methods of branding that you have used, and make adjustments for next campaign.

5. Prepare a document stating the results of 1–4.

CHAPTER REVIEW

In this chapter we covered:

1. The MarCom Matrix, and the strengths and weaknesses of each MarCom discipline;

2. Guidelines and Idea Starters in the various disciplines;

3. Message Windows, both traditional and nontraditional – with particular attention to the Target's Personal Media Network and the way MarCom programs can reinforce each other;

4. Some basic good advice for Budgeting;

5. How to create a Media Flow Chart and Marketing Calendar; and

6. CRM and an Evaluation program for your brand's marketing activities.

REVIEW QUESTIONS

1. On judgment, which MarCom disciplines seem like they will be the strongest for your brand? Why? Which seem to be least effective? Why?

2. Quick. Write down some of your favorite creative thoughts for your brand. (We'll be doing more of that in the next chapter.)

3. On judgment, which Message Windows seem to make the most sense for your brand?

4. How do your preferred Message Windows connect with your Target's Personal Media Network?

5. How would you describe your brand's ideal Message Window?

6. What's the biggest budget you think you can afford? What will be your probable budget?

7. If you had extra dollars, what would you add?

8. If you only had money for one thing, what would you do?

9. Describe the CRM program you think your brand should implement.

10. Initially, how will you evaluate your brand's activities?

RESOURCES

http://www.dtsf.com

Downtown Sioux Falls Association

http://www.blackhillscorvetteclassic.com//links.htm

Black Hills Corvette Classic

Bendinger, B. (2009). *The Copy Workshop.* The Copy Workshop, Chicago, IL.

CHAPTER 11:
MESSAGE WINDOWS 2:
Creative Executions

In Chapter 9, you decided on your Message Strategy – and your Message. Then, you gave a bit more thought to your Target and your most cost-effective Message Windows. Now, we're going to be doing some Window Decoration.

We'll be designing and determining the best way to combine your brand's Message and those Message Windows. That's the purpose of this chapter. You'll want to do four things: 1) deliver the Message, 2) to the right person, 3) using the appropriate Message Windows, 4) to build on your brand equity.

Whether you're working with a student team, for your own company, or for a non-profit, the process is the same. What is your Message? How will it look? In what windows will your message appear?

In this chapter we'll discuss how to manage all the details involved in getting it right. You'll have to consider things such as which images, layout, font, and design elements will deliver the highest impact to increase the chances of your message getting onto someone's radar in the marketplace.

The decisions you made in the previous chapter will now have a face.

LEARNING OUTCOMES

Specifically, after studying this chapter you will be prepared to:

1. Manage teamwork on message development and implementation

2. Craft messages that fit your Message Windows

3. Evaluate the Message production process

WORKING WITH YOUR TEAM

Brand Building is a team sport. The team kicks into high gear here. At this point, there should be something for everyone to do, even if it's offer an opinion.

The kind of teamwork we're talking about is a meshing of many disciplines. Sometimes it's a group of specialists, and sometimes we have to be Swiss Army Knives, wearing different hats as we become strategists, communicators, and production specialists late at night in front of the computer screen or driving over to the copy shop to get the invitations printed.

Team Duties

It will be quite common for your brand-building to be done as part of a creative team – either as students or as a small "start-up agency." Figure 11.1 gives you a picture of a typical six-person team. If you have five, someone takes two duties. If you have four people on your team, sets of two people should have two sets of tasks. If you have seven, you have an extra designer, or writer, or producer.

A One-Person Team

We're all Swiss Army Knives. Some of our blades are better and sharper than others. If you are an entrepreneur, you may find some of the skills you need are not your strength. You know what I mean. The good news is that entrepreneurs are usually excellent at making other things happen around them. You have developed something that is unique, and this book has found its way into your hands to help you market your brand. Here's what to do.

If you are the business person, find an artist or graphic designer. If you are the artist or designer, find the best writer to work with. If you're creative, find a good business person.

You might also need others, but you'll figure that out as well.

As you go, you'll probably have to start adding to your team. As we grow, we need to find those who can add their skills – good designers, smart communicators, tough-minded marketers, and those "worth-their-weight-in-gold" project managers.

Bringing out the Creativity in Your Organization

Finally, if you're a non-profit organization, you may have a committee assigned to the same functions, or have a group of media specialists calling on you. This chapter may be helpful in identifying the things that need doing as you develop your communications program. It will help you identify the skills needed – either from people already involved with your organization, or those you need to recruit – so you can design your own persuasive messages.

Here, in a general sense, are the skills needed.

Designers and Writers

We'll put designers first, writers second. Your brand will need good graphics. That means a good graphics person or a good graphics firm – with a great lead designer and able assistants to handle the details. This is a capability that will be critical to your brand's success. You need someone on the team who specializes in the "look" of your messages, such as an ad or a brochure, as well as all the other things a brand needs – from the logo to the menu to the sign on your store to your business card, to the look of your website. Sometimes this will be one talented individual, sometimes it will be a team with specialties.

In general, your Message will have both a visual and a verbal component. We like to have both kinds of thinkers working on the problem. Often, the two put their heads together and come up with a concept that connects on both levels.

Then again, sometimes, the only head is yours, and you have to use both sides of your brain to connect with whatever talent you can find. Just remember that a good message will tend to work both visually and verbally. It will look good and it will contain, in some way, persuasive words. They might even "bristle."

Strategists, Project Directors, Media Professionals, and Production Experts

As we move to the implementation stage of our program, it helps to understand some of the other skills you need. It would be nice to have one specialist for each skill, but it's unlikely to be practical. You'll probably need to use more than one blade on your Swiss Army Knife. Whatever and whomever, let's look at what's involved.

Strategists. Strategy isn't just about Messages, it's about business and it's about prioritizing. After all, "Strategy is about choice." Every team and every business needs at least one person who's good at this.

Project Director. If you've ever thrown a big party, a wedding, or an important fund-raising event, you know that a lot of things need to be done to make it happen. It may vary from project to project and event to event, but it all adds up to a lot of things that need to get done. You need someone with good project management skills. That's why many good teams have a smart get-it-done project manager at the center of projects and events. There are many different titles for this important skill, but the key point is that there is someone keeping on top of things.

Media Professionals. Every medium has something special about it – whether it's a TV commercial or a bus bench. Often, the media company can help – they're usually glad to help as they take your money. But once you decide on the Message Windows you want to use for your brand, you may need to develop some specific expertise – it may be as simple as getting flyers and brochures printed, or it may be as complex as getting the coding on your website right so you can capture those e-mail addresses and then send out that electronic coupon.

Production Specialists. That visual may look good on your computer screen, but you may need an electronic pre-press person to make sure that the image shining out of the screen doesn't end up looking dark and dull when you print it. Each kind of production has its "tricks of the trade." Again, you want your team to capture that expertise – either from team members, or from outside specialists who provide you with the critical skills you need to get the job done right.

So now let's talk about what it takes to do that job right.

CRAFTING MESSAGES
Strategy > Message > Message Window

That's the sequence we've been building towards throughout the book.

At each stage you have to get it right. At this point, we'll assume you're fairly well focused on your Business Goals, your Target, and, as far as it goes, your Strategy. We'll also guess that your Message is still a bit fluid – particularly because you probably understand, without our mentioning it, that different Message Windows may frame your Message differently. Well, you're right, they do.

For example, the Message you have to deliver will be very different on a billboard than when it's in a personalized fund-raising letter. That press release will be a lot different than the Special Grand Opening Offer on the windshield flyer.

So, to begin, let's use a more specific word than Message. Let's call it a **Selling Idea**. What's that? An idea that sells. Simple. We'll bet that your Message does that. At P&G, a big company that understands Selling Ideas very well, they observe that good ones seem to have three things going for them:

1. **Substance** – The idea is meaningful or desirable to the consumer;

2. **Credible** – The idea is believable. It's okay if it's a bit of a challenge;

3. **Provocative** – The idea is "a thought provoking method of expression."

At the same time, it's worth repeating that your Selling Idea is going to be a lot different in a long fund-raising letter than it will be on a poster or a bus bench. So, as we get ready to craft our Messages and decorate those different Message Windows, let's add a few more thoughts to your already overstuffed brain:

- **Dramatize the Benefit.** It can be a practical benefit or something a bit more over the top, like Old Spice's "The Man Your Man Could Smell

Like." A simple idea that dramatizes the benefit of your brand is probably a good thing. It's better yet if it's a visual idea.

- **A Distinctive Selling Personality.** Brands you like, such as Apple, Nike, Starbucks, and Target have developed a personality that goes across many different products and services. Some of it is graphics, and some of it is a result of being very smart about how they present themselves. One more thing related to that. Your brand was started by people. When we read about Starbucks, we read about Howard Schultz. When there's a story about any of the Virgin brands, you can bet that there's a photo or an interview with Richard Branson. Our bank had a very important brand asset – our President. When you think of that Nike swoosh, it's a pretty good bet you also remember a commercial featuring one of its star athletes. People. Personality.

- **A Unique Selling Environment.** Often, our brands are part of a place – an Apple store, a Starbucks, or any of a whole range of retail environments. If this is a part of your brand, realize that it's part of your message and your message should project that selling environment. Another quick question to ask. "What color is your brand?" Fine artists get to paint with a wide pallette. We usually get just a few crayons. Choose them wisely.

- **Something Else.** The mnemonic rhythm of Subway's Five Dollar Footlongs. The Mascot at a sporting event. The way Geico surrounds a simple claim ("Switching to GEICO could save you 15% or more") with a wide range of executions. The Geek Squad at Best Buy.

There are lots of different ways to build your brand. It can be frustrating, but it can also be satisfying and fun.

Some Final Questions

You can keep evaluating your efforts. And you can keep asking questions.

But if you're getting it right, we bet you'll be answering "yes" to more and more of those questions. Here are a few more:

1. **Is it clear and good-looking?** Is the language clear and is the piece a good-looking reflection on your brand? Now you know why writers and designers are so important.

2. **Does it communicate the benefit?** Benefits are good. What is yours? Does it solve a problem? Does it make people feel better? Does it taste really really good? See how memorably you can deliver that benefit as part of your message.

3. **Does it reinforce awareness?** A lot of brands compete for attention. If people are more aware of your brand, it's a step in the right direction.

4. **Can it be used across all Message Windows?** There are more message opportunities every day. If your message can stay consistent no matter what the window is, that's probably a good thing.

5. **Does it develop drama?** We remember stories. Story development is based on some sort of dramatic structure. Tell us a story.

6. **Is it faithful to the Strategy?** In the beginning, a strategy is an hypothesis, a "best guess" on how to persuade. Which leads you to another thought: What if you don't have a strong Message that sells? You might not have a strong Strategy. You might need to go back and tweak the Strategy. That's fine. This is an art. Do it until you get it right.

Let's Review Your Writing

Still need work on your message? Here are two more lists of good advice for you on writing your messages from Bruce Bendinger's *Copy Workshop Workbook* (2009).

Collect Vocabulary for Your Brand. Remember how we worked our way to the three best words for our Chamber Music Group? That was all part of building our brand vocabulary. Here are four categories for your brand vocabulary.

1. **Find your Verb** – active verbs persuade
2. **Add Adjectives** – clarify, inform, relate to strategy
3. **Pick up the pieces** – clichés and puns, endorsements, reasons why, etc.
4. **Organize your Thinking** – Take your time. Think. Incubate. Think and write.

Bruce wanted to share a story. Years ago, a girl walked into his copy class and she was having trouble with one of his standard assignments – developing a campaign for a vegetable. She had chosen baby corn. Bruce told her to "find your verb."

A week later she came back with a big smile on her face and a lovely campaign: "Adopt Baby Corn!"

Good Copy Has Rhythm. We need to enjoy what we read. After all, nobody's making us do it. So how do we add more enjoyment to the things we write?

Here are a few more tips.

1. Short simple sentences
2. Active verbs and positive attitude
3. Parallel construction (Easy to read, easy to understand)

4. Alliteration, Assonance, Rhyme
5. Puns, double meanings, and word play
6. Good copy vs. good grammar. Let's face it, messages to teen-agers might not get an A+ from an English teacher. Make the language fit the Target – and, if there's a reason for it, a slight bit of variation from totally proper English usage might get more attention. As they say, Think Different.

Now it's your turn. You're probably pretty much there. You just need to go over these things one more time to make them that much better. Here's a worksheet to help you do that. And, of course, you can download these from our website.

BRAIN BUILDER EXERCISE 11.1: Collecting Vocabulary

This exercise will help you and your team collect vocabulary for your ads.

Instructions:

1. Put your thinking hats on! It's time to put a collection of words together that would fit with your product and brand.

2. Follow the steps below and list at least five (5) words per category, but feel free to go beyond five.

3. Each person in the group should do the exercise alone, then bring all the words to the table to discuss in a group setting.

Write down some words and phrases.

Collecting Vocabulary		
	Find your verb	
	Add Adjectives	
	Pick up the pieces	
	Organize and incubate	

Now write long constructions – try for something in every category.

Good Copy has Rhythm	
Short and simple	
Active and positive	
Parallel construction	
Alliteration, Assonance, Rhyme	
Puns	
Good copy or good grammar	

THE IMPORTANCE OF VISUAL COMMUNICATION

This book is full of words, and, when we think and write our strategies and memos, we're usually using words. But a lot of powerful communication comes from pictures and symbols.

See what you can do to make your messages more visual – a strong logo, maybe an iconic figure for your brand, a nice graphic for a promotion – these are all things that can make your brand's messaging more effective.

Your selling message and visual ideas begin the process, which is followed by adding additional images, color, and design elements. Finally, select the best Message Windows your client's money can buy and deliver the best possible return for their money. Simply put, you want your Messages to look wonderful.

The Process

In general, you'll want to go through these three steps.

1. **Determine Your Selling Message.** That includes the Visual. In a basic way, you should know what your message is – the key theme line, the logo, often with your slogan (the "slogo," remember?), the key visual element or elements – and, in the back of your mind, the Mission and Strategy.

2. **Select Message Windows.** How and where will your Target best connect with your brand? Are there key locations? Are there favorite broadcast channels? Are there print media that are particularly effective? Is there an event or similar connection point? These Message Windows will, in many ways, help define the look of your brand communications. In general, you'll have more good ideas than your budget will accommodate – but have them ready, you never know when opportunities will arise.

3. **Design the Messages to fit the Message Windows**. It's a busy world. If you can find a moment where you can deliver a lengthy message, terrific. But, we're usually grabbing people on the run, with other things on their minds. That said, try to include a response-generating offer. Have a restaurant? Can you offer a free item of enough value to generate a visit? Have a service to offer? How can you get someone to "sample" your service? Is there a new store we should visit? What does it take to get us to go to the trouble? Remember, you only have one time to make a first impression.

How it happened for the Learning Center – Connect Yourself
On Message and Logo Design

Remember our library group? Their Message was created strong and simple – "Connect Yourself." It took a lot of work to get there, but we all agreed it was the best fit for the target and client. It also worked with the current messaging for the college branding campaign. A logo design had also been requested. And, no surprise, this logo had to please a lot of people.

The team worked hard to develop a logo that librarians, the dean of the Learning Center, and academic services staff were pleased with. They would own it. The logo would be a big part of the creative work (it dominated one member's time and energy). In this case, the team consisted of eight students – two were graphic design majors, three advertising majors, two business majors, and one with a business cluster.

Design Elements

With an approved logo and message, "Connect Yourself," the brainstorming and sketching began. We looked to decorate those Message Windows. The logo went on mugs, T-shirts, pens, and stationery. Then another designer sketched out "Connect Yourself" as a headline. Those Message Windows had pictures of students connecting with the Learning Center staff members. After some class feedback, a final design was accepted.

We knew it was a strong message when students began to come up with more and more ways to execute "Connect Yourself." It worked with games, promotions, faculty events, and at freshman orientation.

That's one of the things that happens when the Message is right. More good ideas and more ways to design those Message Windows keep showing up. You can feel when you've got it right. It's a great feeling.

Rough Layout

Even with the computer, the design process generally goes from rough layout (sometimes "thumbnails" drawn by hand) to a finished graphic file – ready to go to the printer or publication.

In this case, the team's designers started with a rough layout for posters and the campus newspaper. They proposed one or two designs with a font, photography, illustrations, and design elements (lines, graphics, etc.) appropriate for the brand and target audience. They also selected a color scheme complimentary for the brand and target. Depending on the designer, the layouts appeared on a sketch pad or computer.

Concept Testing

Score-keeping doesn't have to wait until after your Message has run.

During class time, students tested their concepts with the target audience – other students and faculty. While their teammates were good critics, others from the campus would offer different perspectives. Concept testing can generate feedback on all areas of the branding campaign. Often, you can make a good thing even better.

Finding members of the target audience is critical at this stage. For a non-profit or art group, have board members or customers on hand. They can really help students find their way through some of the clutter that gets in the way of their design.

You might want to find a way to host a small focus group get-together to conduct the concept testing. Ask some tough questions during testing: What do you like best? What don't you like at all? Present your target group with your sales promotions, event ideas, print series, and TV concept all at once. Let them tell you what they think the message is. If they can't see it right away, the audience will not see it. Is it clear what the benefit is? It should be!

THE PRODUCTION PROCESS:
Creating Communications in Traditional and New Media

The advertising legend Howard Gossage had a phrase he liked to use. *"People read what interests them. Sometimes it's an ad."* In this world of over-communication, with a blizzard of messages surrounding us, this is a useful thought.

As we get caught up in the production logistics of designing Messages to fit our Message Windows, we need to remember that we need to be interesting. Sometimes that interest is due to what we have to say, and, if your target is a hungry teenager, "FREE FRENCH FRIES" might be a very interesting message indeed.

Across Message Windows

Ideally, your visual and messaging should appear in an appropriately consistent way across a number of Message Windows.

Even if you only end up with a few Messages in your initial budget, it can be useful to kind of overdo it in the beginning. You might uncover some interesting ways to serve up your message and if you're limiting yourself at the beginning, you'll miss out on that exploration time. Also, it is not uncommon for new opportunities to pop up at the spur of the moment – often with short closing times ("We have a spare page in the program. How would you like a free ad?" "Sure, you can put a poster in our window."). With that in mind, here are Message Windows I usually suggest:

- **Two or three print ads** (both color and black and white)
  Remember, that print ad might also be a door hanger or a flyer under a windshield wiper. Can it work as a bold, simple poster? You never know when an opportunity like that can come up.

  Is there something that's easy to hand out and save? Great! And don't forget the power of an "Introductory Offer" to stimulate that all-important first visit.

- **One TV spot – usually six frames**
  Once upon a time, TV was unaffordable for smaller brands. But now, with YouTube, FinalCut, and local cable channels, that might not be the case. I like a six-frame storyboard – but, if you're developing a lot of TV ideas, you might want to try Key Frames – that's one key visual, with the script pasted underneath. (If you're going to be presenting, you'll also want to paste the script on the back. Hold up the Key Frame and read the script on the back.)

- **Radio – two scripts**
  Radio can be a great way to work out your proposition. It's 60 seconds – a long time – you can stretch out and maybe figure out a new way to dramatize

what's interesting about your brand. Sometimes local radio personalities can get involved if you provide them with "talking points." And, don't forget that "Introductory Offer." What will it take to get the casual listener to decide to visit you? Want more tips on writing radio? They're waiting for you in *The Copy Workshop Workbook.*

- **Billboard – two**
  Here's a medium that's changing with technology – so look at something old and something new. For something old, look for a plain old poster, bus bench back, or some other fairly traditional place to post your message. Then, see if there is some newfangled outdoor going on in your market – big video screens, for example. Why not call your local outdoor company and ask, "What's new?"

- **Press Releases – two**
  This is a good discipline. It forces you to think about what's newsworthy. Think of some story angles that will get the local news to feature you. And don't forget the human element. Lots of stories about Apple, Microsoft, and Starbucks are stories about Steve Jobs, Bill Gates, and Howard Schultz. Often, the human angle is what makes it newsworthy. And maybe you'll get a better deal at the bank if you mention you featured their President. Probably not.

- **Internet – website / social media**
  Here, we want to think about the range of possibilities. How can we get e-mail addresses so that we can connect inexpensively. Can we use the Internet to deliver added value? Digital images? Content? A catalog? E-commerce? A printable coupon? Get the idea? The Internet is just waiting to help you give your brand new brand exciting new ways to connect with your Target.

STEPS TO TAKE

Typically the print ad will be the first creative piece you execute. It will have the Message (Selling Idea), the visual, the logo, design elements, illustrations, photography, and the copy. The pieces of the puzzle will start to take shape. While you are getting the print ready, consider all forms – magazine, newspaper, billboard, posters. And don't forget those buttons and bumper stickers.

After print, think about broadcast. Write your radio and television scripts. TV is typically presented in a six-frame storyboard. Radio is often written to correspond with an event or promotion.

Create promotional posters and collateral material for all events. Then, plan internet presence, social media, event, direct marketing initiatives, sponsorships, e-mail marketing, public relation, etc.

There's a lot to do, isn't there? These are the steps you would typically take, though, you might not choose to take them in that order. Or you might choose to do more. I've found that once we get going, this can be one of the most fun times. Everybody has good ideas – even they don't all get used – and everyone feels like they've made a contribution. This is a good thing. It also encourages everyone to stretch out into new areas. When your Message is strong, it can have a life of its own.

"Echonomical," "Echological" and "Echocentric"

Here's an example of taking a Message and expanding it into a variety of Message Windows. This was student team work for the AAF competition – a Toyota Echo campaign with an *Echonomical, Echological and Echocentric* messages. The word "Echo" repeated itself as one of the graphic elements.

The word "Echo" was a playful element, and the three words were very simple to execute across many Message Windows. Those three words also emphasized strong customer benefits, reinforced name recognition, and served as the taglines for the product introduction.

The Message Windows chosen were banner ads, a magazine ad, the website, and an event: Echo Night at the ballpark. Some of the Echo campaign ideas were right on – and maybe a few were just over the edge. But for college students to work as a team to produce that level of work way back in 1999, it was hard to beat. And it was a lot of fun.

Banner ad

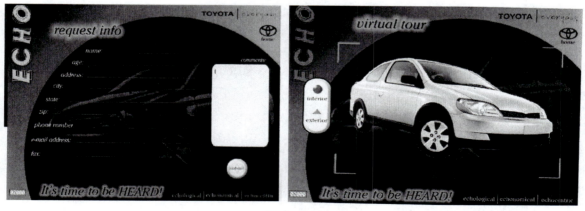

Web work

Echo Night at the Ballpark

The ideas kept on coming…

>A co-branding event with Rock the Vote was "It's Time to Be Heard".
>The DVD test drive was named "Echoactive."
>A new discount card – "Echonomic Incentive."
>Co-branding with *Sports Illustrated* for a campus festival was "Echomania."
>Unexpected Places: "Echooooooooo" wrapped portions of large buildings. Small ads were placed on ATMs.

Toyota used similar messages and visuals that fall; we found one in *Maxim* magazine – "Echological."

Security National Bank. A Variety of Message Windows.

For Security National Bank (SNB), the student teams presented ideas to the management team to promote additional SNB products to the Young Professional market.

SNB is a medium-sized organization that just celebrated over 125 years of service to the community. This work shows how a single Message can be executed across various windows.

Simple selling idea – Confident. Reliable. Distinguished.

You might notice a similarity in this campaign with one we showed you much earlier for our Chamber Music group. In each case, we used three words that were meaningful to our Target. They were based on research, and that research showed that we clearly and persuasively positioned the brand. Was it the most creative Message ever created? Probably not. But it was clear, easily understood by the Target, and easy for decision-makers to understand. This might not be the cleverest and most creative approach, but it does have a few advantages.

First, you don't need a creative genius. Smart people paying attention to the problem can determine those Factors That Influence Purchase Behavior. Research with the Target can identify – with reasonable clarity and confidence – what's meaningful. Then, with some confidence, you can write a theme that does the job. Perhaps you won't win the Golden Lion at Cannes, but it's a responsible way to communicate your brand's essence.

Here are some examples of how we extended that theme across message windows.

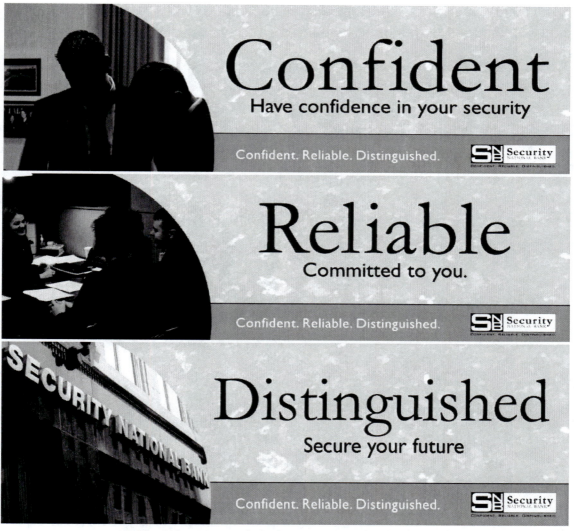

Billboard campaign / also cross over to in bank posters

Print ads

Events and Community Outreach

One area where small local brands can compete powerfully is at the community level. We found a number of ways to leverage that advantage.

At the top decision-maker level, we had a series of "Coffees" with SNB President Rich Waller. At the future decision-maker level, we got involved with schools – another advantage you can implement locally. We provided a curriculum and lesson plans on financial literacy to schools and teachers. There was a contest on YouTube and promotional products such as savings banks and T-shirts. There was also a game that taught financial literacy with game boards and game cards.

Finally, the bank connected to Social Network sites, with Facebook, Twitter and YouTube. How will those Message Windows work out? Stay tuned.

The Production Process

After you've been through the process, you start to appreciate what's involved. When you look at the professionally finished materials, you begin to realize that there is a production process that contributes to a quality look for your brand.

As you develop your plan for these various Message Windows, you will also have to collect or develop the skills you need to achieve those results. Let's run through a quick review of what's involved.

Print Media. Here, the skills are initially visual – good layouts with handsome proportion and well-handled typography. But, you'll also need to develop skills in print production so art and photography are reproduced well. Whether you use original art and photography or buy "stock photography" there may be a bit of legal housekeeping involved. Make sure proper payments are made and rights secured.

Broadcast Media. Each medium involves a range of skills. In addition to having the idea, getting that idea produced in video and/or audio involves specialized equipment (and knowing how to use it). It also involves skills such as shooting video, recording audio, and then assembling all the different elements, possibly with a special effect or two. In many cases, broadcast suppliers, such as your local television station, cable provider, or radio station can be valuable contributors to the broadcast production process.

Other MarCom Disciplines. Whether it's designing and implementing a direct mail campaign, producing an event (or just setting up a booth at someone else's event), printing a cardboard display, or getting your website to do everything you want it to do, your team may need additional specialties – or people willing to learn them. In many cases, there are suppliers ready, willing, and able to help. For example, in the area of promotional products, most suppliers are able to help you get your client's image on a T-shirt, cap, or balloon.

Project Management. As your team moves from ideas in the room to Selling Ideas in the marketplace, you'll find that many of your team's activities will evolve to project management. This requires a slightly different set of skills – and it's a set of skills that is very highly valued in the marketplace. Remember, after you develop and sell the idea, a whole new range of opportunities will open up.

But, wait a minute. Before you can produce it, you have to sell it.

In the next chapter, we'll look at how The Pitch comes together.

BRAIN BUILDER EXERCISE 11.2: Reflection

One last chance to reflect on your Message.

Instructions:

1. Evaluate how well you think your Message fits with your product and brand.

2. How well does your Message fit in each Message Window?

3. Are the values of the company and the brand imprinted through the Message and creative work?

CHAPTER REVIEW

We've covered quite a few very big topics as we move to pulling your final brand-building program together.

1. Teamwork is necessary for message development and implementatio.

2. There are three big things to remember in the process of crafting messages to fit Message Windows.

    a. **The Brand Builder Matrix**. This simple system locks in the key building blocks for your brand communication

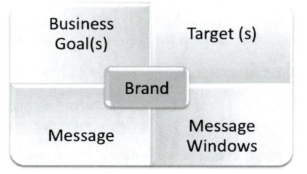

    b. **The MarCom Matrix**. This graphic reminds you of the variety of opportunities we now have for brands in today's marketplace.

c. **Improve Performance with Research**. You have to keep learning – even when things are going well. Every step of the way, you should keep checking with your Target to see how you're doing. In most cases, they'll tell you.

3. The Production Process is important. As you move from ideas for your presentation to actual programs in the marketplace, you will discover an increased need for the specific production skills that are key to a professional result. This includes the important team skill of Project Management.

REVIEW QUESTIONS

1 How is your team organized? What skills would you like to add? Will you do it with new team members, current members adding skills, or by bringing in outside suppliers?

2 Have you filled in your Brand Builder Matrix recently? If not, let's do it. Any changes?

3 Now, let's review the elements.

a. **Business Goals**. Is there anything else you can do to leverage your core values with Cause Marketing or some community involvement?

b. **Target**. What is most important to your Target in this Category? Do you have a Secondary Target with potential?

c. **Message**. Why is this the best Message for your brand? Are there any alternative messages you're still considering? What would an alternative strategy look like?

d. **Message Windows**. What are the strongest matches of Message and Message Window? Hold that thought. Anything you want to test?

4. **MarCom Matrix Review**. Let's review each of the areas below:

a. **Advertising**. Are there any interesting advertising opportunities for your brand? A medium where you can dominate? Any low-cost opportunities?

b. **Public Relations**. Quick, what's newsworthy? Are there any values that your brand represents? Like fashion? Maybe you can publish a local best-dressed list. Health? Institute an award for healthy places to eat.

c. **Sales Promotion**. What's the bribe? What offer can we make that will stimulate someone to become involved with our brand? What are some effective ways to deliver that offer?

d. **Direct**. How's our database? Do we already have a list of potential Targets or, better yet, existing Customers? What are we doing with that data? How are we continuing to capture names for the database? What will we do when we do get their name? Do we have offers for them? What are we doing for CRM? Do you remember what CRM stand for? How about referrals? Do you have a referral program?

e. **Other**. Let's focus on Events and Promotional Products.

i. What Events do you think are a particularly good match for your brand? Are there any aspects of Cause Marketing that are a good fit with your Mission and Business Goals?

ii. What Promotional Products make sense for your brand?

f. **New Media**. How's our website? Do we have the best possible addresses? How are we using the Internet to deliver our brand messages? Does our site reinforce our brand experience? How? Do you have a "wish list?"

g. **Guerrilla Media**. Any unique local opportunities where you can make some unique impact quickly, easily, and at a low cost?

5. **Improve your Message with Research**. Let's think ahead to our client presentation. When they ask how we know we have an effective message, what do we tell them?

6. **The Production Process**. What production skills do we need to add? What will our first projects be? Who will be the Project Manager?

CHAPTER 12:
THE PITCH

There are always next steps. One of the most critical is the presentation you make to final decision-makers. It may be a CEO, a venture capitalist, an investor, a bank, your rich Aunt Ethel, the director of marketing, or the professor grading your final exam. In every case, all the work you've done to this point is on the line.

This is The Pitch. It's the meeting where your work is sold to the next level. The purpose of this chapter is to help you prepare, polish, and sell your work. A second purpose is to help schedule your work so that when it's time, you're ready.

We'll start with backdating your work flow. Simply put, backdating is planning ahead. You do it all the time. If the theater is 20 minutes away, you leave early, factoring in the possible amount of time necessary for traffic, parking, buying tickets, and – optional – getting popcorn. If it's spring break, you may plan early to get the best fares, or hop in a car with friends and hope for the best. Life is like that. Only some things are more important than others. The Pitch is important.

Next we'll talk about one more piece of production – the "book." This is the entire campaign wrapped up in a binder, so that executive decision-makers can see how you're recommending they spend their money.

Finally, there's the presentation itself. We really should capitalize it, because, for you, it's The Presentation. Then there's one more thing – you also have a longer-term objective. You are not only selling your work, but yourself. Presentations such as the one you're going to make are also the stuff of winning portfolios, impressive résumés, and getting the job. So when it's time for that important interview, you'll have a little extra – actually, a lot extra – to add.

LEARNING OUTCOMES

After studying this chapter you will be able to:

1. Backdate your workflow
   a. Organize workflow with the end in mind
   b. Assign team responsibilities
   c. Build a practical schedule

2. Publish your "book"
   a. Write the presentation book
      i. Proofread and edit
      ii. Style

   iii. Table of Contents
  b. Design the presentation book
   i. Cover
   ii. Layout and design
   iii. Software
   iv. Budget
  c. Print the presentation book
   i. Scheduling
   ii. Color and font proof
   iii. Budget
   iv. Shipping and binding

3. Pitch your campaign
  a. Outline and write your presentation
  b. Build Slide Show
   i. Integrate creative work into slideshow
   ii. Design Slides to compliment book's design (Maximum of 30 slides)
  c. Assemble the presentation team
  e. Practice Makes Perfect
  f. Pitch the campaign to client

4. Build your portfolio

BACKDATE YOUR WORKFLOW

We all have a triangle of work factors – quality, time, and money. In my world, I have a fixed amount of time and very little money, but expect superior quality. Sound familiar? You can use this triangle in a number of ways. Right now, you need to use it to plan your workflow and backdate your time.

Backdating is a technique where you start with the endpoint (the day you plan to Pitch your work) and then go backwards to create deadlines for each step. If you haven't done it before, it should help your productivity. (By the way, this has *nothing* to do with backdating documents!)

TIP: Microsoft Project is a tool that is very powerful in this area. It can help you manage many resources and responsibilities along the way.

Look at all the steps we need to take (Fig. 12.1). Take a look at the end point and the date for the Presentation.

Now, how much time will it take for you to get to that step from here? And don't forget to factor in the time to make the CD, plans book, and any other "leave behinds."

Campaign Development

Situation Analysis	Research Plan	Primary Research	Target Audience	Goal Setting	Creative Strategy	Prioritizing	Creative Executions	The Pitch
Define the Problem advertising can solve	10 Step Research Process	Brand, Purchasing Behavior, Target Audience	Target Sketch Demographics and Psycho-graphics	SWOT	Creative Tool Chest	Marketing Services	Traditional Media: Radio, Television, Magazine, Newspaper, Outdoor, Transit	Book
Conduct Brand Audit. Use Brand Analysis. Answers the question, "Where are we?"		Quantitative and Qualitative Methodology		Marketing Objective	Big Idea	Media: Traditional and New Media	Nontraditional and New Media: Internet, Social Media, Nontraditional outlets	CD
Complete Competition Analysis	Literature Review of Industry, Target, Competition	Designing questions		Positioning Statement	Tagline	Evaluation		Pitch
		Research Proposal and Report						

Fig. 12.1: Campaign Development

Be realistic. Work backwards – from the Book, back to the Creative Executions, back through the Marketing Services, Creative Strategy, etc. Then, if it's your first time, factor in a little more time. See? You're already behind schedule – and you've barely started. Don't worry. Just use your best judgment.

After all, the only way you will truly know how long it takes is if you've done it already. So it should be no surprise that the more experience you have, the better you'll be at knowing what needs to be done. And the better you'll be at doing it.

If you're part of a student team working in a semester system, your Pitch will most likely be delivered during the week of finals. The book is usually due the week before at roughly the same time as the rehearsal (Mock Pitch). But, of course, if it's a "real world" client, that might change. In case you haven't heard, the "real world" doesn't run on the semester system. Sometimes, every day is a final exam.

The more you understand your strengths and specific skills, the better you will be able to backdate and schedule. If, for example, you know how to do research and write a SWOT analysis, you can tell me how long it should take.

If you're a good copywriter and have good data from the research section, you and the Art Director should be able to estimate how long it should take to complete your Message brainstorming session. But, again, if you've never done this before, it'll be a "best guess." So hang on, it will be a fun ride trying to see how this baby flies for the first time.

When my students are in a competition, the timeline follows the competition schedule. For example, if the competition call-for-entry deadline is February 16th, we'll put it on the calendar for February 2nd. With backdating, that means we should actually have something in pretty good shape before winter break. And, if we're not ready, we all know how we're spending our winter break.

Planning Your Work

Here are two scenarios for you:

1. Planning a *semester* brand building campaign, and
2. Planning a campaign for *your own* non profit.

Semester Schedule for a Brand Building Campaign

Here's a sample 15-week plan for those of you working within a semester system.

For entrepreneurship courses, your marketing team should be able to backdate the activities as well. You can find additional support material or links to ask questions at www.brandbuilderworkbook.com.

With a little coaching, and a lot of organization, the brand building plan delivers.

To date, the following schedule has worked well for our student teams. Though, as more real world clients – both start-ups and non-profits – become part of the process, you will find that their schedules don't always fit the school calendar.

Date	Day	Reading /Activity for Class	BRAND BUILDING ASSIGNMENTS
Week 1	Th	Course introduction, team development discussion	Show previous Student Branding Campaigns
	T	Chapter 1	Brand Campaign Assignments
	Th	Chapter 1	
Week 2	T	Chapter 2	
	Th	Chapter 3	
Week 3	T	Exam Review	
	Th	Exam I	
Week 4	T		Meet Client -- Situation Analysis - Brand Analysis
	Th	Chapter 8	
Week 5	T	Chapter 11	Research Plan

	Th	Chapter 9	
Week 6	T	Exam II	
	Th	Advertising Workshop	Situation Analysis, Research Plan, Primary Research
Week 7	T	Advertising Workshop	Situation Analysis Report due
	Th	Advertising Workshop	Primary Research Report due
Week 8	T	SPRING	
	Th	BREAK	
Week 9	T	Advertising Workshop	Target Audience Report
	Th	Advertising Workshop	SWOT, Marketing Objective, Positioning Statement Reports
Week 10	T	Advertising Workshop	Creative Strategy
	Th	Chapter 7	
Week 11	T	Chapter 6 & 10	
	Th		Media Plan, Marketing Services, Evaluation plan
Week 12	T	Advising Day	Creative executions, Book, CD, Pitch
	Th	Exam III	
Week 13	T	Advertising Workshop	Book, CD, Pitch
	Th	Easter Break	
Week 14	T	Advertising Workshop	Book, CD, Pitch
	Th	Write, Rewrite, Proofread, Edit	Book, CD, Pitch
Week 15	T	Creative Workshop a	Creative executions finalized
	Th	Advertising Workshop	Book published, CD burned, Pitch Finalized
Week 16	T	Mock pitch to Instructor	
Finals	M	Final Exam Period - The Pitch!	

Fig. 12.2 Sample schedule

While school's out, your business or non-profit is still going – so you may have to plan a transition. There are lots of good agencies out there – with a little legwork, you can probably find one that's a good fit. Also, it's not uncommon for one of the key team members to graduate and continue the relationship with the client.

In general, there's never enough money – so use time as your tool to dial up the quality. When you have a specific time frame (an opening, a launch, a holiday), you need to be disciplined with your scheduling. Meanwhile, don't forget that other businesses, particularly media, have their own back-timing needs.

The daily newspaper and the local radio station can react fairly quickly. That monthly city magazine (check their schedules) may be quite a bit different. You may need one or two months lead time.

Now you're starting to see why I recommend that teams read this chapter early on.

Scheduling and Team-Building

If you're planning to brand your non-profit, artistic venture, or small business, think about that Time/Money/Quality Triangle again. How much money do you have?

It takes time to build and grow a brand. And it usually takes a team. Some of this advice may seem obvious, but it is worth stating and then worth repeating.

It's a noisy world. You must promote yourself if you are not able to pay someone else to do it. Even if you do pay, you must make sure that third party does it right. And you want your money spent in areas that will yield returns.

Remember that saying, "*When all you have is a hammer, every problem looks like a nail.*" Well every communication professional will believe – often sincerely – that the best expenditure of your limited budget is with them. Don't be too trusting – and try to pay for performance rather than promises.

Business Plans

One more question. Do you have a business plan? Even if you're a non-profit, you need a set of financial guidelines to help you move ahead.

Did you write your entire business plan? Or did you have someone else write part of it for you? Were you pleased with the quality? For example, did a lawyer write the incorporation section, and your accountant the tax liability section?

How long did it take you to write the Business Plan? Two weeks, six weeks, or one year?

Often, there's a spreadsheet section where you project expenses and income. Is this section realistic or did it suffer from a bit of wishful thinking?

One more thing about a good business plan. You're never done. You're always changing it and improving it.

Assuming you have an initial Business Plan, let's look at a schedule for doing some brand-building. If you don't have a Business Plan, you can still go ahead, but don't be surprised if certain business situations arise that set back your starting point or generate major changes. That's just the way it is sometimes.

A Brand-Building Worksheet

Based on the process in this workbook, here's a rough outline of what you have to do. You fill in the blanks for the timeline.

Stage	Time Frame	Deliverables	Due Date
Start-up: Situation Analysis/Brand Analysis			
Research – Secondary*			
Research – Primary			
Target Audience Report			
Goal-Setting: SWOT, Marketing Objective, Positioning			
Business Goals/Goals			
Message Development: Creative Strategy/Message			
Message Windows 1: MarCom, Media, Recommendation			
Message Windows 2: Creative Executions, Media Flow Chart, Marketing Calendar, Production			
The Pitch: Presentation & Presentation "Book"			
Putting Your Plan into Action: Production, Evaluation, Score-Keeping			

You can begin your Secondary Research at the same time you're doing your Situation Analysis and Brand Analysis.

Putting Your Schedule into Action

Before leaving this section, think about putting your schedule into action. By that, we mean your Goal, Target Audience, Message, and Message Windows need to be prioritized and executed. If you have a Media Flow Chart ready, a budget set for the year, and messages that are ready, you're in a position to put your plan into action.

And, of course, once you're rolling in Year One, it's time to do some Evaluation, take a look at your results (Score-Keeping), and start planning for Year Two. With brains, hard work, and a little bit of luck, you'll be building your brand.

PUBLISH YOUR BOOK

We call it "The Book," but it often has other names and other forms. PowerPoint print-out, "Leave Behind," Business Plan, Marketing Plan, Marketing Presentation, Plans Book, or The Binder.

Basically, it's a fairly comprehensive presentation of your communications plan for the brand. If it's a more comprehensive book – like a full-blown marketing plan or business plan, this chunk will be an important section in that larger "Book."

Whatever your circumstance, whatever you call it, you will be pulling your program together into some sort of coherent form – and even if there are slides on a screen and dancing hamsters on the website, there will usually be some sort of "Book" involved that holds it all together.

The "Leave Behind." Sometimes you leave the entire book with those you've presented to – and sometimes the situation calls for a shorter, condensed, more promotional piece used to "sell" the program. Depending on the presentation and the circumstances, you may need to do both a Book and a leave-behind.

It's also worth mentioning that executives like to read Executive Summaries. Often, this is the first thing read. Sometimes the only thing. You need to make your point quickly while showing the decision-maker that you respect his (or her) time.

Write the Book

The Book is all of your work put together in one place and it serves as the Pitch in your absence. It's a formal documentation of all of your proposed brand building activity. It deserves your best efforts and attention.

The Small Business Institute, a college consulting arm of the Small Business Administration (SBA) helps publish similar documents. If you are applying for a loan with the SBA, the completed loan package looks very similar to the plans book we are discussing in this section. After helping clients prepare their SBA loan packages, those documents look very similar to this manuscript.

It should be no surprise that bankers love a well organized and professionally written document. Competitions sponsored by the AAF describe the "Book" as a "Plans Book." In the AAF competition, submissions of the Plans Book are required a month before the presentations. Judges score them. Teams have been known to win or lose by half a point.

Proofread and Edit

The need for a good editor and good proofreaders cannot be understated. Your book is almost ready, but there's a bit more to do. You don't want any "misteaks." See how they can ruin things?

Create a proofing system within your team. One or two goofy typographic errors can take away from the credibility of your work, and it will make all your hard work seem like the work of amateurs.

One more point. When you get to this stage, you discover that you really do know a lot about your brand, and you may be feeling pretty good about yourself, your team, and all the work you've done. You're also tired. This is when some of those big, goofy, stupid mistakes are made. Those mistakes, like a typo in the third frame of the PowerPoint you put in at the last minute, take away from your credibility and devalues all the good hard work you've done.

Find a fresh pair of eyes for your final proofing. Check the math, too. We've seen programs off by a factor of ten. Those little decimal points can slide around.

Style

Decide on the "readability" of your proposal. You might want your proposal to compliment the tone of your branding campaign. Make it professional and accurate.Spelling does count. And you should document your sources. Also, use a Style Manual: APA (American Association of Psychology) is the style used most in the social sciences. Others are Chicago and MLA. The point here is to have your team agree on a style and use it. It is another mark of professionalism.

Table of Contents

Figure 12.3 illustrates the contents of the book. It begins with the Executive Summary, usually a two-page summary of the entire document. One page might even be better.

You might not be familiar with the Executive Summary. It is critical. The busier and more important the people to whom you're presenting, the more important it is to start with an Executive Summary that "tells 'em what you're going to tell 'em."

The headings of each of the sections should sound very familiar to

| Executive Summary |
| Table of Contents |
| Situation Analysis |
| Research Plan |
| Primary Research |
| Target Audience |
| SWOT Analysis, Marketing Objective, and Positioning Statement |
| Creative Strategy |
| Media, Marketing Services, and Evaluation |
| Creative Executions |
| Acknowledgements |
| Bibliography |
| Team/Agency Member Recognition |

Fig. 12.3: Sample Book Contents

you. These are the chapters that we have discussed. And, of course, if your plan varies, so should the Table of Contents. Here is a general description of what's in these sections – it should be quite familiar to you by now.

Executive Summary

Naresh Malhotra (2009) author of *Basic Marketing Research,* describes the Executive Summary as follows:

> *"The Executive Summary is an extremely important part of the document, because this often is the only portion of the report that executives read... The Executive Summary should be written after the rest of the document, because it is much easier for the writer to read though the body of the report and then summarize the most important points."*

Concisely describe the problem your program will solve, the target audience you address, the creative strategy you developed, your major messages, message windows, and the media you recommend. It should be a maximum of two pages. Preferably it will be one page.

Acknowledgements

Always say thank you and recognize anyone who helped you along the way – from printers to department members to student government funding, and sometimes even family members. Acknowledging them shows class. Don't forget to do it. But no need to get carried away – be heartfelt, but businesslike. You can do both.

Team members and Agency members

You are a team. Include who you are either in the back pages or the very front. Your client should know who did all this work…and for your own portfolio a few years from now, you might enjoy remembering.

Common Questions Regarding the Book

1. How long should each section be?
    As long as it takes to get your point across.

2. How much of the Competitive Analysis do I include?
    Again, as long as needed to get the point across. But keep in mind that you are selling your idea in the Pitch. Position yourself and your plan to build to your idea. Those decision-makers are very aware of the competition and value any intelligence you can provide. There might also be some information that will set up the problem you solve. It is an opportunity to establish a bit of drama.

3. How long should the book be?

   Most AAF Plans Books are between 30- and 40-pages. This length shows you have been thorough and have a professional proposal. Longer than that it sort of shows you don't have the discipline to edit. Incidentally, keep Addendums to a relevant minimum. Then again, for busy entrepreneurs, you might want to make the Book a bit shorter. There are many types of decision-makers. Some feel better seeing stacks of marketing data and others just want to get to it. Think about that very important target. You be the judge.

4. Are bibliographies really necessary?

   I don't know if they're necessary, but I do know they're occasionally helpful. Some clients benefit greatly from the secondary research. Documentation allows them to find the original sources if they so choose.

Designing the book

Now, a few suggestions about designing your book. We'll talk about the cover, illustrations, layout and design, software, and a budget.

Cover

The cover is the *face of your campaign*. Your book will likely be passed from desk to desk and to those who weren't at the meeting. People will talk about your work, what you said, and look at the Message you recommend.

Ideally, the design of the cover will compliment the branding ideas that follow.

Here are examples from the Sioux Bee Honey campaign for Buzz, the Security National Bank campaign, and the competition for the National Case study for Cadillac in 2007. In many cases, the Plans Book and the PowerPoint were connected – so the horizontal formats can go together well.

Fig 12.4: Plans Book Cover: Sue Bee Honey, Buzz, Regional Case Study

Fig 12.5: Plans Book Cover: Security National Bank, Regional Case Study

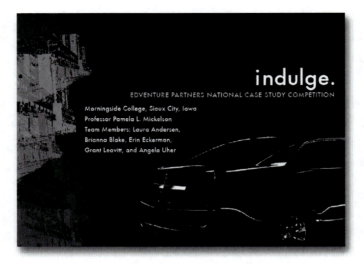

Fig 12.6: Plans Book Cover: Cadillac National Case Study, 1st Place National Winner

Layout and Design

With publishing software such as InDesign and presentation programs like PowerPoint and Keynote, we're all now used to very professional looking work. Yours should be no exception. Though we call it a Book, it is often in the horizontal format. Often, these books are compatible with the PowerPoint presentations they accompany. The horizontal format can also be useful for things like Media Flow Charts. Last but not least, the format encourages a minimum of writing. The layout format forces you to be brief. This is a good thing.

You might want to go to aaf.org and locate the education link. There, you can order the Plans Book from the winning campaigns. Seeing how others performed can offer some great insight and provide great examples.

Some Hard Truths about Software

In general, people will be working with up-to-date software on the Mac platform. As we indicated, most work with InDesign (along with the rest of the Adobe Creative Suite) and, usually, the Microsoft Office programs such as Word, Excel, and PowerPoint (though some are moving to Keynote for the presentation). For major competitions like the AAF, you will be seeing flashy Flash animations and other more advanced things, including well-produced videos. Today, this is the kind of thing people have come to expect. (Incidentally, if you're competing in the AAF/NSAC, you should also be using Avery's *Advertising Campaign Planning*.)

Do you need additional software to complete your book or presentation? Is there an upgrade that would help you do your work more efficiently? If there is, start planning ahead and you might be able to request funds to purchase it.

Is your software compatible with other packages belonging to members of your team? If you are using a Mac and others are PC users, make sure to test how the files go back and forth. What if you need to send someone a file to proofread?

What is your system? Doc and Docx are different versions of Microsoft Word. Can everyone read and write in all file formats?

Oh yes, and one more thing – BACK UP! Back up regularly and backup often. The more you add to your book and your presentation – graphics, video, text, sources from here and there – the greater the chance that whatever software and storage you're using could have a problem. These days, it's somewhat less of a problem, but still… somehow the files know when things are really, really critical – and that's the time your file, or your disc, or your program decides to crash on you. A back up is better than a crack up.

Budget

Your budget should include consideration of the following:

- Printing, binding
- Software and Hardware
- Research, photography, video
- Travel – field studies and travel to the competition, if appropriate
- Creative executions, if necessary

Plan your budget so you know what your expenses will be and what client expenses should be. If you are in a college setting, you should write a proposal to request its support. You're in a position to help brand some community organizations, and colleges like to help students who help others. Sometimes it can be factored in as part of the fee for the class.

In some cases, a bit of fund-raising ends up being part of the team project.

Printing the Book

Locate a reliable printer who can deliver a beautiful book for you when you need it. Kinko's can be pricey, but they have the capability to produce great quality work, and they're used to quick turnaround times. For about $25 you can get 35 or so nice color pages. But, you might want to shop around and have a test run conducted.

Scheduling

Scheduling with the printer is sometimes a problem. Kinko's has positioned themselves as a very reliable printer that delivers high quality printing on short notice. But you pay for that (Time, Money, Quality – remember?). Scheduling with other printers can save you a great deal of money, but you can expect a longer lead time.

Color and font proof

Printing is still an art – particularly with graphic files. Bring your files with fonts, photos, and illustrations with you to the printer. You can call to get instructions on how to save your file and what you need to do to save your files to travel with them. In today's world, notebook computers make it very easy to transfer files for printing; but even so, proofing your color and pages is still needed.

Budget

The printing budget can vary by as much as the number of printers in town. Asking for a bid is very common and not offensive to anyone. It's how people do business. If you plan ahead, some colleges might be able to assess a course fee so that your work is attached to your university bill.

Shipping, Binding, Covers

If you're in a competition, you might have to ship your work somewhere. Overnight shipping can be costly, so add that into your budget, too. It would be nice if things were done early. But, somehow, things are always revised, polished, and given that one final improvement at the last minute. That's just the way it is. Binding is extra as is extra heavy card stock for the front and back covers. Extras can add up and creep into the final costs.

THE PITCH

Now let's talk about the Pitch. The day has come for you to present your work to the client. Have you made presentations before? Maybe so. But you might not have made a presentation with this much on the line. For example, do you know how long it takes to make an impression? Seven to seventeen seconds. Every second counts.

You may be dealing with clients you've come to know well, and it may be a comfortable meeting. Or, you could be standing across the room from suspicious strangers you barely know. There are as many different situations as there are clients.

Some of you may have given important presentations before. But, right now, the most important one is the one you're about to make. It deserves all the attention you can give it.

Outline and Write Your Presentation

Simply put, your presentation is a sales pitch. Begin with an outline. I've read a number of stories about Steve Jobs, the co-founder of Apple. He wrote and practiced everything he said before making public presentations.

If you have a speech or theatre department on campus, you might want to ask someone there to assist you, or at least read your speech. But ask far enough in advance so you are not putting people in a bind, they are pros at this, and can help you.

But here's the thing. DON'T JUST STAND THERE AND READ THE SLIDES. You've done all this work and there's a lot there. Don't ruin it by boring busy executives by reading aloud what they can easily read themselves. To be successful, your presentation needs to involve some salesmanship and some show business.

Building Your Slide Show

These days, it seems we're as good as our PowerPoint presentation. PowerPoint is a wonderful program and it's given us all some terrific tools for communicating. But it's also a mixed blessing. You pretty much need to work within its limits, and chances are, your audience has seen a PowerPoint presentation or two – so you may be compared to some pretty good presenters. That said, with our previous advice in mind (DON'T JUST STAND THERE AND READ THE SLIDES), do your best.

As a general "rule of thumb," aim for a 20-minute presentation with a maximum of 30 slides. This should keep the interest of the audience, but that is never guaranteed. You have to take steps to ensure that interest. Plan to play with the timing a bit, and find a pace that is comfortable for the audience.

And, again, a presentation is NOT just reading the slides. Did we mention that?

Some write their presentation and then build the slides. Others work out the outline and the slides and then create their presentation. Either way can work. And, of course, the more you do it, the more you'll be developing your own approach and your own style. Here are some general good guidelines:

- 6 x 6 rules – Try for no more than 6 lines and no more than 6 words per line.
- The slide should follow the speaker and look professional.
- The slide should have limited animation. Builds are fine. Don't bounce around.
- A few short videos can really brighten a slide presentation. For example:
  - A short video interview with a Target;
  - A piece of animation from the website;
  - A TV commercial (if there is one) will look good in your PowerPoint.

These days, there is a lot of advice on the general topic of "How to avoid boring someone with a PowerPoint presentation." There are even some good, short videos on YouTube to help. We're guessing that you've had to sit through enough bad ones to know you don't want to do one.

Integrate your creative work into your slide presentation

This can be a chance to provide a little relief from standing in front of a screen. You can hand out a mock-up of the brochure. A bumper sticker with your theme. Put a button on your lapel – or sip from a cup of coffee with your logo on the cup. Your creative work also offers an opportunity to be a bit theatrical. Steve Jobs held that iPad in his hand and demonstrated. Even if it's just putting a big mock up on an easel, creative work gives your team something to do.

Speaking of big, don't be afraid to be a bit oversize. There's nothing like pulling a big letter out of a big envelope four-times normal size. Get a handle on the proportions of the room and see what you can do to "own the room" with your work.

Design slides to compliment your book's design

Basically, brand communications should have a family look. So it makes sense that your book, your messaging, and your presentation should share many graphic aspects. In general, the presentation, the book/binder/leave behind – whatever you call it – and your Messaging campaign should have a compatible look and feel.

Assemble the Presentation Team

This is all part of a learning experience. Presenting can be a part of that. However, when you make the presentation, you should open and close with your strongest person. That person will "frame" the presentation. Then, various team members can present based on their specialty.

This isn't youth soccer where everyone gets a trophy for showing up, but it is an opportunity for everyone to learn and get better. So, without jeopardizing the impression you want to make, make a sincere effort to maintain involvement of all the people who worked so hard to put this brand-building campaign together.

That said, you may find that some of the big national contests, such as the AAF/NSAC, have turned into Show Biz Extravaganzas, with beautiful people making very polished presentations. If you're in that competition, you'll have to play that game. Watch the videos of the winning teams. Pretty impressive.

But let's remember to be real when we get together in a conference room in our own hometown and show someone, who is also our neighbor, how hard we've worked to help their business or non-profit succeed. Let's be good team members. Let's look them in the eye, shake their hand, and show them how we can help build their brand.

Practice Makes Perfect

Start by making a mock pitch a few days before the real deal. We call it the Mock Pitch. It's a dress rehearsal. Dress in your business attire, come with your note cards. If possible, be in the room you are going to use and have all the props you plan on using. You might even want to video the whole thing.

If you're in a competition, find out how large the room is. Simulate it as closely as you can. Have an audience of people you don't know asking questions coming from all over the place so you have to think on your feet.

Consider the strongest and the weakest elements of your campaign. Think about how you are going to answer questions about those areas. Who is going to answer? For example, designate John for the target audience, Martha for the competition, LaRae for the message windows, etc.

Sometimes, people ask questions just to see that you actually did the work. But most of the time, they want to know more of 'why' you did it a certain way. Be ready.

Show Time! Pitch Your Campaign to Your Client

The day you pitch to the client, greet them with that handshake and a great smile. Show up early and well prepared. Check equipment at least an hour before the scheduled time – or the night before if possible.

Do not read. Use note cards, but DO NOT read. Every person should have their own set of notes. One person can advance slides, or you can take turns. Just make sure that someone is not in the way of the screen.

Look at the audience and the decision-makers. The screen is not making the decision, so no need to look at the screen – it's not going anywhere. Look at them.

Smile at your client with confidence. Support your team members.

Done and done!

On our site, we've uploaded the slide show the Cadillac team put together.

Here are a few of their slides.

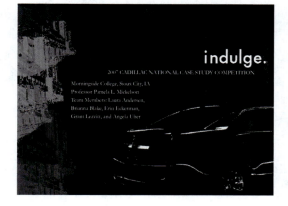
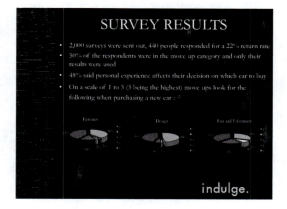

Time to take a deep breath. You've done something special. You got involved in an enterprise – whether business or non-profit – looked under the hood, kicked the tires, and figured out how it worked. You identified the Goals needed to achieve success. You got to know your Target. Then, you figured out how and where to talk to them with your Message and Message Windows.

You did all that. Along the way, you developed some skills, some insights, and some ways of looking at how the world works that will benefit you and the people you work with for years to come. How about that?

BRAIN BUILDER EXERCISE 12.1: Building Your Pitch

OK, by now you should know what to do.

1. Design and produce your 'Book.' Don't forget to proofread. Twice.

2. Write the outline for your Presentation.

3. Design the slides and write your accompanying comments. Rehearse like heck.

4. Produce the accompanying creative materials. Make them look terrific.

5. Give yourself and your team members a pat on the back for a job well done.

BUILDING YOUR PORTFOLIO

All the time you've been working to build a brand, you've been building something else – your own skills and capabilities. This kind of entrepreneurial effort is one of the best learning experiences you can have – because you're learning a skill that will be valued in the world you enter after graduation.

As you wrap-up this experience, don't forget to have a specially gift-wrapped version for your resumé and your own portfolio. Then, when you're at an interview and someone who's hiring wants to know what you can do, you can show them.

FEEDBACK AND REFLECTION

Let's stay in touch. If you have some lessons learned or some great brand building examples you want to share, get in touch with us through our website.

We mean it. If you have more thoughts and comments, or perhaps a suggestion or two, we'd love to hear from you.

OK, go build those brands and best of luck. The world needs you, your talent, and your hard work. Go get 'em.

BRAIN BUILDER EXERCISE 12.2: Reflection

The purpose of this last exercise is to give you the chance to do one final reflection. The questions will help you realize what kind of experience you have had.

This questionnaire is also available as a .doc file on our website. Fill out as much as you want and send it to us. We'd love to hear from you. Did we mention that?

1. Think about how the entire branding process went for you. Jot down a few quick thoughts

2. How do you think it went for your team?

3. How effective and inspiring was the entire experience?

4. How successful do you think your campaign can become?

5. Was there any one thing you could change about your experience? What would that be and why?

6. What sections would it be helpful to revisit and learn more about?

7. What sections were toughest? How might they be improved?

8. What do you think you learned from this project (personal or work-related)?

9. What has been the best part of the project? Why?

10. What was the hardest part of the project? Why?

11. What have you learned that you didn't know at the beginning of the project?

12. What is the most valuable information you gained?

13. How do you feel about your overall project?

14. What information did you find most useful? Why?

15. What have you learned from the people involved in this project?

16. What have they learned about you?

17. Are there ways that you could stay involved in this project in the future?

18. Do you think differently about advertising after completing this project? How?

CHAPTER REVIEW

In this chapter we reviewed:

1. How to backdate the workflow of your branding campaign;

2. How to put together a book containing the entire branding campaign;

3. How to outline, write, and create a Pitch that sells, including a slide show and accompanying presentation materials; and

4. The value of brand-building skills and the work you've done on this project as you set out to build your own career.

REVIEW QUESTIONS

1. What is the Time/Money/Quality triangle?

2. What types of issues (software, hardware, file sharing, people, schedules, etc.) could arise with multiple writers and multiple designers working on a branding campaign? What can you do to plan ahead to avoid those issues?

3. If you had a 40-page, full-color book and needed 15 copies by the following two deadlines, how much would it cost? How would you pay for it?
   a. Next week

   b. Tomorrow

4. What additional materials might you produce in addition to the Book and presentation to make your Pitch more interesting and persuasive?

ACKNOWLEDGEMENTS

I'd first like to thank publisher Lorelei Bendinger. She and Eugenia Velazquez took me to a wonderful lunch in Greek Town in Chicago. It was there that she saw The Learning Center, Sioux City Chamber Music, Tyson Event Center, Pizza Hut, Yahoo, and Cadillac campaigns – following selected works from *Advertising The Business of Brands*. She called Bruce Bendinger on her cell phone, excited about the potential of this project. Later, Bruce joined us and, if the truth be told, we chatted as much about farming as we did about advertising.

I'd like to thank Dr. Sam Clovis for recognizing the greatness that my students have produced and recommending that I document the process.

I am most appreciative to the faculty and their students who are lead users and reviewers: April Hearne, Pulaski Technical College; Renee Gravois Lee, Sam Houston University; Zina Taran, Pennsylvania State University, Harrisburg; and Sharon Alpi, Millikin University. Their early adoption and reviews provided rich feedback to help develop this work. I am grateful to Stephanie Rude who served as a preceptor for me during her senior year when we first used the manuscript in the classroom. She continued working with me to read and edit the exercises. The examples in the instructor's manuals are hers. Later, Mallory Lowe, another outstanding preceptor, further edited the exercises. Thank you to colleagues Jim Fisk and John Kolbo – for always collaborating on improving students' brand building expertise, and again to Jim for a line by line editing of the book.

I want to acknowledge the many Ad Club members, classroom teams and clients over the last 25 years. They've inspired me more than they will ever know. Security National Bank, Wells Blue Bunny, Kellogg's, Hearst, VISA, American Airlines, Kodak, Saturn, Hallmark, Neon, American Red Cross, Pizza Hut, Matrix, New York Times, Echo, Banc America, Daimler Chrysler, Visit Florida, Yahoo, Postal Vault, Cadillac, Cadillac CTS, Sioux Bee Honey, Security National Bank, Conservation Districts of Iowa/AGRON, Palmer Candy, Sioux City Chamber Music, Tyson Event Center, Human Rights Commission, Jessica and John Page – Page Portraits, Jack FM, The Learning Center, Mid America Aviation and Transportation Museum, Sober Driving Saves, HardPressed Fruit and Nut Bar, and Palmer Candy.

I want to thank Bruce Bendinger for his leadership in the project, Pat Aylward for his hard work editing and improving the look of this book. Being part of The Copy Workshop team has been a pleasure.

Most of all I want to thank Al, John, and Martha; for being the greatest family supporters ever!